“NAMING THE BOOK *PORTICO* IS MY WAY OF SAYING, ‘WELCOME. I’M GLAD YOU ARE HERE.’”

A leading authority on Jewish food, Leah Koenig celebrates *la cucina Ebraica Romana* within the pages of her new cookbook. *Portico: Cooking and Feasting in Rome’s Jewish Kitchen* features over 100 deeply flavorful recipes and beautiful photographs of Rome’s Jewish community, the oldest in Europe. The city’s Jewish residents have endured many hardships, including 300 years of persecution inside the Roman Jewish Ghetto. Out of this strife grew resilience, a deeply knit community, and a uniquely beguiling cuisine. Today, the community thrives on Via del Portico d’Ottavia (the main road in Rome’s Ghetto neighborhood)—and beyond.

Leah Koenig’s recipes showcase the cuisine’s elegantly understated vegetables, saucy braised meats and stews, rustic pastas, resplendent olive oil–fried foods, and never-too-sweet desserts. Home cooks can explore classics of the Roman Jewish repertoire with Stracotto di Manzo (a wine-braised beef stew), Pomodori a Mezzo (simple and sumptuous roasted tomatoes), Pizza Ebraica (fruit-and-nut-studded bar cookies), and, of course, Carciofi alla Giudia, the quintessential Jewish-style fried artichokes. A standout chapter on fritters—showcasing the unique gift Roman Jews have for delicate frying—includes sweet honey-soaked matzo fritters, fried salt cod, and savory potato pastries (burik) introduced by the thousands of Libyan Jews who immigrated to Rome in the 1960s and ’70s. Every recipe is masterfully tailored to the home cook, while maintaining the flavor and integrity of tradition. Suggested menus for holiday planning round out the usability and flexibility of these dishes.

A cookbook for anyone who wants to dive more deeply into Jewish foodways, or gain new insight into Rome, *Portico* features the makers and creators who are keeping Roman Jewish food alive today, transporting us to the bustling streets of the Eternal City while also making us feel—as we cook and eat—very much at home.

Portico

ALSO BY LEAH KOENIG

The Jewish Cookbook

Modern Jewish Cooking

Little Book of Jewish Appetizers

Little Book of Jewish Feasts

Little Book of Jewish Sweets

The Hadassah Everyday Cookbook

Portico

Cooking and Feasting in Rome's Jewish Kitchen

LEAH KOENIG

Photography by Kristin Teig

Half-title image: *Mixed Fried Vegetables, 130, and Fried Fresh Anchovies, 138*

Printed in China
First Edition

For information about permission to reproduce selections from this book, write to Permissions, W. W. Norton & Company, Inc., 500 Fifth Avenue, New York, NY 10110

For information about special discounts for bulk purchases, please contact W. W. Norton Special Sales at specialsales@wwnorton.com or 800-233-4830

Manufacturing by Imago
Book design by Laura Palese Design
Production manager: Julia Druskin

ISBN: 978-0-393-86801-2

W. W. Norton & Company, Inc.
500 Fifth Avenue, New York, N.Y. 10110
www.wwnorton.com

W. W. Norton & Company Ltd.
15 Carlisle Street, London W1D 3BS

1 2 3 4 5 6 7 8 9 0

AI MIEI AMORI

Yoshie, Max, and Beatrice

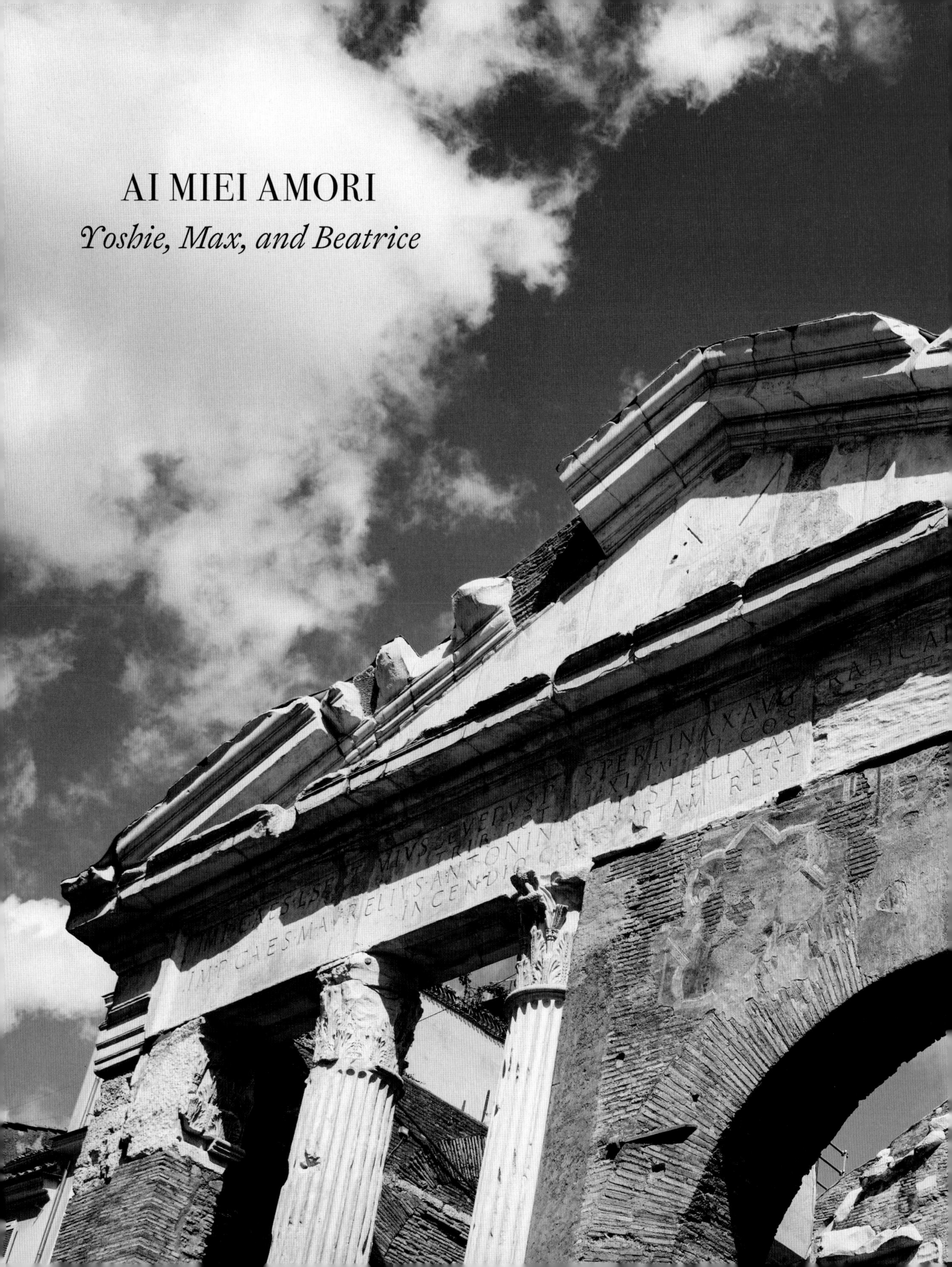

INTRODUCTION

Inside the bakery—a corner storefront no larger than a university dorm room—customers jostle at the counter for service. Just outside the doors, the line of hopefuls stretches half a dozen deep. Two display cases hold the array of sweets these folks are after: double-crusted ricotta and sour cherry tarts, chubby amaretti, and bar cookies studded with almonds and candied fruit, all blistered and molten from the bakery's ancient ovens.

The shop's swirl of sugar and good-natured chaos could easily be found in Brooklyn or down a Jerusalem side street. But this bakery, the 200-year old Pasticceria il Boccione, is on Via del Portico d'Ottavia—the main drag in Rome's Jewish Ghetto neighborhood. And it is not alone. Up and down the street, restaurants and shops serve up classic dishes from la cucina Ebraico-Romanesca (Roman Jewish cuisine), including sultry beef stew spooned over rigatoni, oil-drizzled tomatoes roasted to the point of collapse, rosemary-scented lamb and potatoes, and whole artichokes deep-fried into crisp, salt-kissed blossoms.

Rome's Jewish community dates back more than 2,000 years, and it is home to three distinct but overlapping communities. The first, the Italkim, date their ancestors' arrival in Rome back to the second century BCE. The second, the Sephardim, arrived after the Spanish Inquisition. And the third, Libyan Jews, immigrated in the late twentieth century. Through the centuries, the community has been shaped by both the creative and determined people who have lived there and vast periods of unthinkable discrimination and hardship. But out of strife grew a resilient, deeply knit community and a beguiling cuisine.

I first visited Rome in 2004, when I was twenty-two. A newly minted college graduate, I was en route to Tuscany, where the plan was to commune with the vineyards at an organic winery for a month and emerge with a greater knowledge of sustainable viticulture and, hopefully, a deeper understanding of myself.

The days I spent in Rome were filled with a mix of marveling at the Colosseum and Sistine Chapel, getting lost in the city's endless labyrinth of tiny streets and charming piazzas, spending my limited euros on rectangles of Roman pizza, and navigating the strange social world that exists only inside youth hostels. I made the briefest of forays into the Jewish Ghetto neighborhood (for 316 years, Rome's Jews were forced to live inside a walled slum; see page 21 for more) and felt some amorphous stirrings of connection. But I was too young and distracted at the time to follow the feeling any further.

I returned to Rome five years later on my honeymoon, and this time, I was ready. My connection to my Jewish heritage was more fully developed, and my interest in the link between food and Jewish history was in full bloom. My husband, Yoshie, and I wound our way up and down Via del Portico d'Ottavia's smooth cobblestones, eating our weight in fried artichokes.

We took a tour of the Ghetto with historian and tour guide Micaela Pavoncello (see page 184) that left me dizzy with wonder at how Rome's Jewish community had managed to survive for twenty-two centuries and find moments of joy and meaning in the most hostile of circumstances. We also lucked into a Shabbat dinner invite at the home of Giovanni Terracina, who founded the kosher catering company Le Bon Ton. Yoshie and I were embarrassingly well fed that evening, and we walked back to our hotel arm in arm, happily tipsy, and overwhelmed by our good fortune.

That Shabbat dinner completely exploded my previous understanding of what Jewish cuisine was. The dishes Giovanni served—including chicken meatballs in tomato-celery sauce and a rich beef stew perfumed with red wine—were unlike anything I had ever eaten for Shabbat before. But around his gracious table, where we talked, laughed, and raised our wineglasses like old friends, rather than people who had met just hours before, they felt deeply familiar. Those dishes were neither Ashkenazi (hailing from Central and Eastern Europe), nor Sephardi (hailing from the Iberian Peninsula). They were uniquely Roman, and they were incredible.

ברוך אתה בבאך וברוך אתה בצאתך

Ristorante Kosher

It is not an exaggeration to say that that trip to Rome solidified a desire to dedicate my professional life to studying and sharing Jewish cuisines from around the world. Time and again over the last decade and a half, I have fallen in love with previously unfamiliar-to-me corners of the Jewish food world. And it all started in Rome. So while I have included a handful of Roman Jewish dishes in my other cookbooks, *Portico* is my attempt to give something back to the city that has been so generous and inspiring to me.

Time and again over the last decade and a half, I have fallen in love with previously unfamiliar-to-me corners of the Jewish food world.

I researched and wrote *Portico* in the midst of the Covid-19 pandemic. For the first many months of the process, I could not travel for research, and so I relied on books, phone calls, and video chats to connect me to the city's people and their kitchens. During those months of learning, I longed for nothing more than the chance to walk down Via del Portico d'Ottavia again.

A few months before my manuscript deadline, the world finally opened up enough for me and the book's photographer, Kristin Teig, to fly to Rome. After settling into our Airbnb and taking a quick nap, we grabbed notebook and camera, respectively, and set off toward the Ghetto neighborhood. It had been years since my last visit, but somehow my feet remembered the way. Despite the presence of face masks, everything—the sunlight glinting off the Tiber River, the majestic dome of the Tempio Maggiore (Great Synagogue) rising into the skyline, the overlapping bustle of tourists and locals stopping into the bakery or twirling spaghetti topped with sautéeed artichokes at one of the tables lining the street—was just as I remembered it.

The Italian word *casereccio* translates as "homemade," and it is used to describe a sense of homeyness—cozy, relaxed, inviting. (Yiddish speakers have a similar word, *haimish*.) Whether you have traveled to Rome a million times or are planning to make your first trip soon, and whether or not you come from a Jewish background, I hope that reading and cooking your way through this book gives you the feeling of simultaneously being transported to Rome and coming home.

A Note on the Book's Title

At one edge of the Ghetto neighborhood stands the majestic remains of an ancient structure called Portico d'Ottavia (Octavia's Porch). Although it was built in the first century BCE by Emperor Augustus, in honor of his sister, and damaged over the centuries by earthquakes and fire, significant portions of the stone and marble structure are still remarkably intact.

The Portico d'Ottavia has had many purposes over the years, from its origin as the site of two ancient Roman temples, to a library, an open-air art museum, and public square. In the twelfth century, it became the home of a fish market (La Pescheria) that operated continuously until Italy's unification in 1871. The market was a major source of nutrition for Rome's Jews during the Ghetto period. Today the ruins' role as a fish market is memorialized in the name of the church that stands beside them: Sant'Angelo in Pescheria, or, literally, "Holy Angel in the Fish Market." And the main street of the Jewish Ghetto is called Via del Portico d'Ottavia, in recognition of the neighborhood's physical and emotional proximity to the market.

I knew I wanted to title this cookbook *Portico* from the earliest stages of my research. Aside from the Tempio Maggiore di Roma (Great Synagogue of Rome), Portico d'Ottavia is the most iconic structure in the Jewish Ghetto neighborhood. It holds symbolic importance for the community as a reminder of its longevity. I also love how the word *portico*, which translates as "porch" or "front porch," evokes the idea of coming in—an entrance. Naming the book *Portico* is my way of saying, "Welcome. I'm glad you are here."

Naming the book *Portico* is my way of saying, "Welcome. I'm glad you are here."

S·PERTINAX·AVG
TRIB POT
INCENDIO
REST

A Note on the Recipes

A couple of years ago, while I was in the kitchen of a Roman Jewish friend, she asked me to help prepare sandwiches. In front of me she laid out Pizza Bianca (page 190), fresh mozzarella, Casalino tomatoes, and a bowl of fried and marinated zucchini, or Concia (page 44). I got to work, diligently layering a bit of cheese, a slice of tomato, and a spoonful of the zucchini into each split wedge of flatbread.

All was going well until my friend glanced over at me. "What are you doing?" she asked with widened eyes. "You don't put everything on one sandwich! It's either mozzarella and tomato *or* mozzarella and zucchini!" I must have looked just as incredulous when I responded, "Why not both?" We laughed, and I happily agreed to make the remaining sandwiches to her specifications. But the moment crystallized something for me: I may adore Rome, but my "more is more" approach to sandwich making is decidedly American.

That moment stuck with me as I gathered and developed recipes for this cookbook. As a journalist and recipe developer with a passion for Jewish cuisine and culture, I strive to share recipes that reflect the uniqueness of the places from which they originate. I also cook in the homes of as many people as possible when I am doing research to make sure I am representing the dishes accurately. And yet to pretend that I do not bring my own American sensibilities or point of view to the kitchen would be misleading.

For the recipes in this book, on the occasions where I have made a subtle tweak to a traditional recipe, or when I have included a more contemporary dish from a Roman or American chef, I have noted that in the headnote. Otherwise, the recipes are closely inspired by what I observed while cooking or eating with members of Rome's Jewish community. Because ultimately, the recipes—and the stories behind them—are theirs to share.

A Glimpse into Rome's Storied Jewish History

The history of the Jews in Rome stretches back more than 2,000 uninterrupted years, making theirs the oldest community outside of ancient Judea (and predating both the Ashkenazi and the Sephardi Diaspora). The community is so longstanding that its traditions evolved alongside, and often overlapped with, Roman traditions. From a culinary perspective, it can be a challenge to untangle which dishes are prepared "alla Giudia" (Jewish style), and which are "alla Romana" (Roman style). In many cases, in fact, they are one and the same.

The earliest Jews arrived in Rome in the second century BCE as diplomatic envoys of Judah Maccabee. They sought protection against the Syrian king Antiochus, who held power in Judea and had desecrated the Holy Temple in Jerusalem with statues of idols while forbidding Torah study, Shabbat observance, and other central tenets of Jewish practice. These Jews were welcomed to Rome by Emperor Julius Caesar and then Emperor Augustus, who granted them protections allowing them to live independently and worship as they chose.

Two centuries later, in 70 CE, Emperor Titus captured Jerusalem during the Jewish-Roman Wars. He destroyed the Holy Temple, functionally ending Jewish ritual in Jerusalem. He also captured thousands of Jews and brought those prisoners of war to Rome as slaves. There the city's existing Jewish community paid ransoms to help free their fellow Jews after they had arrived.

These early Roman Jews, who are called Italkim, established religious rites and customs that drew from what they knew in Jerusalem, but evolved to be uniquely Roman. The liturgical styles, many of which continue to this day, offer a peek into the liturgy of ancient Israel. One stunning example is that Romans sound the shofar (a ram's horn blown like a trumpet on Rosh Hashanah and Yom Kippur) as it was done in ancient Jerusalem. Instead of the call-and-response blasts familiar to most Ashkenazi and Sephardi Jews, the shofar is blown in a continuous, rippling wave that is quite extraordinary to hear.

From the fall of Rome through the rise of Christianity and the early Middle Ages, Jews maintained their presence in Rome.

שָׁלוֹם
שָׁלוֹם
שָׁלוֹם
שָׁלוֹם
שָׁלוֹם
שָׁלוֹם
Hand painted ceramic tile
€8,00

The Arrival of Sephardi Jews to Rome

While Spain and Italy are more than 1,000 miles apart, the Spanish Inquisition and its aftermath drastically changed the makeup of Rome's Jewish population. Before Italy became a unified country, it was broken up into a tapestry of independent states with their own customs and dialects. For many centuries, some of the largest and most vibrant Italian Jewish communities were located in the southern part of the country, in places like Sicily, Calabria, Apulia, and Sardinia.

Their arrival was met with suspicion and derision at first, but over time, the two communities merged into a largely unified whole.

In 1492, following centuries of rising antisemitic sentiment and violence toward Jews (as well as Muslims and other non-Catholics) in Spain, King Ferdinand II and Queen Isabella I issued the Alhambra Decree, which resulted in the expulsion of more than 150,000 Jews from the Kingdom of Spain. At that time, much of southern Italy was under Spanish rule and therefore subject to the same decrees. So in subsequent years, as the Inquisition's ripples reached Sicily and other southern Italian regions, tens of thousands of Jews were expelled from these regions, all but wiping out the southern Italian Jewish population.

The majority of Sephardi Jews fled to countries throughout the Ottoman Empire. But approximately 9,000 Jews from Spain, Portugal, and the south of Italy fled to northern Italian cities that were not under Spanish rule—including Rome. Pope Alexander VI accepted these persecuted Jews, declaring that they were permitted "to continue in their own rites, to gain wealth, and to enjoy many other privileges." The Sephardi Jews joined Rome's existing Italkim community. Their arrival was met with suspicion and derision at first, but over time, the two communities merged into a largely unified whole.

The Ghetto Period

The Sephardi Jews who landed in Rome did not, unfortunately, find the respite from persecution they sought. After Alexander VI, papal attitudes toward Jews tended to oscillate between tolerance and distaste. Then in 1555, Pope Paul IV, a particularly cruel man, came into power. One of his first acts was to create the Roman Ghetto—an undertaking that would inexorably transform the city's Jewish community. The word *ghetto* originated in Venice in 1516, with the institution of the first Jewish Ghetto. Likely derived from a copper foundry, or ghèto, that existed in the area, the name came to mean an enclosed (often gated and locked) neighborhood in which Jews were forced to live.

Prior to 1555, the center of Jewish life in Rome was in the Trastevere neighborhood on the west side of the Tiber River. If you visit Trastevere today, you can make your way to Vicolo dell'Atleta 14 and see a building that housed a synagogue in the eleventh century, thought to be Rome's oldest remaining synagogue structure. (The building is currently home to a restaurant named Spirito Divino, or "divine spirit," in acknowledgment of its history.) With the Ghetto's establishment, the Jewish population was forcibly moved across the river and compelled to live in a four-block-wide gated slum in one of the city's most undesirable, and virtually uninhabitable, locations.

According to historian and tour guide Micaela Pavoncello, the area was approximately "250 steps wide and 200 steps long" and housed 9,000 people at its peak capacity. The buildings were packed tightly together, blocking out the sunlight. As the population in the Ghetto grew, the buildings were forced to expand vertically, often in a haphazard and structurally unsound manner. The streets were cramped and bombarded with the odors emanating from the fish market at Portico d'Ottavia. And every winter, when the Tiber River swelled after heavy rains, the streets of the Ghetto would flood and exacerbate the existing mess.

The gates to the Ghetto were kept locked every day from dusk until dawn. (The noble Roman Mattei family held the keys and were the Ghetto's official gatekeepers.) During the day, Jews could travel throughout the rest of the city, but they had to wear humiliating identification. The men

were forced to don yellow hats, and Jewish women had to wear yellow kerchiefs, similar to those then worn by prostitutes. This distinctive apparel left the Jews vulnerable to their Christian neighbors, some of whom would taunt or even beat them in the streets.

From a financial standpoint, Jews were forbidden from owning property and from engaging in virtually all professional trades except for money lending, peddling used clothing and rags, and street vending. The women of the community became very skilled seamstresses, transforming scraps of cloth and old dresses into beautiful creations, including extraordinary covers for Torahs. A vast collection of these Torah covers is displayed today at the Museo Ebraico di Roma (Jewish Museum of Rome).

Italian Jews were also limited in terms of what they could buy—both by their extreme poverty and by papal decree. Roman Jews, for example, were not permitted to purchase larger species of fish. In the fish market, sellers used a marble slab to measure a fish's size. If the head and tail extended beyond the edges of the slab, Jews were not allowed to buy it. Instead, Jewish families subsisted on fish scraps (particularly heads and spines) and smaller fish like anchovies, mackerel, and sardines.

The Ghetto was allowed a synagogue, but only one. Yet Rome's Jews hailed from many different places, including Jerusalem, Spain, Sicily, and Portugal, and each community had its own liturgical rites and customs. Since a single congregation could not accommodate the residents' diverse backgrounds, the community created five tiny synagogues (Cinque Scole) inside the larger building, offering five different prayer services in one space. The building burnt down in an accidental fire in 1890, but it is memorialized in the Piazza delle Cinque Scole.

If life in the Ghetto seemed impossibly hard, that was by design. The Vatican hoped to make things so difficult for Jewish residents that they would convert to Catholicism. Churches were erected directly outside the Ghetto's gates ("They stood like neon flashing signs saying, 'Convert!'" said Pavoncello), and every Saturday, which was Shabbat, Jews were required to attend mass. Local legend claims that many of them stuffed their ears with wax or cotton to avoid hearing anything the priests said.

Ultimately, the Vatican's plan backfired rather spectacularly. Some Roman Jews did choose to convert to Catholicism, and others (particularly children) were forced to undergo unwanted baptisms. But the isolation and hardships ultimately strengthened the community's identity. Roman Jews developed their own dialect—a mix of Hebrew, ancient Roman, and Spanish called *Giudaico Romanesco*. Older members of the community still speak it today and, as with Yiddish, certain phrases and words made their way into wider use. For example, the Giudaico Romanesco word *devare*, which is derived from the Hebrew word *ledaber* ("to speak"), is used to tell someone to be quiet or stop talking.

While the majority of Roman Jews in the Ghetto were desperately poor, they still practiced tzedakah (the Jewish commandment of charity and societal justice), setting up organizations to aid one another in times of need. Along one side street in the Ghetto neighborhood, you can find a coin slot carved into a stone wall accompanied by a sign reading "Give to the orphans" in both Hebrew and Italian.

Meanwhile, a distinctive take on cucina povera emerged during Ghetto times. "Throughout their history, Jews have demonstrated considerable creativity in handling food dilemmas—often in challenging situations," writes historian Ariel Toaff in an article on the cuisine of Italian Jews. From the small fish they were permitted to purchase at the market came endive and anchovy pies, as well as rustic stews that melted anchovies into the soffritto (a base of aromatics, similar to the French mirepoix). Using the inexpensive "throwaway" parts of cows and lambs (animal offal was collectively referred to as the *quinto quarto*, or "fifth quarter"; see page 244 for more), they simmered enticing dishes that would become classics of Roman cuisine. And with the abundance of locally produced olive oil, they created an entire canon of deep-fried dishes.

The Sephardi Jews who arrived after the Spanish Inquisition brought their own culinary customs to the mix. These included desserts made from ground almonds, abundant use of pine nuts and raisins in both sweet and savory dishes, and a fondness for vegetables like eggplants and artichokes.

Inside the Ghetto walls, these influences mingled with local Roman tastes and ingredients, resulting in a cuisine unlike any found elsewhere on earth—including other Italian Jewish communities. As an example, Jewish cooking styles that emerged in northern Italy were influenced

by Ashkenazi foodways that arrived with immigrants from neighboring countries like Germany, Austria, and France. In his book *Mangiare alla Giudia*, Toaff dedicates an entire chapter to goose, which he identifies as "the Jews' pig." But while goose salami and sausages, goose fat (used for cooking), and foie gras were commonplace on Jewish tables in northern Italy, they never became a significant part of Roman Jewish cuisine.

Walking through the neighborhood today, it is impossible to get a true sense of what it must have been like to live there during the Ghetto period.

In 1871, the individual papal states of the Italian Peninsula were consolidated into a single unified country, called the Kingdom of Italy. Rome was designated the kingdom's capitol, and the Ghetto was disbanded. After more than 300 years spent cloistered inside gated walls, Rome's Jewish community was free.

Walking through the neighborhood today, it is impossible to get a true sense of what it must have been like to live there during the Ghetto period. In 1888, the walls and gates were torn down and many of the squalid buildings were demolished, with newer ones erected in their place. The streets were widened, allowing sunlight to penetrate where it once could not, and, perhaps most important, embankments were built to keep the Tiber River from flooding the streets.

In 1901, the community broke ground on a new synagogue, and three years later, the Tempio Maggiore di Roma (Great Synagogue of Rome) opened its doors—a majestic symbol of the future. Today the synagogue houses two congregations and is home to the Museo Ebraico di Roma (Jewish Museum of Rome), which houses stunning artifacts, Jewish ritual items, and exhibits about the city's Jewish history. In 1986, Rome's synagogue would also become the site of a historic moment: the first-ever visit by a Pope (Pope John Paul II) to a Jewish house of worship. During that emotional visit, the pope embraced Rome's chief rabbi, Elio Toaff, in front of a thousand people and publicly apologized for the Church's treatment of the Jews in Italy.

Italian Racial Laws and World War II

In 1938, only a few generations after the unification of Italy brought an end to the Roman Ghetto, the National Fascist Party, led by Benito Mussolini, introduced the Leggi Razziali (Racial Laws), a series of laws designed to enforce discrimination against Italian Jews. They prohibited Jewish children from attending school and stripped Jewish doctors, accountants, journalists, artists, and university professors, among others, of their professions. And non-Jewish Italians were forbidden to see plays or listen to music created by Jews.

Life under Mussolini's cruel laws must have felt like whiplash for a community that had so recently been allowed to fully participate in general society. Suddenly, their daily existence was harsh and severely limited once again. And yet, because Italy was an ally to Hitler's Nazi regime in Germany, Italy's Jews were relatively protected from the worst of the death camps—until 1943.

On October 13, 1943, less than three months after Mussolini was ousted and replaced by General Pietro Badoglio, and one month after Italy surrendered to the Allied forces, the country officially switched sides and joined the war against Nazi Germany. "Many of Rome's Jews were naive enough to think the Pope would save them from any trouble with the Nazis," Pavoncello said. But on Saturday October 16, the Gestapo parked their trucks in the Ghetto at sunrise and began collecting families for deportation. "They were told they had twenty minutes to pack a suitcase and gather food for a week," she said. More than 1,000 Roman Jews were taken to Auschwitz—only sixteen returned after the war.

The remaining members of Rome's Jewish population managed to escape the Gestapo and go into hiding. Their efforts were aided by Catholic neighbors who objected to the deportations. Many Jews hid in Vatican City or were sheltered in convents and monasteries. Pope Pius XII officially maintained strict neutrality, refusing to publicly condemn the Nazi's actions. Behind the scenes, however, he instructed the clergy to open their sanctuaries to those in need of refuge.

When I interviewed Michele Pavoncello, the co-owner of Nonna Betta restaurant in the Ghetto neighborhood, he shared the story of how his grandmother managed to slip through the Nazis' fingers by appearing to be desperately poor (which she was, in fact). "They assumed she was a street beggar and did not stop her," he told me. "She hid in convents until the occupation ended." Her story is one of thousands.

The Germans occupied Rome for a total of nine months, until the Allies liberated the city on June 4, 1944. At that point, Jews came out of hiding and participated in a ceremony of liberation held at the Great Synagogue in the heart of the Ghetto neighborhood. Families were reunited and, in the years that followed, the community attempted to re-create some semblance of normalcy after generations of trauma.

The Arrival of Libyan Jews in Rome

The makeup of Rome's Jewish community changed yet again with the arrival of several thousand Jews from Libya in 1967. In what was called the Six-Day War, the State of Israel fought an armed conflict against a coalition of Arab countries. Relations between Jews living in Arab nations and their neighbors had already been strained over the creation of the Jewish state, but in the aftermath of the war, attacks against Jews intensified. Nearly all of Libya's Jewish community, which had lived in cities such as Tripoli and Benghazi for centuries, fled the violence and persecution with little more than a suitcase or two and the clothes on their backs.

Libya was an Italian colony from 1911 to 1943, and afterward, the two countries maintained a shared relationship that made Italy an accessible landing spot for Libyan refugees. (Many Libyans were already conversant or fluent in Italian.) In the days and months following the Six-Day War, approximately 6,000 Libyan Jews were evacuated to Rome with the help of the Italian airline Alitalia and the Italian Navy. Some then emigrated from there to Israel or other countries, but more than 2,000 remained in Rome, largely settling in the Piazza Bologna neighborhood.

Daniela Gean, who co-owns the Middle Eastern and North African restaurant Mezè Bistrot, arrived in Rome with her family as a baby. While she has no memories of Libya, she said, "I can build Tripoli in my mind

EMMA DI VEROLI

QUI ABITAVA
GRAZIA AJÒ
NATA 1917
ARRESTATA 16.10.1943
DEPORTATA
AUSCHWITZ
ASSASSINATA 23.10.1943

from everything my parents have told me. I know it was a beautiful town by the sea. I could take my mother to the most wonderful restaurant on the most beautiful beach in Italy, and she would say, 'This is nice, but the fish in Libya was really something else.'"

The Libyan Jews' arrival in Rome was largely met with skepticism and xenophobia by the existing Jewish population. "I remember the local people used to see us as strange and uncivilized because we were coming from Africa," said Gean. "We were considered a little primitive," recalled Hamos Guetta, who created a YouTube channel focusing on Libyan and Roman Jewish cuisine (see page 78). "They did not know that Tripoli was a cosmopolitan city with wonderful architecture and people from all over the world."

Rome's Libyan Jews have held fast to many of their traditions. They founded a synagogue, Centro Beth El in Piazza Bologna, that maintains Libyan prayer styles. Many families also keep customs alive at home, serving Libyan dishes for Shabbat and holidays. And yet, over the past five decades, the community has also established its own place in Rome and built connections with the city's historic Jewish community. "Step by step, the community is now more integrated," said Gean. "We have many mixed Libyan and Roman Jewish families."

The Roman Jewish Community Today

Approximately 16,000 Jews currently call Rome their home—a fraction of the city's nearly 3 million residents, but meaningful all the same. There are approximately 30,000 Jews living across Italy (with concentrations in Milan, Venice, Turin, Florence, and Livorno), making Rome's population the largest in the country. The city is also home to nearly a dozen active synagogue congregations, more than thirty kosher (or otherwise Jewish-focused) restaurants and eateries, and a Jewish day school that instructs 800 students every year. Jewish residents are widely spread throughout the city, with higher populations in neighborhoods like Monteverde and Piazza Bologna.

A handful of Jews still live in the Ghetto neighborhood, primarily elderly residents whose families did not have the means to move elsewhere when it was dissolved. But as is true of other formerly impoverished Jewish neighborhoods around the world (e.g., Le Marais in Paris, Mile End in Montreal, and New York City's Lower East Side), the neighborhood has become gentrified in recent decades and, ironically, now accounts for some of the most fashionable, and expensive, real estate in Rome.

Although the majority of Roman Jews no longer live in the Ghetto neighborhood, the area is still an active hub of Jewish life. The day school's presence means that every weekday, in the early afternoon, the streets fill with the delighted shouts of children getting out of class. And beyond being home to a major cluster of Jewish restaurants, Via del Portico d'Ottavia also serves as a gathering spot—particularly for the Jewish elders who park themselves on benches or folding chairs to chat. "It is like an open-air JCC [Jewish Community Center]," said Pavoncello.

Most of the city's Jews identify as Orthodox, but that does not necessarily mean they are religious in terms of Shabbat observance or keeping strictly kosher. In recent decades, Rome has also become home to a small Hasidic (Chabad-Lubavitch) community, which runs a synagogue and offers resources about kosher food and Shabbat-observant accommodations to tourists and visiting students. It also helped get the Jewish school up and running. But because Rome's Jewish community identity was already so strong and solidified, Chabad's local influence has been relatively muted.

Today's Jews live as equal members of Roman society, with full protection and rights under the law, though ignorance and prejudice still exist on the margins. The community also collectively shares the trauma of October 9, 1982, when terrorists carried out a violent attack on the Tempio Maggiore (Great Synagogue). The attackers threw hand grenades and opened fire on the crowd leaving the synagogue after Shabbat morning services, injuring more than thirty people and killing a two-year old boy. As an act of both nonviolent protest and community healing, Rabbi Toaff led a silent march through the city in response to the attack. Heightened security measures for worshippers and visitors were also put into place, and they exist to this day.

Roman Jews are deeply aware of their history and proud of everything their community has overcome throughout the centuries.

Roman Jews are deeply aware of their history and proud of everything their community has overcome throughout the centuries. They are also proud of their long-standing customs and believe that honoring tradition is paramount. Still, today there are kosher sushi and hamburger restaurants in the Ghetto neighborhood. And at home, Roman Jewish children are nearly as likely to be served chicken schnitzel as Stracotto di Manzo (page 235).

Giovanni Terracina, the chef who runs the kosher catering company Le Bon Ton, put it this way: "What is traditional to my parents won't be the same as what is traditional to my son." Every Friday, for example, his wife, Yael, makes pasta with butter and Parmesan for their son because, like many busy parents, she is preparing for Shabbat and does not have time to prepare a more elaborate lunch. "Because this is what my son eats every Friday," Terracina said, "he will think this is tradition."

Terracina's anecdote represents the experience of many Roman Jews. Tradition matters, but neither the community nor the cuisine is stagnant—both are alive, evolving, and creating new traditions for the generations to come.

THE ROMAN JEWISH PANTRY

With these staples, you can stock your pantry and refrigerator like a Roman Jew.

Anchovies (Fresh and Cured)

During the Ghetto period, Rome's Jews were prohibited from buying larger and more desirable species of fish. As a result, their cuisine ended up incorporating scraps left behind at the fish market (particularly heads and spines) and smaller fish including anchovies and sardines. From these meager ingredients, they developed a variety of appetizing dishes. The restrictions also had the unintended benefit of providing the impoverished community with important nutrients like B vitamins, zinc, and omega-3 fatty acids.

Artichokes

Artichokes, particularly the regionally-grown purple and green variety, carciofi romaneschi, are the king of the Roman Jewish kitchen. See page 54 for more information on their history, their significance, and how to prepare them.

Baccalà (Salt Cod)

Traditional Roman cuisine, both Jewish and not, features plenty of salt cod (baccalà). Fresh cod fillets are thickly coated with salt and dried into stiff, well-preserved planks that have to be rehydrated before using. To do so, place the baccalà fillet in a large bowl and cover with water. Refrigerate for at least 24 (ideally, closer to 48) hours, changing the water several times, until the fish is pliable and most of the salt has been washed away.

Bottarga (Dried Fish Roe)

Bottarga is fish roe sacs (most often from mullet or tuna) that are salted, pressed to extract liquid, and dried until firm. It can be shaved or grated over dishes, and adds an umami-rich, seawater-like taste to dishes.

Caraway Seeds

Rome's Libyan Jews incorporate plenty of spices into their cooking, including caraway seeds, which lend an earthy, almost citrusy, anise-like zing to dishes.

Carne Secca

Rome's Jewish community developed a variety of cured meats (salumi) made with beef instead of the more common (but not kosher) pork. Carne secca—a fat-streaked side of beef that is rubbed with salt and pepper and cured for more than a month, until it turns silky—is arguably the most beloved. Carne secca (also called prosciutto di manzo) is primarily sold either thinly sliced at kosher butcher shops for snacking or cubed for cooking. It is difficult to find outside Rome, so be sure to try it when you visit. Beef bacon or pastrami can be substituted in some recipes.

Casalino Tomatoes

Romans love their tomatoes, particularly this variety, which grows around Rome. The tomatoes are round and slightly flattened, with distinct ribbing that makes them look like dark red mini-pumpkins. Their sweet and gently acidic flavor makes them equally good for sauces and for slicing and layering on top of bread. If you cannot find or grow them, substitute medium-sized red heirloom tomatoes.

Cicoria

Cicoria is a bitter green related to dandelion greens (the two are often used interchangeably). It grows wild around Rome and has become a central part of Roman Jewish cuisine, usually served boiled or sautéed, and sometimes topped with shaved or grated bottarga.

Curly Endive

This hearty green, which is (rather confusingly!) also marketed under the names frisée and chicory, is defined by its abundance of frilly leaves. It has a very light, yellow-white core that gradually turns green at the top of the leaves. Curly endive's flavor is quite bitter when eaten raw, but its sharpness mellows considerably when cooked.

Hot Paprika

This fire engine–red powder, which is made from dried ground hot chile peppers, is a staple in Rome's Libyan Jewish kitchens. It has a warm aroma and is significantly spicier than sweet paprika, though with less heat than cayenne. It is often sold in stores under the name Hungarian hot paprika. If you are unable to find it, you can approximate it by mixing equal parts sweet paprika and cayenne (adjust the ratio to your desired heat preference).

Mentuccia Romana

This Mediterranean herb is central to Roman Jewish cuisine, and it pairs especially well with artichoke dishes. The leaves are small and tender, and the flavor is delicate, with subtle woodsy notes. If you cannot find (or grow) it, a combination of fresh or dried spearmint leaves and oregano makes a decent approximation.

Olive Oil

All Romans share an obsession with olive oil, but for Roman Jews living during the Ghetto period, the local fruity, green-gold oil, which was inexpensive and readily available, provided a rare source of comfort. The general rule, as I was told many times while cooking with Roman Jews, is when you see the oil floating on top of the soup, that's when you know you have added enough!

While Roman Jewish fritter recipes traditionally call for olive oil, I recommend using a neutral vegetable oil with a higher smoke point, such as sunflower or grapeseed oil, instead. If you want a hint of olive taste, opt for light olive oil, which is refined enough to be suitable for deep-frying.

Passata (Tomato Puree)

Passata is an uncooked tomato puree from which all of the seeds and skin have been removed, with no added flavorings or other ingredients. The name means "passed" in Italian, and it refers to passing the tomatoes through a sieve. Passata is popular all across Italy (where it is typically sold in tall glass bottles) and can be found in many other Europe countries. It is less commonly known in the United States, though it is available in specialty food stores and larger grocery stores, as well as online. If you cannot find it, substitute ordinary canned tomato puree.

Peperoncino (Red Chile Peppers)

If you have ever strolled through an open-air market in Rome, chances are you have seen long strings of slender red chile peppers hanging above produce displays like fiery streamers. These peperoncini share a name with the pickled green peperoncini that often top pizza and Italian sandwiches in the United States—but don't confuse the two. The red peperoncini are sold fresh or dried (rather than pickled), and add heat to a variety of savory dishes. If you cannot find them, substitute red pepper flakes or another type of fresh chile.

Rice

Pasta is the primary starch for Roman Jews, but rice shows up too, thanks to the influence of Sephardi and southern Italian cuisines. Most recipes call for either Arborio (short-grain) or Carnaroli (medium-grain) rice, Italian varieties that have a relatively high starch content and maintain an al dente bite when cooked. In general, long-grain varieties like jasmine and basmati do not have the right texture to be substituted in Roman Jewish recipes.

Ricotta

Several traditional Roman Jewish recipes, including tarts and pies, incorporate ricotta, which comes from the whey left after making other cheeses. Roman Jews most commonly use sheep's-milk ricotta, which tends to have a rich, full-bodied flavor. If you cannot find it, a high-quality cow's-milk ricotta makes a worthy substitute.

Romanesco Broccoli

When autumn rolls around in Rome, the markets fill up with Romanesco broccoli. It has a rather stunning appearance, with bright chartreuse coloring and florets that spiral out in a majestic fractal pattern. Romanesco broccoli has a milder flavor than regular crown broccoli, and a crisp bite more akin to cauliflower. In the United States, it can typically be found in farmers' markets from mid- to late fall.

Sour Cherry Jam

Sour cherries cooked with sugar into a thick, sweet-tart jam, are used for several iconic Roman Jewish cakes and crostata. The jam is available at specialty food shops, larger grocery stores, and online.

Zucchine Romanesche

These Italian squash are typically smaller and lighter green than standard zucchini, with thick ridges running the length of the vegetable. They have a low moisture content, which means they don't turn mushy during cooking, and a light, nutty flavor. If you can find them, use them in any Roman Jewish recipe that calls for zucchini. Otherwise, small regular zucchini work as a substitute.

Zucchini Blossoms

Zucchini blossoms, fiori di zucca, are the bright yellow-orange flowers that are harvested from zucchini plants. The petals are fragile and velvety-soft and pack a distinct summer squash flavor. Roman cuisine makes good use of the blossoms, most famously stuffing them with mozzarella and frying them. They can be found in farmers' markets from June to September. If desired, you can reach into the center of each flower and twist off and remove the stamen or pistil at the center, which can be bitter.

VEGETABLES

Verdure

BUCCIA
EDIBIL
MOCCIA FRUTTA
Ingrosso frutta e ortaggi freschi
MOCCIA F
4.00
PALLOTT

SILKY MARINATED ZUCCHINI

Concia

SERVES 4 TO 6

"If you keep a jar of concia in the refrigerator during the summer, you will always have something delicious for making sandwiches and pasta," said Daniela Gean, a restaurateur in Rome's Monteverde neighborhood. She's right. This dish of fried zucchini marinated in vinegar, garlic, and fresh herbs is ubiquitous in Roman Jewish homes because it is equal parts tasty and useful. What's not ubiquitous, however, is the way home cooks choose to slice their zucchini. Some insist it must be cut into long planks, while others argue that thin coins are the only option. (Call me a peacemaker, but I like both methods!)

The dish's name stems from a word in the ancient Roman dialect for hanging clothes out to dry in the sun, the same way the sliced zucchini is dried before it is fried. Some cooks leave the zucchini in the sun for half a day or more! But an hour or so stacked between paper towels will also do the trick. Roman Jews exclusively use zucchine romanesche for their concia—a prominently ribbed, light green variation of the squash. It tends to be available at farmers' markets during the summer months, but if you cannot find it, regular zucchini makes a fine substitute. Serve concia as an appetizer or side dish, toss it with cooked pasta, or layer it with sliced fresh mozzarella in a satisfying sandwich.

5 medium zucchini (about 2½ pounds / 1 kg), *ends trimmed*

¼ cup (5 g) fresh basil leaves, *chopped*

¼ cup (5 g) fresh mint leaves, *chopped*

1 medium garlic clove, *finely chopped*

⅓ cup (80 ml) extra-virgin olive oil, *plus more if needed*

¼ cup (60 ml) red wine vinegar

1 teaspoon kosher salt, *plus more if needed*

½ teaspoon freshly ground black pepper

Slice the zucchini into ¼-inch- (6 mm) thick planks or rounds. Lay the zucchini out in a single layer on one or two paper towel–lined baking sheets and top with another layer of paper towels. Let stand for at least 1 hour to draw out some of the moisture.

Meanwhile, stir together the basil, mint, and garlic in a small bowl; set aside.

Heat the oil in a large frying pan over medium heat. Working in batches, fry the zucchini, turning once, until softened and lightly browned on both sides, 3 to 5 minutes per side; if the pan begins to look dry, add more oil as needed. As each batch of zucchini is done, transfer to a small baking dish, sprinkle with a bit of the herb mixture and some of the vinegar, salt, and pepper, and gently toss to combine. Continue layering the fried zucchini and the remaining ingredients until everything is used up.

Let the zucchini sit at room temperature, basting it occasionally with the juices in the baking dish, for at least 30 minutes (ideally, an hour or more) to allow the garlic to soften and the flavors to meld.

Just before serving, taste and add more salt if needed. Store leftovers, covered, in the fridge for up to 3 days.

CIRCOLO 48
VENDITA
PROMOZIONALE
VENDITA
PROMOZIONALE

Silky Marinated Zucchini, 44

ROMAN-STYLE BRAISED ARTICHOKES

Carciofi alla Romana

SERVES 4 TO 6

These fragrant, brothy artichokes are packed with garlic and herbs and simmered gently in a bath of oil and white wine until lusciously tender and flavorful. The dish is more traditionally Roman than Jewish, but it is beloved by Roman Jews and frequently served in their homes. Carciofi alla Romana is typically made with mentuccia, a mild-flavored wild herb found in the Mediterranean. If you can get it (or grow it), use it! If not, the combination of oregano and mint in this recipe mimics mentuccia's flavor. Serve the artichokes as an appetizer with crusty bread for dipping in the broth, or as a side dish to fish or meat dishes.

1 teaspoon kosher salt, *plus more as needed*

½ teaspoon freshly ground black pepper

½ teaspoon dried oregano

6 large artichokes, *cleaned according to the instructions on page 58*

½ cup (10 g) fresh flat-leaf parsley leaves, *finely chopped, plus more for serving*

¼ cup (5 g) fresh mint leaves, *finely chopped, plus more for serving*

3 medium garlic cloves, *finely chopped*

3 tablespoons extra-virgin olive oil, *plus more for serving*

½ cup (120 ml) water

¼ cup (60 ml) dry white wine

Stir together the salt, pepper, and oregano in a small bowl, then sprinkle and rub the cleaned artichokes evenly inside and out with the mixture. Combine the chopped parsley, mint, and garlic in a small bowl and sprinkle it evenly inside the artichokes, packing it into the cavities and spreading it between some of the leaves. (It is okay if some of the herbs fall out of the artichokes; just pack them in as best as you can.)

Heat the oil in a medium deep pot over medium heat. Place the artichokes cut side down in the oil, and allow to sizzle for about 1 minute. Add the water and wine and bring the liquid to a bubble, then cover the pot and reduce the heat to low. Cook the artichokes, undisturbed, until very tender, 25 to 30 minutes. You should be able to pierce the flesh of the heart with a knife without any resistance.

Transfer the artichokes to a serving plate or shallow bowl. Spoon a generous amount of the cooking liquid over the top and serve warm or at room temperature, sprinkled with more salt and chopped herbs and drizzled with a little more olive oil.

למען היתומים
DATE
PER GLI ORFANI

ARTICHOKE CARPACCIO

Carpaccio di Carciofi

SERVES 4

A vegetarian play on beef carpaccio, this dish dresses shaved raw artichoke hearts with a lemony vinaigrette, then showers them with shaved Parmesan. When I watched chef Giovanni Terracina make it in the kitchen of his Rome-based kosher catering company, Le Bon Ton, he told me he likes the artichoke slivers to be quite crunchy. For more tender artichokes, you can let them marinate in the dressing for longer. Giovanni also recommended experimenting with flavors to make the dish your own; he particularly likes to add crushed pink peppercorns, toasted coriander seeds, or a splash of Cognac. The dish serves four as part of an appetizer spread, but I could eat it all myself in one sitting with some crusty bread. It scales up well if you are serving a crowd.

2 tablespoons fresh lemon juice

2 tablespoons fresh orange or blood orange juice

2 tablespoons extra-virgin olive oil

1 small garlic clove, *minced, grated, or pushed through a press*

¼ teaspoon kosher salt, *plus more for serving*

⅛ teaspoon freshly ground black pepper, *plus more for serving*

4 large artichokes, *cleaned according to the instructions on page 58, and halved lengthwise*

Chopped fresh flat-leaf parsley and shaved Parmesan *for serving*

Whisk together the lemon juice, orange juice, olive oil, garlic, salt, and pepper in a large bowl.

Using a sharp knife or a mandoline, slice the cleaned artichoke halves very thin, ideally 1/8 inch (3 cm) thick or thinner. Add the slices to the citrus juice mixture, tossing well to coat. Let the artichokes marinate, tossing occasionally, for at least 30 minutes, or up to 1 day. (The artichokes will continue to soften as they sit.)

Transfer the artichokes to a serving platter, sprinkle with a little more salt and pepper, and top with parsley and wide slices of shaved Parmesan. Serve immediately.

Artichokes: A Roman Jewish Love Affair

THERE IS PERHAPS no greater love affair on earth than the flame that burns between Roman Jews and artichokes. The ancient Mediterranean thistle, which sits at the center of cucina Ebraico-Romanesca (Roman Jewish cuisine), serves as a totem of the community's identity and offers a great source of pleasure and pride. I have found that most food-related conversations I begin with Roman Jews eventually wend their way back to artichokes—the love simply runs that deep.

History

Artichokes, which are native to the Mediterranean, are likely a domesticated variety of the wild cardoon. They were known to ancient Romans (first-century aristocratic Romans ate artichokes preserved in honey and vinegar), but they seem to have disappeared from the cuisine after the fall of Rome. During the medieval period, they were prized by the Moors, who began cultivating them in earnest in Spain and Sicily. (The name *artichoke* derives from the Arabic word *al-kharshuf,* which means "ground thorn.")

Like other vegetables introduced to Spain and Sicily through Arab cuisine (most notably eggplant and fennel), artichokes were at first regarded with suspicion or distaste by the general public. But the region's Sephardi Jews generally had limited means and fewer culinary options, and so they took to these vegetables and created a variety of dishes that eventually helped raise their profiles. Non-Jewish Italians in the South originally dismissed artichokes as "the Jewish vegetable." They eventually caught on to the thistle's hidden pleasures, but, as the Italian Jewish historian and scholar Ariel Toaff wrote in his essay "The Cuisine of the Jews of Italy," "It takes time to engage the palate of a society."

Catherine de' Medici is widely credited with introducing artichokes to France (and beyond) in the sixteenth century, following her marriage to Henry II. But what interests me more is how, during that same period, Sephardi Jews fleeing Spain and the South of Italy after the Spanish Inquisition brought their beloved thistle to Rome. There, in the Roman Ghetto, the artichoke encountered the locals' fondness for deep-frying foods (see page 132), and the famous deep-fried artichokes, carciofi alla Giudia, were born.

Artichoke Season

True Roman artichokes, called carciofi romaneschi, are large and globe-shaped, with vibrant leaves stained purple and green. Unlike many other artichoke varieties, they grow with almost no fuzzy choke, which makes them ideal for frying or braising whole.

Carciofi romaneschi are only in season for a few short months each year, typically from late February to early April. In spring, the restaurants lining Via del Portico d'Ottavia, the main street of the Jewish Ghetto neighborhood, display majestic towers and tightly bundled bouquets of the beautiful thistles, beckoning customers inside. The rest of the year, restaurants import other varieties from Sicily, Sardinia, and Normandy. They are still supremely delicious, but locals insist they are not as sublime as the homegrown version.

Kosher Controversy

In the late 2010s, artichokes became a major source of controversy for Roman Jews. Israel's chief rabbinate decreed that because an artichoke's tightly interlocking leaves might be host to small insects (which would not be kosher), the plant itself should also be treated as unfit for consumption.

Needless to say, locals did not take well to a ruling that effectively banned their most culturally important foodstuff—particularly a ruling coming from outside their own community. Defining artichoke consumption as unkosher would have a devastating financial impact on Rome's Jewish restaurants, many of which had built their reputations around carciofi alla Giudia. They also simply found the notion insulting—both to their centuries-old culinary traditions, and to the people who skillfully uphold them. "Jewish Roman women know how to inspect the artichoke, and better than the rabbis," said Rabbi Umberto Piperno in a 2018 *New York Times* article on the subject.

In Milan, where artichokes are not as central to local Jewish cuisine, the local rabbinate relented. There only the bottom part of artichokes are served, and only after thorough cleaning and inspection. In Rome, however, the chief rabbi supported his community by pushing back against the ruling from Israel. "As a result," said Michele Pavoncello, who runs the kosher-style restaurant Nonna Betta, along with his father, Umberto, "artichokes remain kosher in Rome."

How to Clean Artichokes

As the old adage goes, "two Jews, three opinions." But when it comes to Roman Jews and artichokes, the ratio of opinions is much higher. On one visit to Rome, I witnessed a spirited argument break out between two Jewish community elders sitting on one of the benches along Via del Portico d'Ottavia. The source of the tension? Artichokes, naturally, and how best to trim away their tough outer leaves in order to prepare them. Both sides made their cases with the precision of Talmudic scholars and the swagger of prizefighters. After all, to Roman Jews, artichokes are so much more than just food—they are central to "la dolce vita."

Watching a skilled artichoke cleaner at work is mesmerizing. Starting at the base and spiraling their way up, they whittle away with astonishing speed, removing an impressive amount of roughage to expose the tender inner leaves and heart. Mastering the technique is not easy, and I would be lying if I said I am an artichoke trimming expert. But even a less-than-elegantly cleaned artichoke is well worth the effort. In other words, don't let the fear of not being perfect stop you from trying.

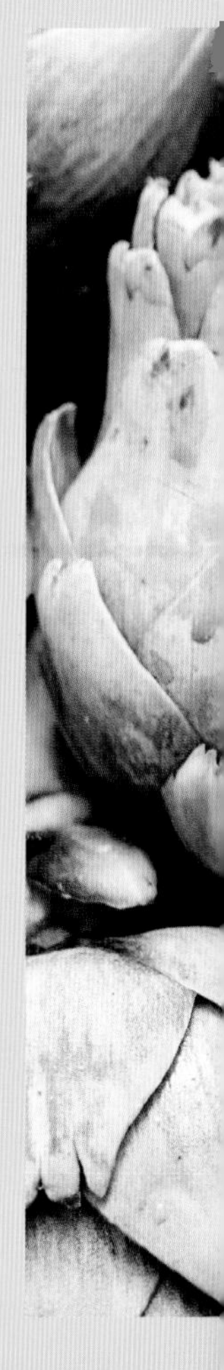

WHAT YOU NEED

A Paring Knife Roman Jews use a curved paring knife (sometimes called a peeling knife or bird's-beak knife) to peel back the woody top layer of the artichoke stems and trim away the tough leaves. The curve is helpful for working around the artichoke's globe-like shape. If you do not have access to one, however, any sharp paring knife will work.

Lemons Artichokes oxidize and turn brown very quickly, but the acidity of lemon juice helps to combat the effect. Before you begin, halve a lemon and keep it at the ready, rubbing the lemon halves over any trimmed areas that are newly exposed to oxygen.

THE PROCESS

Step 1: Begin by pulling off the tough dark green outer leaves from the artichoke. Keep removing the leaves until you expose the tender, lighter-colored inner leaves **(A)**.

A

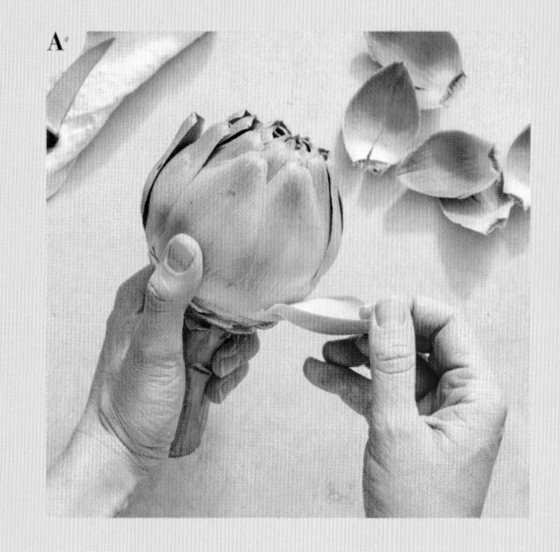

Step 2: Using the paring knife, gently trim away the woody outer layer from the stem and the thicker bright green parts at the base of the artichoke **(B,C)**, rubbing the exposed areas with lemon **(D)**. If you are making Carciofi alla Giudia (page 128), trim off all but about ½ inch (1.25 cm) of the stem. For other dishes, you can leave the stem longer.

D

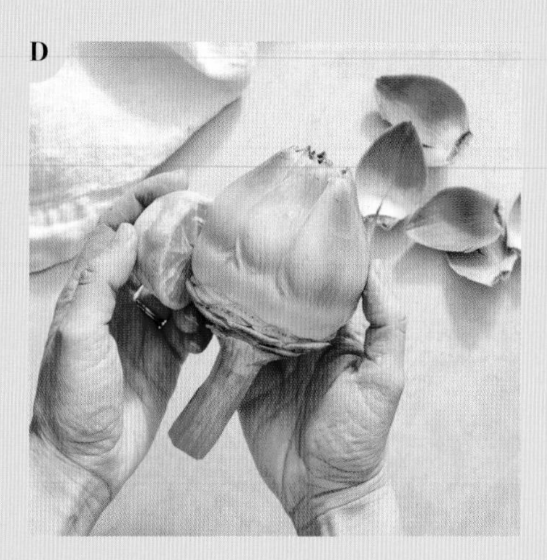

Step 3: Use the knife to make a horizontal cut to remove the top half of the remaining leaves **(E)**, and generously rub the exposed areas with more lemon. The artichoke should look like a closed flower **(F)**.

Step 4: Using a melon baller or sturdy spoon (a serrated-edged grapefruit spoon works particularly well), scoop out and discard any hairy choke in the center of the artichoke **(G)**.

G

Step 5: If you need to store the cleaned artichokes for a while before using them, drop them into a bowl of cold water that has been acidulated with the juice of a couple of lemons **(H)**. Remove the artichokes and pat dry before using them **(I)**.

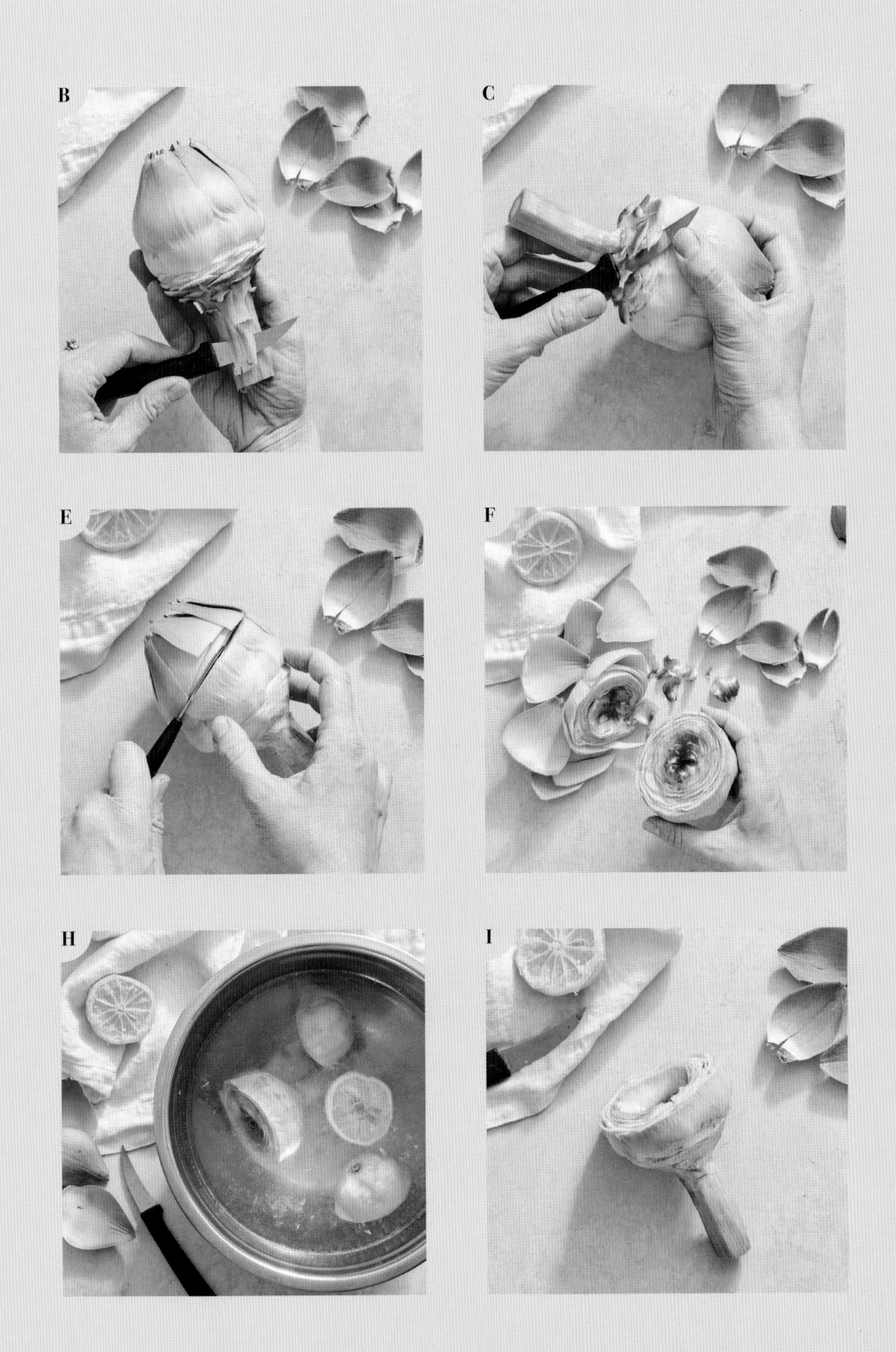
B
C
E
F
H
I

CRISP AND LEMONY PICKLED VEGETABLES

Msaiier

SERVES 6

This simple Libyan Jewish dish of lemony, lightly pickled vegetables serves as both an appetizer and a refreshing palate cleanser between courses. Msaiier is readily customizable—you can swap in or add other vegetables like cucumber, bell pepper, radish, and kohlrabi. My friend and the owner of Mezè Bistrot in Rome, Daniela Gean, told me she prefers to use a mix of fennel, cauliflower, and carrots because they stand up to the lemon juice without getting too quickly "cooked" or wilted. The fresh chile peppers are optional but add a nice kick.

3 medium fennel bulbs (about 1½ pounds / 680 g), *quartered, cored, and thinly sliced lengthwise*

1 small head cauliflower or half a medium head (about 1 pound / 454 g), *cored and cut into small florets*

2 medium carrots, *peeled and cut into thick matchsticks*

1 to 2 fresh red chile peppers, *seeds removed and thinly sliced (optional)*

2 tablespoons fresh lemon juice, *or more if needed*

1 teaspoon kosher salt, *or more if needed*

Combine the fennel, cauliflower, carrots, and chile peppers, if using, in a large bowl. Drizzle with the lemon juice, sprinkle with the salt, and toss well. Taste and add more salt and/or lemon juice, if desired.

Let the mixture sit for at least 15 minutes before serving to allow the flavors to meld and the vegetables to soften slightly. Leftovers can be stored for up to 3 days in the fridge. The longer the mixture sits, the more the vegetables will soften.

ROASTED TOMATO HALVES

Pomodori a Mezzo

SERVES 4 TO 6

No Roman Jewish Shabbat table is complete without pomodori a mezzo—halved tomatoes generously drizzled with olive oil and roasted until they are candy-sweet and lusciously soft. The dish is traditionally made with ruby-colored Casalino tomatoes, a regional variety that is round, slightly flat, and ribbed, like a mini-pumpkin. If you cannot source them, swap in the best-quality ripe tomatoes you can find. Serve pomodori a mezzo with crusty bread as an appetizer, or as a summery side dish alongside just about anything.

¼ cup (60 ml) extra-virgin olive oil

6 medium ripe tomatoes (about 2 pounds / 907 g)

2 small garlic cloves, *finely chopped*

1 teaspoon granulated sugar

1 teaspoon kosher salt, *plus more if needed*

¼ teaspoon freshly ground black pepper

Finely chopped fresh basil *for serving (optional)*

Preheat the oven to 375°F (190°C). Brush a 9 × 13-inch (23 × 33 cm) baking dish with about 1 tablespoon of the olive oil. Halve the tomatoes crosswise and gently squeeze the halves over a bowl to remove most of the seeds and liquid; use a spoon if necessary. (Discard the liquid and seeds or reserve for another use.)

Place the seeded tomato halves cut side up in the baking dish. Sprinkle evenly with the garlic, followed by the sugar, salt, and pepper. (Do not be tempted to combine the garlic with the seasonings first, or it will be clumpy and difficult to sprinkle.) Drizzle the tomatoes evenly with the remaining olive oil.

Roast the tomatoes for 30 minutes. Give the baking dish a gentle shake, then continue roasting until the tomatoes are very tender and beginning to collapse, 40 to 45 minutes, depending on their size and ripeness.

Remove from the oven and transfer the tomatoes to a serving dish to cool. Serve slightly warm or at room temperature, sprinkled with chopped basil, if using, and a little more salt, if desired.

The Matriarch of the Ghetto

WHENEVER I WALK down Via del Portico d'Ottavia, the main street that runs the length of Rome's Jewish Ghetto neighborhood, I look out for the Jewish nonnas (grandmothers). And there they are, without fail—small clusters of women (and sometimes men too) ranging in age from around seventy to over ninety, sitting on benches and folding chairs, shooting the breeze and keeping watch over the streets they grew up walking.

Of this group, Italia Tagliacozzo stands apart. When I first heard of Italia, who was described to me as "the grandmother of Roman Jewish cooking," I envisioned a housecoat, a graying bun, and glasses framing a face creased with wisdom. But meeting Italia changed my admittedly oversimplified expectations. She is an entirely different kind of grandmother—think the elegantly coiffed, Italian gold-bedecked glamour of Sophia Loren meets the take-no-prisoners, girl-boss energy of Anna Wintour.

Born in 1938, only a few years before the Nazi occupation of Rome, Italia survived the war by hiding in a convent. Her determination and fiery spirit led her to a prosperous career in fashion (she owned a leather goods store). At the same time, she gained a reputation within the community as an excellent home cook. "I would have people over for dinner, and they would say, 'Why don't you open a restaurant?'" Italia told me.

So she did. In 1999, she partnered with her son-in-law Rafael to open La Taverna del Ghetto in the heart of the the neighborhood. Italia has personally trained nearly all of La Taverna's cooks in cucina Giudaico Romanesco

(Roman Jewish cooking), ensuring that the dishes coming out of the kitchen meet her exacting standards. If, say, too many carrots made it into the sauce ("Too sweet!" she'd insist), that batch would not make it to customers' plates.

"When I make the sauce, people wipe their plates clean," she told me. Italia still comes to the restaurant several times a week, dressed to the nines and ready for business, to check on the kitchen and make sure that diners are satisfied.

SAVORY TOMATO SPREAD

Merduma

SERVES 4 TO 6

A cousin of Moroccan matbucha (a cooked tomato condiment), this Libyan Jewish tomato spread tastes like concentrated sunshine. This recipe was inspired by one I watched Ghily Guetta (whose father, Hamos, hosts a Libyan Jewish culinary channel on YouTube; see page 78) make in preparation for her family's Shabbat dinner. Guetta recommends using a nonstick frying pan to make sure the tomatoes do not cling to the bottom of it as they turn concentrated and jammy toward the end of the cooking process. Serve the spread with warm challah or other bread for unparalleled dipping.

¼ cup (60 ml) extra-virgin olive oil, *plus more for serving*

5 medium garlic cloves, *minced, grated, or pushed through a press*

1 fresh red chile pepper, *seeds removed, if desired, and finely chopped*

3 pounds (1.4 kg) ripe red tomatoes, *cored and chopped into approximately ½-inch (1.25 cm) pieces*

2 tablespoons tomato paste

1½ teaspoons kosher salt, *plus more if needed*

1 teaspoon granulated sugar

Hot paprika *for serving (optional)*

Heat the olive oil in a large frying pan over medium heat. Add the garlic and chile pepper and let sizzle, stirring, until fragrant, about 1 minute. Add the tomatoes, tomato paste, salt, and sugar and cook, stirring often to prevent sticking, until the mixture turns thick and jammy, 40 minutes to 1 hour. (The timing will depend on how juicy your tomatoes are to start.) If the mixture seems to be close to burning toward the end of cooking, nudge the heat down to medium-low and stir more frequently.

Remove the pan from the heat, taste, and stir in a little more salt if needed. Transfer the spread to a serving bowl and let cool until warm or room temperature.

Just before serving, drizzle the merduma with a little more olive oil and sprinkle with hot paprika, if desired. Store leftovers, covered, in the refrigerator for up to 3 days.

SAUTÉED SPINACH WITH PINE NUTS AND RAISINS

Spinaci con Pinoli e Passerine

SERVES 4

Raisins and pine nuts are two hallmark ingredients of Sephardi cuisine that traveled with the Spanish and Sicilian Jewish refugees who resettled in Rome in the wake of the Spanish Inquisition. Here they lend jammy and buttery notes to an otherwise basic dish of sautéed spinach. While *uvetta* is the commonly used Italian word for raisin, the word *passerine* in the recipe's name comes from the term *uva passa*, which translates roughly (and charmingly!) as "fainted grape." The shower of lemon zest added at the end of cooking is not traditional, but it adds an extra hint of brightness.

3 tablespoons plus 1 teaspoon extra-virgin olive oil

¼ cup (30 g) pine nuts

Kosher salt and freshly ground black pepper

1 small yellow onion, *finely chopped*

1 pound (454 g) spinach leaves (not baby spinach), *rinsed and drained (do not pat dry)*

¼ cup (35 g) dark or golden raisins

1 packed teaspoon grated lemon zest *(from about 1 medium lemon)*

Heat 1 teaspoon of the oil in a large frying pan over medium heat. Add the pine nuts and cook, stirring occasionally, until golden and fragrant, 2 to 3 minutes. Transfer the pine nuts to a small bowl, sprinkle with a little salt, and set aside.

Add the remaining 3 tablespoons oil to the pan and heat over medium heat. Add the onion with a sprinkle of salt and cook, stirring occasionally, until softened and lightly browned, 6 to 8 minutes. Add the spinach (if necessary, add it in two batches, allowing the first batch to cook down a bit before adding the second), cover the pan, and cook until the spinach wilts, about 2 minutes.

Uncover the pan, raise the heat to medium-high, and continue cooking, stirring or tossing with tongs occasionally, until the spinach leaves are tender and silky and most of the liquid has evaporated, 3 to 5 minutes.

Remove the pan from the heat and stir in the raisins, half of the toasted pine nuts, the lemon zest, ¼ teaspoon salt, and a generous amount of black pepper. Taste and add more salt, if desired.

Use the tongs to transfer the spinach mixture to a serving dish (leaving behind any excess cooking liquid) and sprinkle with the remaining pine nuts. Serve hot or warm.

BRAISED PEAS WITH ONION

Piselli in Tegame

SERVES 4 TO 6

I first came across a recipe for this verdant springtime dish (the name translates, rather sweetly, as "peas in a pan") in Giuliano Malizia's cookbook *La Cucina Ebraico-Romanesca*. Then, on a visit to Rome, virtually everyone I spoke to mentioned it, along with their views on whether or not it should contain sugar. My version does (just a little) and also includes two less traditional additions—red pepper flakes and lemon zest—that help make the combination of peas and onions sing. These simple peas make an effortless plus-one to just about anything you are serving.

3 tablespoons extra-virgin olive oil

1 medium yellow onion, *finely chopped*

4 cups (500 g) shelled fresh or frozen peas *(see Note)*

⅓ cup (80 ml) water or vegetable broth

¾ teaspoon kosher salt, *plus more if needed*

½ teaspoon granulated sugar

¼ teaspoon freshly ground black pepper

½ cup (10 g) fresh flat-leaf parsley leaves, *finely chopped*

¼ teaspoon red pepper flakes

1 packed teaspoon grated lemon zest *(from about 1 medium lemon)*

Heat the oil in a large frying pan over medium-low heat. Add the onion and cook, stirring occasionally, until softened but not browned, 6 to 8 minutes.

Add the peas, water or broth, salt, sugar, and black pepper, turn the heat up to medium, and cook until the peas are tender and most of the liquid has evaporated, about 5 minutes. (If starting with fresh peas, this might take a few minutes longer; cover the pan for the first few minutes of cooking to help soften them.) Stir in the parsley and red pepper flakes and cook until the parsley wilts, about 1 minute.

Remove from heat and stir in the lemon zest. Taste and add more salt if needed. Serve hot or warm.

NOTE: *If starting with fresh peas in the pod, you will need approximately 4 pounds/1.8 kg peas.*

ROASTED CIPOLLINI ONIONS

Cipolline al Forno

SERVES 4 TO 6

This dish of roasted cipollini onions will perfume your house with the intoxicating scent of sweet, caramelized alliums and woodsy rosemary. And it tastes just as good as it smells. Giulia Bassan, a Roman Jew currently living outside Philadelphia, told me her family often serves these as part of their Yom Kippur break fast meal, but they are also a welcome addition to any weeknight or Shabbat dinner. If you can't find cipollini, pearl onions can be substituted.

Kosher salt

2½ pounds (1.1 kg) small cipollini onions

¼ cup (60 ml) extra-virgin olive oil

2 tablespoons red wine vinegar

1 tablespoon *finely chopped* fresh rosemary, *plus 2 small rosemary sprigs*

1 teaspoon granulated sugar

¼ teaspoon freshly ground black pepper

Preheat the oven to 400°F (200°C).

Bring a large pot of generously salted water to a boil over high heat. Add the onions and blanch for about 2 minutes, then drain in a colander, rinse with cool water, and drain again. Trim the root and stem ends from the onions, then slip them out of their skins. If any of the onions are thick, halve them horizontally.

Transfer the onions to a 9 × 13-inch (23 x 33 cm) baking dish. Drizzle with the olive oil and vinegar, then sprinkle with the chopped rosemary, sugar, 1 teaspoon salt, and the pepper and toss to coat. Tuck the rosemary sprigs into the baking dish.

Roast, shaking the baking dish and stirring a few times, until the cipollini are golden brown and tender, 35 to 40 minutes. Remove from the oven, transfer to a serving dish, and serve warm.

ROASTED SUMMER VEGETABLES

Verdure al Forno

SERVES 4 TO 6

Roasted vegetables make a frequent appearance on Roman Jewish tables, especially when there is an abundance of summer produce. The recipe may seem quite basic, but the resulting flavors are much more dramatic than the ingredients suggest. I like to swap vegetables in and out, depending on what I have around, and I occasionally toss in hearty chopped herbs like fresh rosemary, thyme, or oregano before roasting. Serve the vegetables as a side for meat and chicken dishes, or dress them up with punchy Salsa Verde (page 75) and enjoy as a light lunch.

1 medium eggplant (about 1 pound / 454 g), *peeled and cut into ¾-inch (2 cm) pieces*

1 large zucchini (about ¾ pound / 340 g), *cut into ¾-inch (2 cm) pieces*

1 red bell pepper (about ½ pound / 227 g), *seeded and cut into ¾-inch (2 cm) pieces*

2 cups (300 g) cherry tomatoes

3 medium Yukon Gold potatoes (about 1½ pounds / 680 g), *cut into ¾-inch (2 cm) pieces*

8 medium garlic cloves, *smashed and peeled*

½ cup (120 ml) extra-virgin olive oil

1¼ teaspoons kosher salt, *plus more if needed*

½ teaspoon freshly ground black pepper, *plus more if needed*

Preheat the oven to 425°F (220°C).

Add the eggplant, zucchini, bell pepper, tomatoes, potatoes, and garlic to a large bowl. Drizzle with the oil, sprinkle with the salt and pepper, and toss to completely coat the vegetables. Divide the vegetables evenly between two large baking sheets and spread them into an even layer.

Roast, tossing or stirring the vegetables and rotating the baking sheets top to bottom halfway through cooking, until golden brown and tender, 25 to 30 minutes.

Transfer the vegetables to a bowl, taste, and add more salt and/or pepper, if desired. Serve hot or at room temperature.

NOTE: *The eggplant soaks up a lot of the oil in this recipe. If you decide to swap the eggplant out for another vegetable, cut back to about ⅓ cup (80 ml) oil.*

GARLICKY PARSLEY SAUCE

Salsa Verde

SERVES 4 TO 6

Serve this verdant parsley sauce over any meat, fish, or vegetable dish that would play well with an extra hit of bright flavor. I particularly like pairing it with the classic Roman Jewish lamb dish Abbacchio alla Giudia (page 248), and with Verdure al Forno (page 74), roasted summer vegetables.

1 medium bunch flat-leaf parsley, *tough bottom stems removed*

1 tablespoon brine-packed capers, *drained and finely chopped*

1 large garlic clove, *minced, grated, or pushed through a press*

1 packed teaspoon grated lemon zest *(from about 1 medium lemon)*

3 tablespoons fresh lemon juice

¾ teaspoon kosher salt, *plus more if needed*

¼ teaspoon red pepper flakes, *plus more if needed*

⅓ cup (80 ml) extra-virgin olive oil

Very finely chop the parsley and transfer it to a medium bowl. Add the capers, garlic, lemon zest, lemon juice, salt, and red pepper flakes and mix well to combine.

Whisking steadily, add the olive oil in a steady stream. Taste and add more salt and/or red pepper flakes, if desired. Serve immediately, or store, covered, in the fridge, for up to 2 days.

SAUTÉED DANDELION GREENS

Cicoria Ripassata

SERVES 4 TO 6

I have a soft spot for "difficult" vegetables, particularly bitter and spicy greens that can challenge the palate as much as they delight. Dandelion greens (called *cicoria* in Italian) are no exception. The greens grow wild in Rome, which made them an easily accessible source of nutrition for Roman Jews confined to the Ghetto. A quick dip in boiling water mellows their sharp bite, while a slick of garlic-scented olive oil and a bit of heat from red pepper flakes transform them into something special. When I enjoyed cicoria ripassata at the gracious Shabbat table of Stefania Gai and Massimo Bassan, Stefania topped the dish with shaved bottarga, which added an extra hit of brine and umami. But even without the dried fish roe, the garlicky greens make a memorable side.

2 pounds (907 g) dandelion greens, *tough bottom stems trimmed*

¼ cup (60 ml) extra-virgin olive oil

6 medium garlic cloves, *thinly sliced*

½ teaspoon red pepper flakes, *or more if needed*

¾ teaspoon kosher salt, *or more if needed*

Grated or shaved bottarga (*optional*)

Bring a large pot of water to a boil over high heat. Meanwhile, thoroughly wash the dandelion greens; drain. Add the greens to the boiling water and cook, stirring once or twice, until just wilted, 3 to 4 minutes. Use tongs to transfer the greens to a colander in the sink to drain.

Heat the oil in a large frying pan over medium heat. Add the garlic and red pepper flakes and cook, stirring, until fragrant, 1 to 2 minutes. Add the drained greens and toss with the tongs to coat with the fragrant oil. Sprinkle with the salt, then taste and add more salt and/or red pepper flakes, if desired.

Transfer to a serving dish and serve hot or warm, topped with bottarga, if desired.

Rome's Libyan YouTube Star

I *HAVE NEVER ENCOUNTERED* anyone else like Hamos Guetta, a Rome and Tel Aviv–based fashion designer who moonlights as a cultural historian and chronicler of Libyan and Roman Jewish dishes on YouTube. Guetta, who fled Libya with his family in 1967 at the age of twelve and found refuge in Rome, had always had an affinity for cooking. "From the age of four, my mother would stand me on a chair in the kitchen to help her form meatballs," he told me. "From there, I saw everything."

He started his YouTube page in 2001 as a way to capture and pass down recipes and heritage to his three daughters. Today the channel hosts hundreds of videos shot and edited by Guetta—many featuring an elder from the community demonstrating how to make an iconic dish—and it has, rather astonishingly, amassed more than 20,000 subscribers. Guetta also founded a WhatsApp chat group for speakers of the Jewish Arabic dialect he grew up with in Libya. With no Jews remaining in Libya today, his work helps to build community and preserve a vanishing world. (He finds many of his videos' subjects through connections from the group.)

Guetta's boundless energy, his strong opinions about food, and his insatiable curiosity jump through the screen, even for those who do not understand Italian or Hebrew. (The majority of the videos are recorded in one or the other of the two languages.) He derives great pleasure from cracking the code for closely safeguarded recipes. "Libyan Jews don't always like to share their dishes," he told me. "But to me, breaking the secrets is my job."

His tireless efforts have paid off, both for his daughters and for his community of followers. I had the good fortune of cooking with one of his daughters, Ghily Guetta, in her apartment in Rome's Piazza Bologna neighborhood. Although only in her early thirties, she has become an accomplished home cook—much, in part, she said, because of her father. "Sometimes, even when I think I already know how to make a dish, I still watch the videos to be sure I get it right," she said. "It is like having a grandma with me while I cook."

FENNEL GRATIN

Finocchi Gratinati

SERVES 6

Sweet and tender baked fennel plays very well with dairy, making it an ideal vegetable to give the gratinati treatment. In her handwritten cookbook *Dal 1880 ad Oggi: La Cucina Ebraica della Mia Famiglia* (see page 152), Donatella Limentani Pavoncello recommends serving fennel gratin for Shavuot, but the dish's decadent flavor makes it a worthy anytime side. I sometimes even eat it alone for dinner, along with a salad and some crusty bread or challah to mop up the flavorful juices at the bottom of the baking dish.

4 medium fennel bulbs (about 2 pounds / 907 g), *quartered, cores removed, and thinly sliced*

4 medium garlic cloves, *thinly sliced*

4 tablespoons (55 g) cold unsalted butter, *cut into small pieces*

½ teaspoon kosher salt

½ teaspoon freshly ground black pepper

¾ cup (180 ml) vegetable broth, *store-bought or homemade (page 109)*

2 cups (140 g) freshly grated Parmesan

Preheat the oven to 425°F (220°C).

Add the fennel, garlic, half of the butter, the salt, and pepper to a 9 × 13-inch (23 by 33 cm) baking dish and toss with tongs to combine, then spread the fennel out in the dish. Pour the vegetable broth evenly over the top. Cover the baking dish with foil and bake, tossing or stirring the fennel pieces once halfway through, until the fennel is tender, about 30 minutes.

Remove the foil and stir about half of the Parmesan into the fennel. Dot the remaining butter pieces over top and sprinkle with the rest of the Parmesan. Bake, uncovered, until the gratin is golden brown and bubbling, 15 to 20 minutes.

Remove the gratin from the oven and let cool slightly before serving.

NOTE: *Grate the Parmesan on the small holes of a box grater rather than with a Microplane so you end up with larger shreds rather than wispy fluffs of cheese.*

CURLY ENDIVE AND ANCHOVY PIE

Aliciotti con l'Indivia

SERVES 4 TO 6

On a recent trip to Rome, I sat down with Michele Pavoncello, who runs the kosher restaurant Nonna Betta with his father, Umberto. From our outside table, we could see the ruins of the ancient fish market at Portico d'Ottavia, about fifty feet away. "The legend is that the famous Roman Jewish recipe of curly endive [also called frisée and chicory] and anchovies was born in the fish market," Pavoncello told me. "In Roman times, when there was no refrigeration, the fish sellers stacked fish between layers of lettuce to keep it fresh." From there, he said, it was only a short leap for home cooks to generously drizzle the whole jumble with olive oil and transform it into a nourishing side dish.

Regardless of the story's historical accuracy, aliciotti con l'indivia is undoubtedly a specialty of the Roman Ghetto. Today it is offered at virtually every restaurant lining Via del Portico d'Ottavia, but it is simple to prepare at home. (Save time by asking your fishmonger to clean the anchovies for you!) While it would hardly be traditional, vegetarians can omit the anchovy layer for a tasty dish of garlicky wilted greens.

3 large heads curly endive (about 1 pound / 454 g), *tough bottom stems removed, leaves chopped*

1 teaspoon kosher salt, *plus more for sprinkling*

¼ teaspoon freshly ground black pepper, *plus more for sprinkling*

2 medium garlic cloves, *finely chopped*

½ pound (227 g) fresh anchovies, *cleaned (see Note)*

⅓ cup (80 ml) extra-virgin olive oil

Soak the chopped endive in a large bowl of cool water for a few minutes, then lift out of the water, leaving any grit or dirt behind, and spin-dry, working in batches, in a salad spinner. Transfer to a large colander set over a large bowl and sprinkle with the salt and pepper. Gently squeeze the greens with your hands to soften them and coat them with the salt and pepper. Let sit for 1 hour to allow some of the bitter liquid to drain off.

Preheat the oven to 350°F (180°C).

Gently pat the endive dry with paper towels. Spread half of the endive in the bottom of a 9-inch (23 cm) square baking dish. Sprinkle the chopped garlic over the endive, then arrange the anchovies evenly on top. Top the anchovies with the remaining endive, sprinkle with a little more salt and pepper, and drizzle evenly with the olive oil.

Bake until the endive is tender and the top is golden, 35 to 40 minutes. Serve hot or warm, scooped onto plates.

NOTE: *To clean fresh anchovies, cut off their heads, then slice vertically down each fish and open them out like a butterfly. Remove the bones and innards, gently rinse the anchovies, and pat dry with paper towels.*

SABEK
EVO

STEWED EGGPLANT AND ONIONS

Malignane Scinicate

SERVES 6

Eggplant is a central vegetable in Roman Jewish cuisine. And malignane (the name is a dialectical variation on melanzane, the Italian word for eggplant), is a traditional dish of the Ghetto. In older recipes, the eggplant is simply stewed with onions in oil and seasoned with salt and pepper. I took a little creative license and dressed up that base with a bit of tomato, vinegar, and herbs to give it depth and balance. The bright, velvety-textured eggplant can be served warm or at room temperature as an appetizer or a side. Or try tucking it into a square of Pizza Bianca (page 190) along with slices of fresh mozzarella for an amazing sandwich.

3 medium eggplants (about 3 pounds / 1.4 kg), *peeled and cut into 1-inch (2.5 cm) cubes*

Kosher salt

½ cup (120 ml) plus 3 tablespoons extra-virgin olive oil, *plus more for serving*

2 medium yellow onions, *halved through the root and thinly sliced*

4 medium garlic cloves, *chopped*

¼ teaspoon freshly ground black pepper

2 tablespoons fresh oregano leaves, *finely chopped*

2 tablespoons red wine vinegar, *plus more if needed*

¼ cup (60 g) tomato paste

1 cup (250 g) tomato puree (passata)

1 cup (240 ml) water

¼ cup (5 g) fresh flat-leaf parsley leaves, *finely chopped, plus more for serving*

Place the eggplant in a large colander, sprinkle with 1 tablespoon salt, and toss to coat. (If the eggplant pieces don't fit into one colander, divide them and the salt between two colanders.) Place a heavy plate on top of the eggplant to weight it down and allow it to sit for 1 hour to drain off some of the bitter liquid.

Preheat the oven to 425°F (220°C).

Divide the eggplant pieces evenly between two large baking sheets and pat dry with paper towels. Drizzle ¼ cup (60 ml) of the oil over the eggplant on each sheet, toss to coat, and spread out on the sheets. Roast, stirring the eggplant and rotating the baking sheets top to bottom halfway through cooking, until golden brown and tender, 30 to 35 minutes. Remove from the oven.

Meanwhile, heat the remaining 3 tablespoons oil in a large frying pan over medium. Add the onions and cook, stirring occasionally, until softened and beginning to caramelize, 10 to 15 minutes. Stir in the garlic, 1 teaspoon salt, the black pepper, and oregano and cook until the garlic is softened, 2 to 3 minutes. Add the vinegar and cook, stirring, until it has evaporated.

Add the tomato paste, tomato puree, roasted eggplant, and water to the pan and stir to combine. Raise the heat to medium-high and bring the mixture to a boil, then reduce the heat to medium-low and cook, stirring occasionally, until most of the water has evaporated and the eggplant is silky and saucy, about 15 minutes.

Stir in the parsley, taste, and add additional salt and/or vinegar, if desired. The flavor continues to develop off the heat, so serve warm or at room temperature, drizzled with a little olive oil and sprinkled with parsley. Leftovers can be stored, covered, in the fridge for up to 3 days.

GARLICKY PUMPKIN SPREAD

Cershi Bel Hal

SERVES 4 TO 6

Watching home cook Ghily Guetta (see page 78) prepare Shabbat dinner in her sunlit kitchen in the Piazza Bologna neighborhood was like observing a master class in multitasking. But of all the pots and pans bubbling simultaneously on her stovetop, this sunset-hued spread—a classic of the Libyan Jewish table—stood out. Guetta fries slices of pumpkin (you can also use butternut squash) until soft and caramelized, then mashes them with copious amounts of minced garlic, hot paprika, and a generous splash of vinegar. The combination of creamy sweetness, bold spice, and tangy brightness is nothing short of magic. Serve alongside couscous or with challah or toasted bread for dipping.

Extra-virgin olive oil *for frying*

1 small sugar pumpkin or medium butternut squash (about 2½ pounds / 1.1 kg), *peeled (see Note), halved, seeded, and cut into ¼-inch- (6 mm) thick slices*

5 medium garlic cloves, *minced, grated, or pushed through a press*

1¼ teaspoons kosher salt, *plus more if needed*

2 teaspoons hot paprika, *plus more if needed*

½ teaspoon granulated sugar

1½ tablespoons tomato paste

2 tablespoons white or red wine vinegar, *plus more if needed*

Heat approximately ¼ inch (6 mm) of oil in a large frying pan over medium heat until shimmering. Working in batches, add the pumpkin slices and fry, turning once, until golden brown and tender, 6 to 8 minutes per batch. Use a slotted spoon to transfer the fried pumpkin slices to a large plate or bowl while you continue to fry the remainder.

Carefully pour off and discard all but about 2 to 3 tablespoons of the olive oil left in the pan, then return the pan to medium heat. (Alternatively, if all the oil has been used up during frying, add a couple more tablespoons of oil to the pan.) Add the garlic, salt, hot paprika, sugar, and tomato paste and cook, stirring, until fragrant, about 1 minute.

Return the pumpkin slices to the pan, toss to coat with the spices, and cook, mashing the mixture with a fork until fairly smooth but still textured, about 5 minutes. Stir in the vinegar. Taste and add more salt, paprika, and/or vinegar, if desired.

Transfer to a serving bowl and serve warm or at room temperature.

NOTE: *To make the pumpkin or squash easier to peel and slice, poke several holes in it with a fork and microwave for 3 to 5 minutes. The skin should peel off more easily after that.*

SPICY GARLIC AND CHILE SAUCE

Filfel Chuma

MAKES ABOUT ½ CUP (125 G)

Libyan Jews use this fiery garlic-forward sauce as both an ingredient in stews, sauces, and other dishes and as a condiment. It lasts for months in the fridge, and the flavor deepens with time, so keep a batch on hand to dollop with abandon on dishes like Shakshuka (page 202) or Vegetable Stew for Couscous (page 204).

1½ teaspoons caraway seeds

3 medium garlic cloves, *smashed and peeled*

1 teaspoon kosher salt, *plus more if needed*

2 tablespoons sweet paprika

1 tablespoon hot paprika

¼ teaspoon cayenne pepper, *plus more if needed*

½ teaspoon granulated sugar

½ teaspoon grated lemon zest

1½ tablespoons fresh lemon juice

⅓ cup (80 ml) vegetable oil

2 tablespoons water, *plus more if needed*

Add the caraway seeds to a spice grinder (or clean coffee grinder) and pulse until finely ground, then transfer to a medium bowl.

Roughly chop the garlic cloves. Sprinkle the salt over the garlic and use the knife to continue chopping, smashing, and scraping the garlic into a paste. (You could also use a mortar and pestle.)

Add the garlic paste to the bowl with the caraway seeds, along with the sweet paprika, hot paprika, cayenne, sugar, lemon zest, and lemon juice, and mix well. Add the oil and water and whisk to combine. Taste and add more salt and/or cayenne pepper, if desired. If the mixture is very thick, stir in a little more water to thin it enough to drizzle.

Transfer the mixture to a glass container with a lid and store in the fridge for up to 3 months.

HOSTARIA KOSHER

SOUPS

Zuppe

Romanesco Broccoli Stew with Pasta, 96

PASTA AND CHICKPEA STEW

Pasta e Ceci

SERVES 4

Roman Jews have a running debate over the desired thickness for this classic dish of small pasta and chickpeas flavored with rosemary and garlic. Some prefer a brothier, stew-like consistency, while others insist it must be so thick that a wooden spoon stuck into the pot should stand straight up! My take: aim for the stewier end, because any leftovers will continue to thicken as the dish sits and the pasta continues to soak up liquid. (For that reason, I tend to serve this for weeknight dinners when we can eat it right away, rather than for Shabbat or a holiday, when I often cook ahead and reheat.) However you like it, a generous glug of olive oil drizzled over top gives the dish a luxurious sheen.

¼ cup (60 ml) extra-virgin olive oil, *plus more for drizzling*

2 medium garlic cloves, *smashed and peeled*

1 large fresh rosemary sprig

¼ teaspoon red pepper flakes, *plus more if needed*

1¼ cups (310 g) tomato puree (passata)

Two 15-ounce (425 g) cans chickpeas, *rinsed and drained*

2 teaspoons kosher salt, *plus more if needed*

½ teaspoon freshly ground black pepper, *plus more if needed*

5½ cups (1.3 l) water

1 cup (140 g) small pasta, such as ditalini or tubetti

Freshly grated Parmesan or Pecorino Romano *for serving* (*optional*)

Heat the olive oil in a large pot over medium heat. Add the garlic, rosemary, and red pepper flakes and sizzle together until fragrant, 1 to 2 minutes. Stir in the tomato puree and cook for another 1 to 2 minutes.

Add the drained chickpeas, salt, black pepper, and 5 cups (1.2 l) of the water and stir to combine. Raise the heat to medium-high and bring to a boil, then reduce the heat to medium-low and simmer, stirring occasionally, until the liquid reduces slightly, about 20 minutes.

Remove and discard the rosemary sprig and garlic cloves. (It is okay if some of the rosemary leaves remain in the soup.) Mash about one quarter of the chickpeas with the back of a spoon or a potato masher until the soup thickens a little.

Add the remaining ½ cup (118 ml) water, raise the heat to medium-high, and bring to a simmer. Add the pasta, partially cover the pot, and cook, stirring frequently, until the pasta is al dente, 12 to 15 minutes. Taste and add more salt, black pepper, and/or red pepper flakes, if desired.

Serve immediately, topped with a drizzle of olive oil and a generous sprinkle of grated cheese, if using. Thin any leftovers with a little water, if desired, when reheating.

שמע ישראל
יהוה אלהינו יהוה אחד
2021

ROMANESCO BROCCOLI STEW WITH PASTA

Minestra di Pasta e Broccoli

SERVES 4

This ancient Roman dish (pictured on page 92) is beloved by Roman Jews as well, who likely contributed the anchovies to the recipe. The vegetable-and-pasta-based stew's star ingredient is Romanesco broccoli—the chartreuse-hued cousin of the standard variation, with florets that spiral out in a majestic fractal pattern. It is available virtually everywhere in Rome during the fall and can usually be found in farmers' markets in the United States starting in mid-autumn. Minestra di pasta e broccoli is the kind of hearty, rustic weeknight fare that demonstrates the true brilliance of cucina povera. My version is relatively brothy, but if you prefer a thicker stew, reduce the amount of water to your liking, decreasing the amount of salt as well.

¼ cup (60 ml) extra-virgin olive oil, *plus more for drizzling*

3 medium garlic cloves, *smashed and peeled*

¼ teaspoon red pepper flakes, *plus more if needed*

1 to 2 oil-packed anchovy fillets, *chopped (optional)*

1½ cups (370 g) tomato puree (passata)

3 tablespoons tomato paste

2 pounds (907 g) Romanesco broccoli, *cut into small florets (5 to 6 cups florets)*

2 quarts (2 l) water

1 tablespoon kosher salt, *plus more if needed*

½ teaspoon freshly ground black pepper, *plus more if needed*

1 cup (140 g) small pasta, such as ditalini or tubetti

Freshly grated Parmesan or Pecorino Romano *for serving* (*optional*)

Heat the oil in a soup pot over medium heat. Add the garlic, red pepper flakes, and anchovies, if using, and sizzle together until fragrant, 1 to 2 minutes. Add the tomato puree and tomato paste and cook, stirring, for another 1 to 2 minutes.

Add the broccoli florets, 7 cups (1.6 l) of the water, the salt, and black pepper and stir to combine. Raise the heat to high and bring to a boil, then lower the heat to medium, cover the pot, and simmer, stirring occasionally, until the broccoli is very tender, 45 to 55 minutes.

Stir in the remaining 1 cup (240 ml) water and the pasta, turn the heat to medium-high, partially cover the pot, and cook, stirring often, until the pasta is al dente, 12 to 15 minutes. Taste and add more salt, black pepper, and/or red pepper flakes, if desired.

Transfer the stew to bowls and serve immediately, drizzled with a little olive oil and topped with grated cheese, if desired. The pasta will continue to absorb liquid as the dish sits. You can thin out any leftovers with a little water, if desired, when reheating.

Rome's Jewish Restaurants

WALKING DOWN VIA del Portico d'Ottavia, the main street in the Jewish Ghetto neighborhood, it is impossible not to notice the abundance of Roman Jewish restaurants lining the cobblestone street. Packed tightly next to one another and overflowing with locals and tourists from lunchtime through late evening, they make a lively and joyful scene. But it wasn't always this way.

In the decades before the current revival of the neighborhood, the streets were decidedly quieter. A few old-school restaurants, like Giggetto, Piperno, Sora Margherita, and Al Pompiere, served a handful of Jewish dishes as part of a larger traditional Roman menu. These spots were (and continue to be) great if you need your fix of Jewish-style fried artichokes, but they are neither kosher nor overtly Jewish.

In 1999, the neighborhood welcomed La Taverna del Ghetto, Rome's first modern kosher restaurant specifically focused on the city's Jewish cuisine. Founded by Rafael Fadlon in partnership with his mother-in-law, Italia Tagliacozzo (see page 66), the restaurant made the bold claim that the city's historic Jewish food was something to celebrate and share with a larger audience. In addition to fried artichokes, their menu features classics like fried and marinated zucchini, salt cod with raisins and pine nuts, and dishes made from cow's offal (brain, lungs, tripe, heart).

La Taverna del Ghetto is a favorite for tourists and locals alike. In recent years, however, the restaurant owners ironically decided to give up their official kosher certification so that they could continue to serve those

"fifth quarter" (quinto quarto, see page 244) dishes, which were increasingly difficult to source with kosher ingredients. "Our goal is to preserve cucina Ebraica as it was traditionally made," said current owner, Angelo di Porto.

Over the last two decades, many other new restaurants have followed La Taverna's example in featuring Roman Jewish cuisine. Nonna Betta, opened by Umberto Pavoncello and currently co-run with his son, Michele, offers education and entertainment—like placemats printed with Jewish phrases and explanations of the different dishes—along with their meals. BellaCarne, owned by Alberto Ouazana, focuses on kosher meat dishes, while Ba'Ghetto, run by Amit Dabush, offers Libyan and Middle Eastern Jewish fare along with Roman Jewish classics.

In more recent years a kosher hamburger joint and a sushi restaurant have opened in the Ghetto neighborhood, catering to those who keep kosher but want to try something different. Meanwhile, new Roman Jewish spots that explicitly merge tradition and innovation have also appeared. There is Casalino Osteria Kosher, which was launched in 2021 despite the hardships brought on by the Covid-19 pandemic. Run by Rachel Zarfati and her father, Mino, who grew up playing ball in the Ghetto's streets, the restaurant is also presided over by Rachel's grandmother, Letizia Della Seta, who comes almost every day to check on the food's quality. "We call ourselves an osteria because we are taking our family traditions and doing them in the best way possible," Rachel said.

A few doors down, Renato al Ghetto, which was founded in 2018 by Menasci and Giorgia Renato, brings creativity to Roman Jewish cuisine. "I wanted to inject something new into a 2,000-year-old tradition," Menasci told me. Dishes like pasta served with sea bass, zucchini cream, and bottarga fit the bill.

Just beyond the Ghetto, Yotvata turns out pastas, fish, and fried goodies. Run by Marco Sed, the restaurant serves the family's mozzarella, ricotta salata, and other high-quality kosher Italian cheeses they started making themselves after they were unable to source them elsewhere. The cheese-making business expanded, and they now ship kosher cheeses across Italy, as well as to France, Germany, Ukraine, and the United States. "The cheese production started as a response to a need for the restaurant," said Marco. "Now the restaurant is a client for the cheese factory."

While the majority of Rome's Jewish restaurants are crowded onto or around Via del Portico d'Ottavia, there are several worthy outliers. In Piazza Bologna, where many of the city's Libyan Jews live, a humble spot called Little Tripoli, run by Maier Babani, turns out shakshuka, mafrum, and other Libyan Jewish dishes.

In the Monteverde neighborhood, the husband-and-wife team Daniela Gean and Roberto Attias serve high-end Libyan and Middle Eastern dishes at Mezè Bistrot. In the Portuense neighborhood, the kosher-style restaurant MeAT serves Roman Jewish specialties in a modern setting. And in Trastevere, Miriam Zarfati and Fulvio di Porto run a kosher fresh pasta shop fittingly called C'è Pasta . . . e Pasta ("There's Pasta . . . and Pasta"). They originally opened it twenty years ago, partly in honor of their pasta-obsessed kids, but they've slowly added stellar versions of traditional Jewish dishes like concia, salt cod in tomato sauce, and fried artichokes. More recently, Miriam and her sister, Tamara, opened a second restaurant in Monteverde called C'è Pasta . . . e Pizza, which boasts the city's only kosher-certified wood-fired pizza oven.

With so many restaurants vying for the same tourists and locals, and trying to make their mark featuring similar dishes, there is naturally some competition. There is also occasionally tension between the restaurants that believe in doing things the old-fashioned way and those that want to bring traditional dishes into the twenty-first century. At the end of the day, though, all of these restaurants have the same goal: to celebrate the glorious flavors of Rome's Jewish kitchen.

STAUB

BROTHY TURNIP AND RICE SOUP

Rape e Riso

SERVES 4 TO 6

Turnips don't get the love they deserve. Unlike flashier vegetables, they don't scream for attention, and they tend to get forgotten in the back of the refrigerator. But in this delicate soup, the humble root vegetable truly shines. Its spicy bite mellows, and the sliced turnips grow silky and luscious as they cook. With its starchy rice and savory broth, the soup is a bowl of pure comfort. If you use vegetable broth, a shower of grated Parmesan or Pecorino Romano finishes it beautifully.

¼ cup (60 ml) extra-virgin olive oil, *plus more for drizzling*

1 medium yellow onion, *finely chopped*

8 small white turnips (about 1 pound / 454 g), *peeled, quartered, and very thinly sliced*

¼ teaspoon red pepper flakes, *plus more if needed*

½ teaspoon kosher salt, *plus more if needed*

Freshly ground black pepper

2 quarts (2 l) chicken broth or vegetable broth, *preferably homemade (page 109)*

¾ cup (150 g) Arborio or Carnaroli rice

Heat the oil in a large pot over medium heat. Add the onion and cook, stirring occasionally, until softened and lightly browned, 6 to 8 minutes.

Stir in the turnips, reduce the heat to medium-low, cover the pot, and cook, stirring occasionally, until the turnips are very tender, 10 to 15 minutes.

Stir in the red pepper flakes, salt, and a generous amount of black pepper, then add the broth. Raise the heat to medium-high and bring to a boil.

Stir in the rice and lower the heat to medium. Partially cover the pot and cook, stirring occasionally, until the rice is tender but the soup is still brothy, 25 to 30 minutes. Taste and add more salt and/or red pepper flakes, if desired. (If you started with unsalted broth, you may have to add quite a bit more salt.)

Divide the soup among bowls and serve immediately, drizzled with more olive oil. Reheat leftovers over medium-low heat, thinning the soup with a little more broth, if desired.

NOTE: *Be sure to peel the turnips (particularly older, tougher ones) thoroughly, going several layers down to remove any thick, fibrous skin.*

CHICKEN AND BEEF BROTH

Brodo

MAKES ABOUT 2 QUARTS (2 L)

Rome's Jews have perfected the art of breaking the Yom Kippur fast. Instead of the bagels and lox platters or noodle kugels that I and other Ashkenazi Jews grew up with, many families begin with brodo, a rich, clear broth made from chicken and beef that is at once hydrating and deeply nourishing. "The first cup you sip plain, and then you add pasta to the second one," said Ghila Ottolenghi Sanders, a Roman Jew who now lives in Atlanta, Georgia.

Broth—of course! What better way could there be to re-enter the realm of physicality after a day-long fast than with a steaming mug of broth? I have made this tradition part of my own family's post–Yom Kippur meal, and I always use this stellar recipe, which I adapted from one graciously shared with me by a member of the Roman Jewish community, Stefania Gai. Stefania's version uses beef shoulder instead of flanken or beef bones. (She shreds the boiled chicken to make chicken salad and serves the beef as a separate course after the broth, sliced and generously topped with Salsa Verde, page 75). I prefer to start with meaty bones, which add great flavor and only leave a little bit of meat to put to another use. (I typically shred it and make Frittata di Carne, page 238.) For Yom Kippur, serve the broth with Carcioncini (page 110), the beef-filled pasta, or the little pasta squares called Quadrucci (page 112).

One 3-pound (1.4 kg) chicken, *cut into 8 pieces and trimmed of excess fat*

2½ pounds (1.1 kg) flanken or meaty beef bones

2 medium yellow onions, *not peeled, halved*

2 large carrots, *peeled and halved*

2 large celery stalks, *trimmed and halved*

4 medium garlic cloves, *smashed and peeled*

2 plum tomatoes, *halved (optional)*

1 tablespoon salt, *plus more if needed (optional; see Note)*

Add the chicken and beef bones to a tall 8-quart (7.6 l) soup pot (not a Dutch oven). Add the onions, carrots, celery, garlic, and tomatoes, if using, then add enough water to cover the ingredients by 1 inch (2.5 cm). Bring to a boil over high heat, skimming any foam from the surface as necessary. As soon as the water boils, immediately turn the heat to low, partially cover the pot, and cook until the chicken and meat are very tender, 2 to 3 hours. (After the initial boil, try not to let the soup boil vigorously again; keep it at a slow and steady burble, adjusting the heat as necessary.) Remove from the heat.

Remove the vegetables from the pot and discard. Remove the chicken and bones and set aside for another use. Strain the broth through a fine-mesh sieve into a large bowl, then return it to the pot. Stir in the salt, if using. Taste and add more salt if needed.

Serve the broth hot, or let cool and refrigerate, then skim off the layer of fat that will have congealed on top. Strain the broth through a sieve again, if desired, and gently reheat before serving. The cooled broth can also be frozen in airtight containers for up to 3 months.

NOTE: *If you prefer to make an unsalted broth to use in other dishes, omit the salt.*

CLAUDIO
AMPO DE'FIORI
DAL 1929

VEGETABLE BROTH

Brodo Vegetale

MAKES ABOUT 2 QUARTS (2 L)

This recipe is not traditional to Roman Jewish cuisine, but I wanted to include an enticing meat-free broth for vegetarians to use in dishes like Rape e Riso (page 105) or Quadrucci in Brodo con Spinaci (page 112). The broth can also be left unsalted and used as the base for soups and other dishes.

2 large yellow onions, *not peeled, quartered through the root*

3 large carrots, *peeled and cut into chunks*

2 celery stalks, *cut into chunks*

1 medium sweet potato (about ½ pound / 227 g), *peeled and cut into chunks*

½ pound (227 g) white or cremini mushrooms, *halved if large*

½ cup (10 g) loosely packed fresh flat-leaf parsley, *including stems*

1 medium fennel bulb (about ½ pound / 227 g), *trimmed and quartered (optional)*

1 tablespoon onion powder

2 bay leaves

10 black peppercorns

3½ quarts (3.3 l) water

1 tablespoon kosher salt, *plus more if needed (optional; see headnote)*

Add the onions, carrots, celery, sweet potato, mushrooms, parsley, fennel, if using, onion powder, bay leaves, and peppercorns to a large soup pot. Add the water and bring to a boil over high heat. Reduce the heat to medium, partially cover the pot, and simmer, stirring occasionally, until the liquid has reduced by a little more than one third and is golden, 1 to 1½ hours. Remove from the heat and let cool slightly.

Carefully strain broth through a fine-mesh sieve into a very large bowl; discard the vegetables and herbs. Stir in the salt, if using. Taste and add more salt if needed. Use right away, or let cool and freeze in airtight containers for up to 3 months.

STUFFED PASTA IN BROTH

Carcioncini in Brodo

SERVES 6

Fans of Ashkenazi beef kreplach will fall in love with carcioncini, homemade pasta squares stuffed with a savory ground beef filling. The dish gets its name from cariscioncini, which is an antiquated word for "pants" (just as pants cover legs, so the pasta covers the filling). Roman Jews traditionally serve the pasta swimming in a clear Chicken and Beef Broth (page 106) to help break the fast for Yom Kippur. You can substitute approximately 2 quarts (2 l) of your favorite chicken broth, if desired.

For the Pasta

2 cups (280 g) all-purpose flour, *plus more for rolling*

2 large eggs plus 2 large egg yolks, *lightly beaten*

2 teaspoons extra-virgin olive oil

1 teaspoon kosher salt

2 tablespoons warm water, *plus more as needed*

For the Filling

½ pound (227 g) ground beef

1 large garlic clove, *minced, grated, or pushed through a press*

2 tablespoons finely chopped fresh flat-leaf parsley

½ teaspoon kosher salt

¼ teaspoon freshly ground black pepper

1 batch Chicken and Beef Broth (page 106)

Finely chopped fresh flat-leaf parsley for sprinkling *(optional)*

MAKE THE PASTA

Combine the flour, eggs, egg yolks, olive oil, salt, and water in the bowl of a stand mixer fitted with the paddle attachment and beat on low speed until a shaggy dough forms. If the dough looks dry, add a little more water, 1 tablespoon at a time, mixing until the desired consistency is reached. Switch to the dough hook and knead on medium speed until the dough is smooth and elastic, 5 to 7 minutes.

Transfer the dough to a work surface and form it into a disk, then wrap tightly in plastic wrap or parchment paper and let rest at room temperature for at least 1 hour, and up to several hours.

MEANWHILE, MAKE THE FILLING

Add the ground beef, garlic, parsley, salt, and pepper to a medium bowl and mix with your hands to fully combine.

ROLL AND FILL THE PASTA

Cut off one quarter of the dough (keep the remainder wrapped) and, on a lightly floured work surface, using a floured rolling pin, roll into a long rectangle approximately 4 inches (10 cm) wide and 1/16 inch (1.5 mm) thick (or use a pasta machine). If the dough is resistant to rolling, cover it with a dish towel and let rest for another 5 to 10 minutes before proceeding.

Place chickpea-sized scoops of the beef mixture down the length of the pasta sheet, about 1 inch (2.5 cm) from the bottom edge and about ½ inch (1.25 cm) apart. Using your finger or a pastry brush, brush a bit of water onto the dough in a grid around the mounds of filling, to help the dough adhere to itself, then fold the dough over the filling, pressing down around the mounds to seal the dough and remove any air pockets. Press the edges firmly to seal.

Using a pizza cutter or a knife, trim the edges of the pasta to even them, then cut between the mounds of filling to create approximately 1 × 1-inch (2.5 × 2.5 cm) squares. Lay the finished carcioncini on a dish towel and cover with a second dish towel. Repeat the rolling and filling process with the remaining dough and filling. (If there is any filling left over, you can reserve it for another use; or form it into small meatballs, panfry them in a little bit of oil until cooked through, 4 to 6 minutes, and add to the broth after the carcioncini are cooked in the next step.)

To serve, pour the broth into a soup pot and bring to a boil over high heat. Add the carcioncini and boil until they float to the surface and are fully cooked through, 4 to 5 minutes, then turn the heat down to low to keep soup at a bare simmer for serving. Transfer to soup bowls and serve immediately, sprinkled with parsley, if desired.

Alternative Method: Make the Pasta by Hand

If you do not have a stand mixer, you can make the pasta by hand: Place the flour on a clean work surface and form a well in the center. Add the beaten eggs, egg yolks, olive oil, salt, and 1 tablespoon water to the well and begin beating the egg mixture with a fork, gradually incorporating the flour from around the edges, until a shaggy dough forms. If the dough feels very dry, add another tablespoon of water. Then knead the dough until it is smooth and elastic, about 5 minutes. Cover the dough and let rest as directed above.

PASTA SQUARES AND SPINACH IN BROTH

Quadrucci in Brodo con Spinaci

SERVES 6

Along with Stuffed Pasta in Broth (page 110), Roman Jews traditionally serve this soup to break the Yom Kippur fast. In my family, it makes an appearance when someone catches a cold or whenever a blustery night calls for something warm and soothing. The pasta dough is rolled very thin and cut into small squares called quadrucci. The soup is served with sautéed onion and spinach (or sometimes peas, but I prefer the spinach version). You can substitute approximately 2 quarts of your favorite chicken or vegetable broth for the brodo.

For the Pasta

2 cups (280 g) all-purpose flour, *plus more for rolling*

2 large eggs plus 2 large egg yolks, *lightly beaten*

2 teaspoons extra-virgin olive oil

1 teaspoon kosher salt

2 tablespoons warm water, *plus more as needed*

For Finishing and Serving

1 batch Chicken and Beef Broth (page 106) or Vegetable Broth (page 109)

2 tablespoons extra-virgin olive oil

1 medium yellow onion, *finely chopped*

½ teaspoon kosher salt

1 pound (454 g) spinach (not baby spinach), *tough stems removed and roughly chopped*

1 packed teaspoon grated lemon zest *(from about 1 medium lemon)*

CONTINUES

MAKE THE PASTA

Combine the flour, eggs, olive oil, salt, and water in the bowl of a stand mixer fitted with the paddle attachment and beat on low speed until a shaggy dough forms. If the dough looks dry, beat in a little more water, 1 tablespoon at a time, until the desired consistency is reached. Switch to the dough hook and knead on medium speed until the dough is smooth and elastic, 5 to 7 minutes.

Transfer the dough to a work surface and form it into a disk, then wrap tightly in plastic wrap or parchment paper and let rest at room temperature for at least 1 hour, and up to several hours.

ROLL AND CUT THE PASTA

Cut off one quarter of the dough (keep the remainder wrapped) and, on a lightly floured work surface, using a floured rolling pin, roll into a large 1/16-inch- (1.5 mm) thick rectangle (or use a pasta machine). If the dough is resistant to rolling, cover with a dish towel and let rest for another 5 to 10 minutes before proceeding. Trim off any ragged edges.

Using a sharp knife or a pizza cutter, cut the rectangle lengthwise into ½-inch- (1.25 cm) wide strips, then cut the strips crosswise into squares. Spread the quadrucci on a large baking sheet lined with a clean dish towel (it is okay if they overlap a little) and repeat the rolling and cutting process with the remaining dough.

TO FINISH AND SERVE

Pour the broth into a soup pot and bring to a boil over high heat.

Meanwhile, heat the oil in a large frying pan over medium heat. Add the onion with the salt and cook, stirring occasionally, until softened and lightly browned, 6 to 8 minutes. Add the spinach and cook until wilted, 1 to 2 minutes. Remove from the heat and stir in the lemon zest.

When the broth comes to a boil, add the quadrucci and boil, stirring occasionally, until they float to the surface and are al dente, 2 to 3 minutes.

Spoon some of the spinach mixture into the bottom of each serving bowl and top with the broth and pasta.

NOTE: *If you would like to make the pasta dough by hand instead of in a stand mixer, follow the instructions on page 111.*

ROMAN EGG DROP SOUP

Stracciatella

SERVES 6

This rustic soup (the name comes from the Italian verb *stracciare*, which means "to shred" and refers to the free-form squiggles of egg that form in the broth) is popular throughout Rome and the larger Lazio region. Roman Jews often serve it on Passover, whisking the egg mixture with matzo meal rather than the bread crumbs or semolina more commonly used. They also omit the traditional Parmesan, to avoid mixing meat and dairy, flavoring the soup instead with lemon and a hint of cinnamon, as I do here. Stracciatella is fragrant and comforting, and the wisps of egg are a delight to spoon up from the bowl. With a soup this simple, it is important to use homemade broth, but you can substitute 2 quarts (2 l) of your own favorite clear chicken broth for the Chicken and Beef Broth, if desired.

1 batch Chicken and Beef Broth (page 106)

6 large eggs

3 tablespoons matzo meal

1 packed teaspoon grated lemon zest *(from about 1 medium lemon; optional)*

½ teaspoon ground cinnamon

½ teaspoon kosher salt, *plus more if needed*

¼ teaspoon freshly ground black pepper, *plus more for serving*

Finely chopped fresh flat-leaf parsley *for serving (optional)*

Lemon wedges *for serving*

Add the broth to a soup pot and bring to a boil over high heat.

Meanwhile, whisk the eggs, matzo meal, lemon zest, if using, cinnamon, salt, and pepper together in a large bowl with a pouring spout. (A large liquid measuring cup also works well).

When the broth comes to a boil, take the pot off the heat. While gently stirring the soup, drizzle the egg mixture into the pot in a slow, continuous stream. Taste and add more salt if needed.

Ladle the soup into individual bowls and serve immediately, sprinkled with a little pepper and chopped parsley, if using. Serve with lemon wedges alongside for squeezing into the bowls.

NOTE: *Dress up this soup by adding some sautéed chopped onion, spinach leaves, chopped fresh basil, or shredded cooked chicken to each bowl.*

MINESTRONE WITH MEATBALLS

Minestrone con Polpette

SERVES 6 TO 8

In her beautiful family cookbook, *Dal 1880 ad Oggi* (see page 152), Donatella Limentani Pavoncello suggests forming tiny meatballs "the size of chickpeas" for her minestrone. I usually go a bit bigger than that, but not much, and there is something delightful about spooning up the miniature meatballs swimming in a sea of vegetables and pasta. Many Roman Jewish minestrone recipes use pieces of broken spaghetti for the pasta. While it is an effective way to use up odds and ends of leftover spaghetti packages, I prefer the consistency of a small pasta shape like ditalini or tubetti. Serve the soup with challah or slices of grilled bread drizzled with olive oil.

For the Meatballs

1 pound (454 g) ground veal or beef

¼ cup (35 g) unseasoned bread crumbs

1 large egg, *lightly beaten*

1 small garlic clove, *minced, grated, or pushed through a press*

¾ teaspoon kosher salt

½ teaspoon freshly ground black pepper

2 tablespoons extra-virgin olive oil, *plus more if needed*

For the Soup

¼ cup (60 ml) extra-virgin olive oil, *plus more for drizzling if desired*

1 large yellow onion, *cut into ½-inch (1.25 cm) pieces*

2 celery stalks, *cut into ½-inch (1.25 cm) pieces*

2 medium carrots, *peeled and cut into ½-inch (1.25 cm) pieces*

1 large zucchini (about 3/4 pound / 340 g), *cut into ½-inch (1.25 cm) pieces*

6 medium garlic cloves, *finely chopped*

3 tablespoons tomato paste

One 14.5-ounce (411 g) can diced tomatoes

7 cups (1.7 l) chicken broth, *store-bought or homemade*

2 medium Yukon Gold potatoes (about 1 pound / 454 g), *peeled and cut into ½-inch (1.25 cm) pieces*

2 bay leaves

1½ teaspoons kosher salt, *plus more if needed*

½ teaspoon freshly ground black pepper, *plus more if needed*

½ cup (70 g) small pasta, such as ditalini or tubetti, or broken spaghetti

Roughly chopped fresh basil *for serving*

CONTINUES

PREPARE THE MEATBALLS

Put the ground veal, bread crumbs, egg, garlic, salt, and pepper in a large bowl and mix with your hands to fully combine. Scoop out rounded teaspoons of the meat mixture and roll into balls the size of marbles, setting them aside on a large plate.

Heat the oil in a large frying pan over medium-high heat. Working in batches, add the meatballs and cook, gently stirring, until browned on all sides and cooked through, 4 to 6 minutes per batch. Transfer the browned meatballs to a plate as they are done. If the pan begins to look dry, add a small drizzle of additional oil. Set the meatballs aside.

PREPARE THE SOUP

Heat the oil in a large soup pot over medium-high heat. Add the onion, celery, carrots, zucchini, and garlic and cook, stirring occasionally, until beginning to soften, about 10 minutes. Stir in the tomato paste, followed by the diced tomatoes and their juices, the broth, potatoes, bay leaves, salt, and pepper. Raise the heat to high and bring to a boil, then lower the heat to medium, partially cover the pot, and simmer, stirring occasionally, until the potatoes are tender, about 20 minutes.

Stir in the pasta, raise the heat to medium-high, and cook, partially covered, until the pasta is al dente, 10 to 15 minutes. Stir in the browned meatballs. Taste and add more salt and/or pepper, if desired. Remove and discard the bay leaves.

Divide soup among individual bowls and top generously with fresh basil and, if desired, a drizzle of olive oil. Reheat any leftovers over medium-low heat.

Variation: Vegetarian Minestrone

Omit the meatballs and swap the chicken broth for vegetable broth. Add one 15-ounce (425 g) can white beans (such as cannellini), rinsed and drained, along with the pasta. Top the soup with grated Parmesan, if desired.

BEEF AND WHITE BEAN STEW WITH CUMIN

Lubia bel Kammùn

SERVES 6

Libyan Jewish cuisine boasts an abundance of meat, vegetable, and legume-based stews—saucy, spicy medleys that pair perfectly with couscous. In one version, called lubia bel selk, spinach or chard is slowly cooked down in oil until it is deeply concentrated and almost black in color. The dish is delicious, but it takes many hours to properly prepare it. This version, with tomatoes, cumin, and hot paprika, is also richly flavored and comes together much more quickly. With its mix of tender beef and white beans swimming in a velvety sauce, it is a staple on Shabbat and holiday tables. After making it for the first time, my research assistant, Megan Litt, astutely commented that it shares a similar flavor profile to beef chili, making it the perfect way to satisfy an autumn stew craving.

3 pounds (1.4 kg) boneless beef chuck, *trimmed of excess fat and cut into 2-inch (5 cm) pieces*

Kosher salt and freshly ground black pepper

2 tablespoons extra-virgin olive oil, *plus more if needed*

1 large yellow onion, *finely chopped*

5 medium garlic cloves, *finely chopped*

2 teaspoons ground cumin

1½ tablespoons hot paprika or ½ teaspoon red pepper flakes

3 tablespoons tomato paste

1 cup (250 g) tomato puree (passata)

Two 14-ounce (400 g) cans cannellini beans, *rinsed and drained*

4 cups (1 l) water

Pat the beef pieces dry with paper towels and season with a little salt. Heat the oil in a Dutch oven or other large pot over medium-high heat until shimmering. Working in batches, add the beef to the pot and sear, stirring occasionally, until browned on all sides, about 5 minutes per batch; transfer the meat to a large plate as it is done. If the pot starts to look dry, add a little more oil as necessary. Set the browned meat aside.

Lower the heat to medium and add the onion and garlic to the pot. Cook, stirring occasionally, until softened and lightly browned, 6 to 8 minutes. Add the cumin, hot paprika, 1½ teaspoons salt, and a generous amount of black pepper and cook, stirring, until fragrant, about 1 minute.

Add the tomato paste, tomato puree, beans, and water to the pot and stir to combine. Return the beef to the pot, along with any juices that have accumulated on the plate, raise the heat to medium-high, and bring the stew to a boil. Then reduce the heat to low, partially cover the pot, and cook, stirring occasionally, until the broth has thickened and the beef is tender, 2 to 3 hours. The broth should be rich and stew-like, but if the pot gets too dry toward the end of cooking, add an additional splash of water.

Taste and add more salt and/or pepper, if desired. Serve hot.

FISH SOUP

Brodo di Pesce

SERVES 4

This soup is part of the legacy of Portico d'Ottavia (see page 14), the ancient ruin-turned-fish market on the edge of the Roman Jewish Ghetto that was a primary source of nutrients for the community. The tomato-based broth, both elemental and comforting, allows the flavor of the fish to shine through. Traditionally only small, oily fish, called pesce azzuro ("blue fish") were used—mackerel, anchovies, sardines, and the like. But some contemporary recipes add white fish, like cod, to the mix. At Casalino Osteria Kosher, a restaurant in the Jewish Ghetto neighborhood, the soup is served with rustic toasted croutons. I love the crunch and contrast they provide, so I include them in my version too.

6 ounces (170 g) rustic white bread, *cut into 1-inch (2.5-cm) cubes (about 4 cups cubed bread)*

½ cup (120 ml) extra-virgin olive oil, *plus more for drizzling*

Kosher salt and freshly ground black pepper

4 medium garlic cloves, *smashed and peeled*

¼ teaspoon red pepper flakes, *plus more if needed*

4 oil-packed anchovy fillets, *chopped*

1½ cups (370 g) tomato puree (passata)

2½ cups (590 ml) water

1½ pounds (680 g) cod, mackerel, branzino, and/or fresh sardine fillets, *cut into 2-inch (5 cm) pieces*

Roughly chopped fresh flat-leaf parsley *for topping*

Roughly chopped fresh basil *for topping*

Preheat the oven to 400°F (200°C).

Place the cubed bread on a baking sheet, drizzle with ¼ cup (60 ml) of the olive oil, sprinkle with ½ teaspoon salt and ¼ teaspoon pepper, and toss to coat, then spread the bread out on the sheet. Bake, stirring once or twice, until the croutons are golden brown and toasty, 8 to 10 minutes. Remove from the oven, transfer to a large plate, and set aside to cool.

Meanwhile, heat the remaining ¼ cup (60 ml) olive oil in a large pot over medium heat. Add the garlic, red pepper flakes, and anchovies and cook, stirring, until the anchovies melt, 2 to 3 minutes. Add the tomato puree, 1 teaspoon salt, ½ teaspoon black pepper, and the water and stir to combine. Bring the mixture to a simmer, stirring occasionally, and cook until it thickens a bit, about 10 minutes.

Season the fish with salt and pepper and nestle into the liquid, then lower the heat to medium-low, partially cover the pot, and cook until the fish is opaque and cooked through, 10 to 15 minutes.

Taste and add more salt and/or red pepper flakes, if desired. Ladle into bowls and serve hot, topped with the croutons, parsley and basil, and a drizzle of olive oil.

FRITTERS

Fritti

JEWISH-STYLE FRIED ARTICHOKES

Carciofi alla Giudia

SERVES 4 TO 6

The first time I tried carciofi alla Giudia ("Jewish-style" artichokes) on a trip to Rome in my early twenties, I gasped. And then, if memory serves, I swore in amazement. The bronzed thistle splayed open like a chrysanthemum, the salt-kissed leaves as crunchy as potato chips, the velvet-soft heart—it was truly unlike anything else I had tasted. I immediately wanted more. Fortunately, nearly every restaurant lining Via del Portico d'Ottavia (and many others beyond) serves a version of this Roman Jewish gift to the world.

Before you attempt to make carciofi alla Giudia at home, a disclaimer: they are a project. The artichokes are fried twice in hot oil—once to cook them through and a second time to crisp up the leaves. The process involves a lot of trimming of the artichokes and a great deal of oil to dispose of afterward. But when you do invest the time, the reward is handsome and the flavor unforgettable (see more, page 54).

Light olive oil or vegetable oil (such as sunflower or grapeseed) *for deep-frying*

6 medium artichokes, *cleaned according to the instructions on page 58*

Kosher salt

Lemon wedges *for serving*

NOTE: *Carciofi alla Giudia are traditionally fried in olive oil, but in practice I have found the oil's smoke point too low for sustained frying. I prefer to use light olive oil, which has been processed enough to handle the heat but still imparts a touch of olive flavor. A neutral oil, like sunflower or grapeseed, works well too.*

Line a large plate with paper towels. Pour about 2½ inches (6.5 cm) of oil into a medium deep saucepan and heat over medium until it reaches 280°F (138°C) on a deep-fry thermometer.

Working in two batches if necessary, add the artichokes to the hot oil and cook, turning occasionally, until the hearts are tender when pierced with a fork, 10 to 15 minutes. Carefully transfer the artichokes to the prepared plate to drain and cool. Set the saucepan of oil aside.

Once they are cooled, gently pull open each artichoke to expose the center (it should resemble a flower). If the artichokes have hairy chokes in the center, use a melon baller or sturdy spoon to carefully remove and discard them.

Put the saucepan back over the heat and bring the oil up to 350°F (180°C). Add the fried artichokes, cut side down, and fry until browned and very crispy, 2 to 4 minutes. Return to the paper towels to drain and sprinkle generously with salt.

Serve immediately, with lemon wedges for squeezing.

SIMPLER FRIED ARTICHOKES WITH HERBED SALT

SERVES 4 TO 6

There is little in the world more heavenly than Carciofi alla Giudia (page 128), the "Jewish-style" fried artichokes that are the heart and soul of Roman Jewish cuisine. This riff on fried artichokes, which starts with jarred artichoke hearts rather than whole fresh artichokes, was inspired by my desire to tap into the salty, fried flavor of the real thing without all the work. The crispy little nuggets that emerge from the oil are hardly traditional, but they are very tasty—especially when sprinkled with herbed salt. Eat them on their own as a snack, or toss them with cooked pasta.

NOTES: *Buy the best-quality canned or jarred artichokes you can find.*

Any leftover Herbed Salt can be saved to sprinkle over popcorn, baked fish, or roasted vegetables.

For the Herbed Salt

½ teaspoon dried rosemary, *crumbled*

½ teaspoon dried oregano

½ teaspoon grated lemon zest

1 teaspoon kosher salt

For the Artichokes

Two 14-ounce (400 g) cans or jars artichoke hearts, *drained and halved lengthwise*

Light olive oil or vegetable oil (such as sunflower or grapeseed) for deep-frying

MAKE THE HERBED SALT
Combine the rosemary, oregano, lemon zest, and salt in a small bowl and rub together with your fingertips. Set aside.

MAKE THE ARTICHOKES
Line a large baking sheet with paper towels or a clean dish towel and lay the halved artichoke hearts in a single layer on it. Cover with a second layer of paper towels or another dish towel and gently pat the artichokes dry. Allow them to dry like this for at least 30 minutes, and up to 2 hours.

Heat 1 inch (2.5 cm) of oil in a medium pot over medium heat until it reaches 350°F (180°C) on a deep-fry thermometer. Line a large baking sheet with paper towels and set nearby.

Working in batches of 4 or 5, gently slip the artichoke hearts into the oil and fry, turning once, until deeply golden brown and crisp, 2 to 4 minutes. Transfer the fried artichokes to the paper towel–lined plate to drain briefly, then transfer to a serving platter and sprinkle with some of the herbed salt. Serve hot.

MIXED FRIED VEGETABLES

Pezzetti Fritti

SERVES 4 TO 6

One of my favorite early memories of Rome is of a food and wine festival thrown by the kosher catering company Le Bon Ton. Members of the city's Jewish community showed up in spades, dressed to the nines and ready to toast one another and go back for seconds and thirds at the abundant food tables. Of all I ate that afternoon, my favorite was the battered deep-fried vegetables, served hot and crisp from the fryer in brown paper cones for easy (and stylish!) nibbling.

Mixed fried vegetables (and sometimes fish), commonly known as *fritto misto*, are beloved by all Romans, but the deep-frying method hails originally from the Roman Jewish kitchen. Roman Jews call the dish *pezzetti fritti* (literally, "fried pieces"), and they fry everything from zucchini and mushrooms to onions, potatoes, cauliflower, sliced artichokes, and parsnips. Feel free to play around with other vegetables when you make this at home. Roman batters are generally quite thick, fully concealing whatever is inside. My version is a little lighter but still coats the ingredients nicely. Serve the fried vegetables piping hot, with lemon wedges alongside for squeezing.

Light olive oil or vegetable oil (such as sunflower or grapeseed) *for deep-frying*

For the Batter

1¾ cups (245 g) all-purpose flour

2 teaspoons kosher salt

½ teaspoon baking soda

2 cups (475 ml) chilled sparkling water

For the Mixed Vegetables

½ pound (227 g) green beans, *ends trimmed*

½ pound (227 g) cremini mushrooms, *halved lengthwise (stems left intact)*

1 medium fennel bulb (about 1/2 pound / 227 g), *trimmed and very thinly sliced lengthwise*

2 small zucchini (about ½ pound / 227 g), *ends trimmed and cut lengthwise into 8 wedges each*

Kosher salt and lemon wedges *for serving*

Heat 1½ inches (4 cm) of oil in a medium saucepan over medium heat until it reaches 350°F (180°C) on a deep-fry thermometer. Line a large baking sheet with paper towels and set nearby.

WHILE THE OIL HEATS, MAKE THE BATTER

Whisk together the flour, salt, baking soda, and sparkling water in a large bowl until smooth and the consistency of a loose pancake batter. (Do not overmix.)

Working in batches, drop the vegetables into the batter to coat, then remove with tongs, allowing the excess batter to drip off, and slip into the hot oil, being careful not to crowd the pan (which can lead to soggy fritters). If you are adding a couple of pieces at once, jostle them slightly with the tongs so they won't stick together in clumps. Fry the vegetables, flipping them once, until crisp and golden, 4 to 6 minutes per batch. Transfer the fried vegetables to the paper towels to drain as they are done. Add more oil to the pan if needed, letting it come up to heat before proceeding.

Transfer the vegetables to a serving platter and sprinkle with salt. Serve hot, with lemon wedges on the side for squeezing.

When in Rome, Fry Like the (Jewish) Romans Do

IF *YOU HAVE* read about or eaten any Roman Jewish food, you have probably come across carciofi alla Giudia—whole artichokes that are deep-fried "Jewish-style" until crisp, golden, and ethereally delicious. But Roman Jews fry so much more than artichokes. From baccalà (salt cod) and fresh anchovies, to mozzarella-stuffed squash blossoms and honey-soaked matzo fritters, deep frying is a specialty of the Jewish Ghetto neighborhood.

Roman Jews typically fry food using one of three methods. The food is slipped into the hot oil completely uncoated, dipped lightly in flour to add extra crispness, or enrobed in a thick batter that fries up light and golden. Each method brings out the best of whatever is being fried.

The Roman Jewish affinity for fried foods was born, like so many other cucina povera traditions, out of necessity. During the Ghetto period, resources were scarce, which meant home cooks were forced to work with whatever ingredients and materials they could find. Homes in the Ghetto rarely had ovens, so food was primarily cooked on the stovetop. And locally produced olive oil was readily accessible and affordable, making deep-frying a relatively cost-effective method for preparing food. (For contemporary cooks, I do not suggest deep-frying in extra-virgin olive oil because of its lower smoke point; see Olive Oil, page 36, for suggested frying oils.)

During the Ghetto period, Roman Jews were prohibited from holding virtually all professions. One exception allowed them to be street vendors, so many became friggitori (literally, "fryers"), selling fried vegetables and fish to passersby. Over time, deep-frying was adopted into the larger Roman cuisine, but it maintains its roots in the Jewish kitchen.

12
13

FRIED SALT COD

Filetto di Baccalà

SERVES 4 TO 6

Deep-fried salt cod is beloved throughout Rome, including the Jewish Ghetto neighborhood. The cod, which has been salted and dried into stiff, well-preserved planks, is desalted overnight (or longer) in water and then drained, cut into pieces, dipped in a thick batter, and deep-fried until golden. The same batter can be used to fry balls of fresh mozzarella—another delicacy that emerged from the kitchens of the Ghetto; see the variation below. Both dishes can be found on virtually every restaurant menu in the Ghetto neighborhood, and are quite a satisfying snack to make at home. Make sure to plan ahead when making fried baccalà, since the fish needs time to soak.

1½ pounds (680 g) baccalà *(boneless salt cod)*

Light olive oil or vegetable oil (such as sunflower or grapeseed) *for deep-frying*

1½ cups (210 g) all-purpose flour

1½ teaspoons kosher salt, *plus more for sprinkling*

½ teaspoon baking soda

1½ cups (355 ml) cold water

Lemon wedges *for serving*

Place the baccalà in a large bowl and cover with water. Refrigerate for at least 24 hours (ideally, closer to 48 hours), changing the water several times, until the fish is softened and pliable and most of the salt has washed away.

Drain the fish, pat dry with paper towels, and cut into approximately 4 × 1½-inch (10 × 4 cm) pieces (think a deck of playing cards cut lengthwise in half). Set aside.

Heat 1½ inches (4 cm) of oil in a medium saucepan over medium heat until it reaches 350°F (180°C) on a deep-fry thermometer. Line a large baking sheet with paper towels and set nearby.

WHILE THE OIL HEATS, MAKE THE BATTER

Whisk together the flour, salt, baking soda, and water in a large bowl, until smooth and the consistency of pancake batter. (Do not overmix.)

Working in batches, dip the baccalà pieces into the batter to coat, then remove with tongs, allowing the excess batter to drip off, and slip into the hot oil, being careful not to crowd the pan. Gently stir and jostle the coated fish pieces as needed to prevent them from sticking together. Fry, flipping once, until crisp and lightly golden, 4 to 6 minutes per batch. Transfer the fried fish to the paper towels to drain and sprinkle with a little salt. Add more oil to the pan as needed, letting it come up to heat before proceeding.

Transfer the baccalà to a serving plate and serve hot, with lemon wedges alongside for squeezing.

Mozzarella Fritta

Instead of baccalà, use 1 pound (454 g) cherry size mozzarella balls (ciliegine), drained and patted dry with paper towels. Proceed as above, frying them for 2 to 3 minutes per batch.

FRIED ZUCCHINI BLOSSOMS

Fiori di Zucca Fritti

SERVES 4 TO 6

Fried zucchini blossoms are found just about everywhere in Rome, particularly between June and September, when zucchini is in season, but the dish has roots in the Jewish Ghetto. The delicate orange-yellow flowers are stuffed with mozzarella and anchovies (you can leave the latter out to keep the dish vegetarian), lightly battered, and fried. The result is extraordinary, the anchovies and creamy cheese playing perfectly off the crackling crust and gently vegetal flavor of the blossoms. I usually eat these sizzling hot from the frying pan, burning my mouth in the process. I am sure they taste great at the dinner table too, but who can wait?

For the Zucchini Blossoms

12 zucchini blossoms *(or other squash blossoms)*

¼ pound (113 g) fresh mozzarella, *cut into 12 pieces*

6 oil-packed anchovy fillets, *halved lengthwise (optional)*

Light olive oil or vegetable oil (such as sunflower or grapeseed) *for deep-frying*

For the Batter

1½ cups (210 g) all-purpose flour

2 teaspoons kosher salt, *plus more for sprinkling*

1¾ cups chilled sparkling water

PREPARE THE ZUCCHINI BLOSSOMS
Gently open the petals of each blossom and remove the pistils or stamens inside. Place a piece of mozzarella and half an anchovy, if using, inside each one and gently close.

Heat 1 inch (2.5 cm) of oil in a medium frying pan over medium heat until it reaches 350°F (180°C) on a deep-fry thermometer. Line a large baking sheet with paper towels and set nearby.

WHILE THE OIL HEATS, MAKE THE BATTER
Whisk together the flour, salt, and sparkling water in a large bowl until smooth and the consistency of a loose pancake batter. (Do not overmix.)

Working in batches of 3 or 4, dip the stuffed blossoms into the batter, allowing the excess batter to drip off, and then, using tongs, slip into the hot oil. Fry, turning once, until crisp and lightly golden, 2 to 3 minutes per side. Transfer to the paper towel–lined plate to drain for a couple of minutes.

Ttransfer the fried blossoms to a serving platter and sprinkle with salt. Serve hot.

FRIED FRESH ANCHOVIES

Alici Fritte

SERVES 4 TO 6

Fried anchovies, alongside many other oil-crisped goodies, are de rigueur on restaurant menus across Rome's Jewish Ghetto neighborhood. The classic dish is traditionally made with fresh rather than cured anchovies, and it tastes best that way. If fresh anchovies are too difficult to find, however, water-packed canned anchovies, which are available at specialty markets and online, can be substituted.

Light olive oil or vegetable oil (such as sunflower or grapeseed) *for deep-frying*

1 pound (454 g) fresh anchovies, *cleaned (see Note),* or three 4.5-ounce (125 g) cans water-packed anchovies, *drained*

1 cup (140 g) all-purpose flour

Kosher salt

Lemon wedges *for serving*

NOTE: *To clean fresh anchovies, cut off their heads, slice down each fish, vertically, and open out like a butterfly. Remove the bones and innards, gently rinse them, and pat dry with paper towels. Or ask the fishmonger to clean the anchovies for you.*

Heat 1 inch (2.5 cm) of oil in a medium pot set over medium heat until it reaches 350°F (180°C) on a deep-fry thermometer. Line a large plate with paper towels and set nearby.

While the oil is heating, pat the anchovies dry with paper towels. If you are using canned anchovies, you can slice them lengthwise in half, if desired. They are delicate, so work carefully.

Put the flour in a large bowl. Working in batches, add the anchovies, and gently toss to coat evenly with flour, then shake off the excess flour. Being careful to avoid crowding the pot, using tongs, slip the anchovies into the hot oil and fry, jostling a few times with the tongs or a slotted spoon to prevent them from sticking together, until lightly golden brown, 2 to 4 minutes per batch. Transfer to the paper towels to drain briefly.

Arrange the fried anchovies on a serving platter, sprinkle with salt, and serve hot, with lemon wedges alongside for squeezing.

MOZZARELLA-STUFFED RISOTTO FRITTERS

Supplì al Telefono

MAKES ABOUT 15 FRITTERS

These cheese-stuffed rice fritters take a bit of time to make, but they are truly one of life's greatest pleasures. The outsides are crisp and crunchy, the risotto inside is creamy, and the mozzarella is molten, with the perfect amount of satisfying "cheese pull." (The dish's name stems from the melted cheese's resemblance to an old-fashioned telephone cord.)

Because they are deep-fried, supplì tend to get lumped together with other fried foods as a descendant of the cuisine of the Roman Jewish Ghetto. In reality, the historical connection is tenuous, but excellent versions of supplì can be found on the menus of Rome's dairy-focused kosher restaurants, including Casalino Osteria Kosher and Ba'Ghetto Milky in the Ghetto neighborhood, and Yotvata, just beyond it. They are also featured on the menu at Che Fico, chef David Nayfeld's San Francisco restaurant that is inspired by cucina Ebraica. Serve them on their own, or with a warmed tomato sauce for dipping.

For the Risotto

2 tablespoons extra-virgin olive oil

1 small yellow onion, *finely chopped*

Kosher salt and freshly ground black pepper

1 cup (250 g) Carnaroli or Arborio rice

¾ cup (180 ml) dry white wine

2½ cups (590 ml) vegetable broth, *store-bought or homemade (page 109), slightly warmed*

1 cup (250 g) tomato puree (passata), *slightly warmed*

½ cup (35 g) freshly grated Parmesan or Pecorino Romano

1 tablespoon *finely chopped* fresh basil

For Assembly and Frying

Light olive oil or vegetable oil (such as sunflower or grapeseed) *for deep-frying*

1 cup (140 g) unseasoned bread crumbs

½ teaspoon kosher salt

2 large eggs

6 ounces (170 g) fresh mozzarella, *cut into thin 1-inch-(2.5 cm) batons (about 15 batons)*

PREPARE THE RISOTTO

Heat the oil in a large deep frying pan over medium heat. Add the onion with a pinch of salt and cook, stirring occasionally, until softened and lightly browned, 6 to 8 minutes. Add the rice and cook, stirring, until coated with oil, 2 to 3 minutes. Add the wine and cook, stirring often, until mostly evaporated 1 to 2 minutes.

Stir together the warmed vegetable broth and tomato puree in a bowl (see Note). Add 1 cup (240 ml) of the mixture to the rice and cook, stirring constantly, until absorbed, 5 to 7 minutes. Continue adding the tomato-broth mixture to the rice about ½ cup (120 ml) at a time, stirring constantly and waiting for the liquid to be absorbed after each addition, until you've added it all. The rice should be creamy and tender, but with a hint of bite.

Remove the pan from the heat and stir in the grated cheese, basil, ½ teaspoon salt, and a generous amount of black pepper. Taste and add more salt, if desired. Spread the risotto out on a large plate and let cool completely, about 1 hour. (*At this point, the rice can be covered and refrigerated for up to 2 days. Bring to room temperature before making the fritters.*)

ASSEMBLE AND FRY THE SUPPLÌ

Heat 2 inches (5 cm) of oil in a medium saucepan over medium heat until it reaches 350°F (180°C) on a deep-fry thermometer. Line a large plate or baking sheet with paper towels and set nearby.

While the oil is heating, spread the bread crumbs on a plate and mix in the salt. Beat the eggs in a shallow bowl.

Scoop out a scant ¼ cup (55 g) of the risotto, form it into an oval, and, holding the oval in your palm, press an indentation down the center. Place a baton of mozzarella in the indentation, then close the rice around the mozzarella. (If the rice feels sticky, moisten your hands slightly with water.) Continue with the remaining risotto and cheese. You should have about 15 fritters.

Working in batches of 4 or 5, dip each fritter into the beaten egg, allowing the excess to drip off, then coat with the bread crumbs. Add to the hot oil and fry, turning once, until the supplì are deep golden brown all over, 3 to 5 minutes. Transfer to the paper towels to drain briefly.

Transfer the fried supplì to a serving platter and serve hot. Leftovers, once cooled completely, can be stored, tightly covered, in the freezer for up to 3 months.

NOTE: *The tomato sauce and broth for the risotto can be warmed together in a microwave or on the stovetop.*

DEEP-FRIED CURLY ENDIVE

Torzelli

SERVES 4

This dish of deep-fried curly endive (which is also called frisée or chicory) follows in the grand Roman Jewish tradition of transforming virtuous vegetables into something truly decadent. Older recipes do not coat the leaves with flour, but I followed chef Joyce Goldstein's advice in her cookbook *Cucina Ebraica* and gave them a light toss in flour before frying, to keep things from getting too heavy. The fried endive turns crisp around the edges and silky and sultry in the middle. I recommend sitting down to enjoy it as part of a larger meal like a civilized human, rather than scarfing it straight from the pan, which is what I usually do.

Kosher salt

1 large head curly endive, *washed and patted dry*

Light olive oil or vegetable oil (such as sunflower or grapeseed) *for deep-frying*

½ cup (70 g) all-purpose flour

Lemon wedges *for serving (optional)*

Bring a large pot of generously salted water to a boil over high heat. Line a large baking sheet with a layer of paper towels. Meanwhile, cut the head of endive into 4 roughly equal pieces, taking care to cut through the core, so that the pieces hold together.

When the water boils, add the endive to the pot and cook until crisp-tender, 1 to 2 minutes. Carefully remove the endive and transfer to the baking sheet to drain thoroughly, at least 30 minutes. (*This can be done several hours in advance.*)

Heat 1 inch (2.5 cm) of oil in a medium saucepan over medium heat until it reaches 350°F (180°C) on a deep-fry thermometer. Line a large plate with paper towels and set nearby. Spread the flour on another plate.

Working in two batches, lightly dredge the endive pieces in the flour on both sides, gently shaking to remove the excess, and slip into the hot oil. Fry, turning once, until golden brown, 4 to 5 minutes per batch. Transfer the fried endive to the paper towel–lined plate to drain and sprinkle with a little salt.

Transfer the endive to a serving platter and serve hot, with lemon wedges on the side for squeezing, if desired.

SAVORY FRIED POTATO PASTRIES

Burik con Patate

MAKES ABOUT 20 BURIK

While visiting Rome, I had the good fortune of dining at the home of Daniela Gean and Roberto Attias. The husband-and-wife team run Mezè Bistrot, a restaurant in Rome's Monteverde neighborhood that specializes in Middle Eastern and North African cuisine. Among the many dishes Daniela (who was born in Libya and immigrated to Rome with her family when she was one) served, her potato burik was the standout. The homemade pastry was ethereally light, with wispy edges that crackled and crunched with each bite. And inside was a filling of creamy mashed potatoes flavored with softened onion, parsley, and a hint of cinnamon.

Making the pastry leaves can be tricky to master, and they require practice and a quick, steady hand. Libyan Jewish grandmothers traditionally spread the batter on the hot pan with their fingertips, but a large pastry brush (or a clean paintbrush) works just as well, without the chance of burning yourself. Be patient, and you will eventually get the hang of it.

For the Filling

3 medium russet potatoes (about 1½ pounds / 680 g), *peeled and cut into chunks*

2 tablespoons extra-virgin olive oil

1 small yellow onion, *finely chopped*

1½ teaspoons ground cinnamon

½ teaspoon kosher salt, *plus more if needed*

3 tablespoons *finely chopped* fresh flat-leaf parsley

For the Burik Wrappers

1½ cups (210 g) all-purpose flour, *plus more if needed*

1 teaspoon kosher salt

1 teaspoon white wine vinegar

1 teaspoon vegetable oil (such as sunflower or grapeseed)

¾ cup water (180 ml), *plus more if needed*

Vegetable oil (such as sunflower or grapeseed) *for cooking the wrappers and frying the burik*

NOTE: *If you are short on time, store-bought square egg roll wrappers make a tasty shortcut.*

CONTINUES

MAKE THE FILLING

Add the potatoes to a medium pot, cover with water, and bring to a boil over high heat, then cook until potatoes are very tender, 20 to 30 minutes.

Meanwhile, heat the olive oil in a medium frying pan over medium-low heat. Add the onion and cook, stirring often, until softened but not browned, 8 to 10 minutes. Stir in the cinnamon and salt, and remove from the heat.

When the potatoes are done, drain, transfer to a large bowl, and mash with a potato masher until creamy.

Add the softened onions to the mashed potatoes, along with the parsley, and stir to combine. Taste and add more salt if needed. Set aside. (*The potato mixture can be made up to 2 days in advance and stored, covered, in the fridge.*)

MAKE THE BATTER

Add the flour, salt, vinegar, and oil to the bowl of a food processor and pulse to combine. Add the water and process until you have a very smooth batter the consistency of a loose (but not thin or runny) pancake batter. If needed, add more water or flour 1 tablespoon at a time until the desired consistency is reached. Transfer the batter to a bowl and let rest for 1 hour.

MAKE THE WRAPPERS

Place an 8-inch (20 cm) nonstick frying pan over the lowest possible heat. When it is hot, add about ½ teaspoon of oil to the pan and use a paper towel to spread it around. (You are going for the bare minimum of oil.)

Pour about 1 tablespoon of the batter into the pan and, using a large pastry brush, quickly brush it into a thin layer all over the bottom. (If the batter is too thick to spread effectively, whisk in a little more water.) Cook until the top of the wrapper is fully dry and the edges are beginning to curl, then carefully transfer to a plate. (It is okay if there are a few small holes in the wrapper.) Continue making wrappers, stacking them with squares of parchment paper between them, until you've used all the batter.

FILL AND FRY THE BURIK

Spoon a heaping tablespoon of the potato filling into the center of one wrapper, fold it in half to make a half-moon shape, and press the edges together to seal. Continue until either all of the filling or all of the wrappers are used up.

Line a large baking sheet with a layer of paper towels and set aside. Heat ¼ inch (6 mm) of oil in a large frying pan over medium heat until shimmering. Working in batches of 4 or 5, gently slip the burik into the oil and cook, turning once, until crispy and golden on both sides, 1 to 2 minutes per side. Transfer the fried burik to the prepared baking sheet to drain. Serve warm.

FRIED ALMOND PASTRIES WITH ORANGE SYRUP

Burik Belluz

MAKES ABOUT 20 PASTRIES

For these Libyan Jewish pastries, spoonfuls of decadent homemade almond paste are encased in delicate rounds of dough. The parcels are fried until golden and crisp, then drizzled with or soaked in a citrus-scented sugar syrup. Prepping the homemade burik wrappers takes time and finesse, but the lacy edges and appealing crunch are worth the effort. If you are short on time, though, store-bought egg roll wrappers make a tasty, if nontraditional, substitute. This recipe was inspired by one I saw Hamos Guetta make on his captivating YouTube channel, which is dedicated to preserving Libyan and Roman Jewish recipes (see page 78).

For the Orange Syrup

1 cup (240 ml) water

1 cup (200 g) granulated sugar

2 packed teaspoons grated orange zest *(from about 2 small oranges)*

For the Almond Filling

1 cup (100 g) blanched almond flour

½ cup (100 g) granulated sugar

¼ teaspoon kosher salt

1 large egg, *beaten*

Water if needed

For Assembly and Frying

1 batch Burik Wrappers (page 143) or store-bought square egg roll wrappers

Vegetable oil (such as sunflower or grapeseed) *for frying*

Sesame seeds *for sprinkling (optional)*

MAKE THE ORANGE SYRUP

Stir together the water and sugar in a medium saucepan set over high heat and bring to a boil. Reduce the heat to medium-low and cook, stirring often, until the syrup thickens slightly, about 5 minutes. Remove from the heat and stir in the orange zest. Set aside to cool. (*The syrup can be made ahead and stored, covered, in the fridge for up to 2 weeks.*)

MAKE THE ALMOND FILLING

Whisk together the almond flour, sugar, and salt in a medium bowl until combined. Add the beaten egg and stir until a thick but spreadable paste forms. If necessary, stir in a little water, 1 tablespoon at a time, to reach the desired consistency.

FILL AND FRY THE BURIK

Spoon 1 rounded tablespoon of the almond filling into the center of a burik wrapper, fold it in half to make a half-moon shape, and press the edges together to seal. (If using egg roll wrappers, fold each one into a triangle and press the edges to seal.) Continue making burik until you've used all of the filling.

Line a large baking sheet with a layer of paper towels and set aside. Heat ¼ inch (6 mm) of oil in a large frying pan over medium heat until shimmering. Working in batches of 4 or 5, gently slip the burik into the oil and cook, turning once, until crispy and golden on both sides, 1 to 2 minutes per side. Transfer the fried burik to the prepared baking sheet to drain.

Arrange the burik on a serving platter. Drizzle generously with the orange syrup (reserving any extra for another use) and sprinkle with sesame seeds, if using. Serve warm.

HONEY-SOAKED MATZO FRITTERS

Pizzarelle con Miele

SERVES 4 TO 6

These sweet fritters are arguably Roman Jews' favorite Passover treat. Made from softened and crumbled matzo mixed with beaten egg, pine nuts, and raisins, they are deep-fried until light and crispy outside and custardy-rich within. The dish is so ubiquitous, it even comes with its own controversy! Some families swear by the addition of a spoonful of cocoa powder to the matzo batter, while others argue that it has absolutely no place in the recipe. Feel free to add a tablespoon or two and see where you land.

5 sheets matzo

4 large eggs, *lightly beaten*

¼ cup (30 g) pine nuts

¼ cup (35 g) dark raisins, *soaked in warm water for 5 minutes and drained*

¼ cup (50 g) granulated sugar

1½ packed teaspoons grated lemon or orange zest *(from 1 to 2 lemons or 1 medium orange)*

¼ teaspoon kosher salt

Vegetable oil (such as sunflower or grapeseed) *for frying*

¼ cup (85 g) honey *for drizzling*

Place the matzo sheets in a baking dish, cover with cold water, and soak until very soft, 5 to 10 minutes.

Meanwhile, add the eggs, pine nuts, raisins, sugar, citrus zest, and salt to a large bowl and stir to combine. Remove the softened matzo from the water, squeeze firmly to remove as much water as possible, and crumble into the egg mixture. Stir to thoroughly combine.

Heat ½-inch (1.25 cm) of oil in a large frying pan over medium heat until shimmering. Line a large plate with paper towels and set aside. Working in batches of 5 or 6, scoop out rounded tablespoons of the batter, carefully slip into the oil, and nudge them with the spoon into an oval shape. Fry, flipping once, until the fritters are golden brown on both sides, about 4 minutes per batch. Transfer to the paper towel–lined plate to drain.

Put the honey in a small measuring cup or bowl and microwave until it is easily pourable, about 30 seconds.

Transfer the fritters to a serving platter and drizzle generously with the warmed honey. Serve warm or at room temperature.

APPLE FRITTERS WITH VANILLA SUGAR

Mele Fritte

SERVES 6 TO 8

For these sweet, crunchy fritters, apple rings are lightly coated with a creamy batter, then fried until crisp and golden outside and tender within. My recipe was inspired by one found in Donatella Limentani Pavoncello's cookbook *Dal 1880 ad Oggi* (see page 152). She served the fritters as part of her family's Hanukkah menu, but they also make great use of an autumnal apple-picking haul.

Donatella sprinkled her fritters with homemade vanilla sugar, as do I. The recipe for the sugar makes a good deal more than you need for the fritters, but it keeps for a long time and is useful to have around for other baking projects. If you would rather skip that step, the fritters are equally tasty sprinkled with regular granulated sugar or cinnamon-sugar.

For the Vanilla Sugar

2 vanilla beans

1½ cups (300 g) granulated sugar

For the Fritters

4 large baking apples, *peeled*

1½ cups (210 g) all-purpose flour

3 tablespoons granulated sugar

½ teaspoon kosher salt

½ teaspoon baking soda

1½ cups (355 ml) milk or non-dairy milk

Vegetable oil (such as sunflower or grapeseed) *for frying*

PREPARE THE VANILLA SUGAR
Split the vanilla beans and scrape out the seeds; set the pods aside. Put the sugar and vanilla seeds in a food processor and pulse until fully combined. Transfer the sugar to a glass jar, add the reserved pods, cover tightly, and set aside. (*The sugar can be used right away, but the flavor will develop over time. It can be stored, tightly covered, for up to 1 year.*)

PREPARE THE FRITTERS
Using an apple corer (or a melon baller or sturdy metal teaspoon), carefully remove the apple cores and discard. Slice the apples into ½-inch- (1.25 cm) thick rings and set aside.

Whisk together the flour, sugar, salt, and baking soda in a large bowl. Add the milk and whisk until smooth.

Heat ½ inch (1.25 cm) of oil in a large frying pan over medium until shimmering. Line a large plate with paper towels and set nearby.

When the oil is hot, working in batches of 4 to 5, dip the apple rings into the batter, let the excess drip off, and carefully slip them into the oil. Fry, turning once, until golden brown on both sides, 2 to 3 minutes per side. Transfer to the paper towel–lined plate to drain.

Sprinkle the fritters generously with vanilla sugar while still hot and serve immediately.

Dal 1880 ad Oggi: *The Cookbook That Changed Everything*

EARLY IN THE process of writing this cookbook, when the world felt very isolated because of the Covid-19 pandemic, I relied heavily on cookbooks to jump-start my research. From Joyce Goldstein's *Cucina Ebraica* to *Popes, Peasants, and Shepherds: Recipes and Lore from Rome and Lazio* by Oretta Zanini de Vita, books served as a portal into Rome's Jewish community when a plane ride to the Eternal City was simply not feasible.

And then I stumbled across Donatella. Donatella Limentani Pavoncello was a Roman Jew born in 1928 who grew up in the Trastevere neighborhood. During World War II, she escaped the Nazis by hiding in Catholic convents, where she could never venture outside for fear of being discovered. After the war ended, as life slowly returned to normal, she reunited with her family and eventually became a professor of literature, got married, and raised three daughters. She also cooked a lot—for weeknight dinners, for Shabbat and holidays, and for the joy it brought her to connect to her heritage and history through food.

After decades of family meals and special occasions, Donatella and her mother decided to write some dishes down as a way of preserving their traditions. Working together, and aided by a list of holiday menus Donatella's great-grandmother had penned many decades before, they began to chronicle their memories and recipes. The result was a handwritten cookbook they called *Dal 1880 ad Oggi*: *La Cucina Ebraica della Mia Famiglia,* or *From 1880 to Today: My Family's Jewish Cuisine.*

The book itself, which was printed in 1982, is stunning. Every recipe is written out in Donatella's impeccable script. And the chapters are accompanied by intricate cut-paper illustrations of kitchen scenes that she made herself. In the introduction, she writes in her trademark lyrical style:

In a large kitchen with tall ceilings, two expert hands that do not know tiredness clean artichokes, slice onions, give the final wise touch to the stracotto that for hours has been basking on the charcoal. Around there is a great ruckus of pots and dishes, the excitement and the smell of the great occasions: Better hurry, it is almost sunset... the party is about to begin...

Locating a physical copy of Donatella's book proved challenging, but my amazing research assistant, Megan Litt, worked with the generous people at torah.it, an Italian organization dedicated to Jewish texts, to source an electronic copy of the cookbook. What a gift it was to see the book in full, even just on my computer screen!

Over the next many months, I turned to Donatella's cookbook time and again as a guide and a comfort. What did she and her family make for holidays? What dishes was her Shabbat table incomplete without? Although she passed away a few years ago, so I never had the opportunity to meet her in person, I leaned on her—and learned from her—in a way that made her feel like family.

In the fall of 2021, the world opened up enough for me to finally return to Rome for a visit. Walking the streets of the Jewish Ghetto neighborhood, which I loved so dearly, was magic enough.

Then one evening, I was invited to dinner at the home of my friend, the Roman Jewish historian Micaela Pavoncello (see page 184). As I was scanning the wall-to-wall bookshelves in her living room, a thin paperback caught my eye. And suddenly, after so many months of virtual everything, I was holding an actual copy of Donatella's book in my trembling hands. I leafed through the pages I already knew so well, and quietly said the shehecheyanu—a Jewish prayer of gratitude. For that brief and beautiful moment, just before we tucked into Micaela's stracotto with rigatoni, Donatella was there too.

1880
1982
DONATELLA LIMENTANI PAVONCELLO
DAL 1880 AD OGGI
LA CUCINA EBRAICA
DELLA MIA FAMIGLIA
CARUCCI EDITORE ROMA
5641
5743

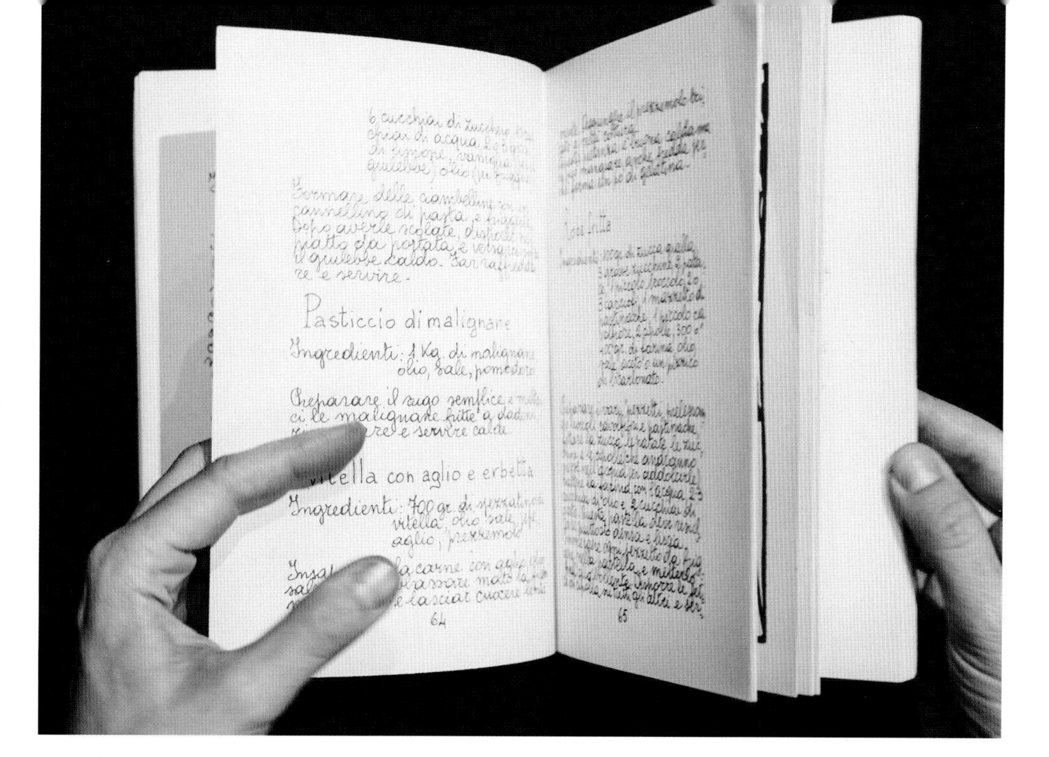
Pasticcio di malignane
Ingredienti: 1 Kg. di malignane
olio, sale, pomodoro
Preparare il sugo semplice
ci le malignane fritte a dadi
e servire calde
vitella con aglio e erbetta
Ingredienti: 700 gr. di
vitella, olio, sale
aglio, prezzemolo
64
65

PASTA AND RICE

Pasta e Riso

PASTA CARBONARA WITH ZUCCHINI

Carbonara di Zucchine

SERVES 4 TO 6

At Nonna Betta in Rome's Jewish Ghetto neighborhood, the father-and-son team Umberto and Michele Pavoncello serve a vegetarian version of classic pasta carbonara that replaces the non-kosher cured pork with sautéed zucchini. Purists would say that the dish is technically no longer carbonara, and that is true—but it satisfies many of the same cravings.

I asked my friend Giovanni Terracina, who runs the kosher catering company Le Bon Ton, to show me how to make the dish. His number one tip? Wait until the pasta has "stopped singing" (meaning actively sizzling, but I like the poetic way he put it better) before stirring in the egg yolks. That way, you end up with a rich, emulsified sauce rather than pasta with scrambled eggs. Carbonara di zucchine is wonderful as is, but I sometimes swap some of the zucchini with sliced mushrooms for an extra hit of meaty texture. This recipe moves fast once it gets started, so be sure to have all of the ingredients prepped and ready.

Kosher salt and freshly ground black pepper

¼ cup (60 ml) extra-virgin olive oil

2 medium zucchini (about 1 pound / 454 g), *halved lengthwise (or quartered if thick) and thinly sliced*

6 medium garlic cloves, *thinly sliced*

6 large egg yolks

2 ounces (60 g) Parmesan, *grated (about 1 cup), plus more for serving*

1 ounce (30 g) Pecorino Romano, *grated (about ½ cup)*

1 pound (454 g) spaghetti or rigatoni

Bring a large pot of generously salted water to a boil over high heat.

While the water is coming to a boil, heat the oil in a large wide frying pan over medium-high heat. Add the zucchini with a generous pinch of salt and cook, stirring occasionally, until softened and lightly browned, 7 to 10 minutes. Turn the heat down to medium, add the garlic, and cook, stirring, until fragrant, 1 to 2 minutes. Turn off the heat.

Vigorously whisk the egg yolks in a medium bowl until no streaks remain, then whisk in the Parmesan, Pecorino Romano, ¼ teaspoon salt, and a generous amount of pepper. (The cheese will not dissolve into the yolks at this stage.) Set aside.

Add the pasta to the boiling water and cook, stirring once or twice, until just shy of al dente; do not overcook. Drain the pasta, reserving about 1 cup (240 ml) of the cooking water.

Turn the heat under the pan of zucchini back on to medium-high. Once the mixture is sizzling, add the drained pasta and ½ cup (120 ml) of the reserved cooking water and cook, stirring or tossing constantly and vigorously, until the water is reduced by about half, 1 to 3 minutes. Remove the pan from the heat.

Whisk ¼ cup (60 ml) of the remaining reserved cooking water into the egg mixture, then slowly stream the mixture into the pan with the pasta and zucchini, stirring or tossing constantly, until the cheese melts and a thick, glossy sauce forms. If the sauce seems tight or thick, add a little more reserved cooking water, about 1 tablespoon at a time, and toss until the desired consistency is reached. (You may not use all of the cooking water.) Taste and add more salt and/or pepper if needed.

Divide the pasta among serving bowls and sprinkle with grated Parmesan. Serve immediately.

NOTE: *Pasta carbonara is traditionally made with only Pecorino Romano, but many recipes also include some Parmesan, which has a milder and less assertively salty flavor. I like the ratio of 2:1 Parmesan to Pecorino Romano, but you can play around with what works for you.*

SPAGHETTI WITH ARTICHOKES AND BOTTARGA

Spaghetti con Carciofi e Bottarga

SERVES 4 TO 6

When Rome's peak artichoke season rolls around in the early spring, Roman Jews waste no time putting them to good use—as in this pasta dish. Starting with fresh artichokes gives it inimitable appeal, but for busy weeknights, canned or frozen artichokes make a good substitute. The pasta is usually finished with plenty of shaved bottarga (dried fish roe), which lends a briny taste of the sea. When I make it at home, however, I tend to go the vegetarian route and use grated Parmesan instead. Either way, the dish tastes like pure springtime.

Kosher salt

¾ pound (340 g) spaghetti

4 large artichokes, *cleaned according to the instructions on page 58,* or two 14-ounce (400 g) cans artichoke quarters, *drained, or* 2 cups (200 g) thawed frozen artichoke quarters

¼ cup (60 ml) extra-virgin olive oil, *plus more for drizzling*

1 medium yellow onion, *finely chopped*

4 medium garlic cloves, *thinly sliced*

½ teaspoon red pepper flakes, *plus more if needed*

½ cup (120 ml) dry white wine

1½ teaspoons grated lemon zest *(from 1 to 2 lemons)*

3 tablespoons chopped fresh basil, *plus more for serving*

Freshly grated bottarga or freshly grated Parmesan *for serving*

Bring a large pot of generously salted water to a boil. Add the spaghetti, give it a stir, and cook until al dente, following the timing on the package. Drain the spaghetti, reserving about 1 cup (240 ml) of the pasta cooking water.

Meanwhile, if you are using fresh artichokes, slice them into ¼-inch- (6 mm) thick slices; set aside.

Heat the oil in a 12-inch frying pan over medium-high heat. Add the onion and cook, stirring occasionally, until softened and lightly browned, 6 to 8 minutes.

Add the artichokes and ½ teaspoon salt and cook, stirring occasionally, until the artichokes begin to soften, 6 to 8 minutes. Add the garlic and red pepper flakes and cook until fragrant, 1 to 2 minutes.

Stir in the wine, bring to a simmer, and cook until the wine reduces by half, about 2 minutes. (If the spaghetti is still cooking at this point, take the artichoke pan off the heat until the pasta catches up. Bring it back up to heat before continuing.)

Add ½ cup (120 ml) of the reserved pasta water to the artichokes and cook, stirring, until it has slightly reduced, 2 to 4 minutes. Add the drained spaghetti and a little more of the pasta water, as needed (you might not use all of it), tossing with tongs until the sauce clings to the noodles, about 2 minutes. Add the lemon zest and basil and toss to combine.

Taste and add additional salt and/or red pepper flakes, if desired. Transfer the pasta to serving bowls and serve hot, drizzled with olive oil and topped generously with chopped basil and bottarga or Parmesan.

SEMOLINA GNOCCHI GRATIN

Gnocchi alla Romana

SERVES 4 TO 6

The name of this traditional Roman dish is a bit confusing because rather than the potato- or ricotta-based dumplings that the term *gnocchi* more commonly refers to, these gnocchi are made from semolina. But after one bite of the creamy, golden brown gratin that emerges from the oven, names will hardly matter. Gnocchi alla Romana is not exclusively a Jewish dish, but it is widely served within the community. In *Popes, Peasants, and Shepherds: Recipes and Lore from Rome and Lazio*, Oretta Zanini de Vita writes that some Jewish families celebrate the holiday of Shavuot (when dairy foods are traditionally eaten) with these gnocchi. Serve with sautéed mushrooms and a salad, or alongside Roasted Tomato Halves (page 65), for a comforting weeknight meal.

3 cups (710 ml) whole milk

1 cup (240 ml) water

1¼ cups (200 g) fine semolina

1½ teaspoons kosher salt

4 tablespoons (55 g) cold unsalted butter, *cut into small pieces*

1½ cups (105 g) freshly grated Parmesan

⅛ teaspoon ground nutmeg

2 large egg yolks, *lightly beaten*

Heat the milk and water in a large saucepan over medium-high heat, stirring occasionally, until the liquid comes to a rolling simmer (just shy of a full boil). Reduce the heat to medium-low and, stirring constantly with a sturdy spoon, steadily pour in the semolina. Cook, stirring constantly, until the semolina plumps and the mixture becomes very thick, with slow bubbles coming to the surface, 2 to 4 minutes.

Remove the pan from the heat and immediately stir in the salt, half of the butter, 1 cup (70 g) of the Parmesan, and the nutmeg. Add the egg yolks and stir vigorously to fully incorporate them.

Lightly moisten the bottom of a 10 × 15-inch (25 × 38 cm) rimmed baking sheet with water. Pour the warm semolina mixture onto the baking sheet and, using a lightly moistened offset spatula or your hands, gently smooth it into a ½-inch (1.25 cm) thickness. Let cool until firm enough to cut, about 30 minutes.

Preheat the oven to 425°F (220°C). Lightly grease a 9 × 13-inch (23 × 33 cm) baking dish.

CONTINUES

Using a 2½-inch (6 cm) round cookie or biscuit cutter, stamp out as many circles of semolina as possible. Use a thin metal spatula to carefully lift the circles out of the baking sheet and arrange them in the greased baking dish, allowing the slices to overlap like roof shingles. (Lightly moisten the spatula as needed to prevent the gnocchi from sticking.) If desired, you can press any scraps of semolina together and stamp out more circles.

Scatter the remaining butter and remaining ½ cup (35 g) Parmesan over the top of the gnocchi. Bake, uncovered, until golden on top and browning at the edges of the baking dish, 25 to 35 minutes.

Remove the gnocchi from the oven and let cool slightly before serving.

Pasta in Roman Jewish Cuisine

C*OMMON LORE SUGGESTS* that the thirteenth-century Italian explorer Marco Polo introduced pasta to Italy (specifically Venice) after returning from travels in China. But pasta, as it is known today, was more likely introduced into southern Italy by Arab traders earlier in the Middle Ages. From there, it caught on quickly. According to Gil Marks's *Encyclopedia of Jewish Food,* "By 1400, commercial pasta production, controlled by guilds, was widespread in Italy." Pasta, he writes, "was so valuable that full-time watchmen were required for protection."

Families made their own fresh pasta dough at home, but the innovation of dried pasta (pasta secca), and the invention of the first mechanical pasta maker in the seventeenth century, allowed it to become an inexpensive staple of daily life in Italy.

Sephardi Jews who were exiled from Sicily during the Spanish Inquisition brought their pasta dishes with them to northern Italy. The Jews in Rome took to those dishes just as their neighbors did. Today, from the rigatoni served alongside wine-braised beef stew and the broken spaghetti traditionally used to thicken simple soups, to sumptuous homemade pasta squares filled with beef, pasta is both central to Roman Jewish celebrations and integral to the everyday table.

Kosher

SPAGHETTI WITH TUNA AND TOMATO

Spaghetti Tonno e Pomodoro

SERVES 4 TO 6

Italo Camerino grew up in Montreal, but his Roman Jewish family maintained many of their food customs in their adopted home. He remembers his father, Enzo, drying his own bottarga and friends clamoring to come eat in his mother, Silvana's, kitchen. "If someone came over, you just added a little more water to the soup," he said. Camerino also recalls his family's spaghetti with tuna and tomato, and for good reason—the mix of bright tomatoes, oil-packed tuna, and spicy red pepper flakes is memorable. I merged Camerino's recipe with the version in Joyce Goldstein's *Cucina Ebraica*, adding capers for an extra hit of brine and lemon zest for sunny freshness. Say hello to your new favorite spaghetti sauce.

Kosher salt and freshly ground black pepper

1 pound (454 g) spaghetti

¼ cup (60 ml) extra-virgin olive oil, *plus more for drizzling*

1 large yellow onion, *finely chopped*

2 medium garlic cloves, *finely chopped*

¼ teaspoon red pepper flakes, *plus more if needed*

One 28-ounce (795 g) can diced tomatoes

Two 5-ounce (142 g) cans or jars good-quality oil-packed tuna, *drained and broken up*

2 tablespoons salt-packed capers, *rinsed, drained, and roughly chopped*

1 packed teaspoon grated lemon zest *(from about 1 medium lemon)*

Chopped fresh flat-leaf parsley *for serving*

Freshly grated Parmesan *for serving (optional)*

Bring a large pot of generously salted water to a boil over high heat. Add the spaghetti, stir well, and cook until al dente, following the timing on the package. Drain well.

Meanwhile, heat the oil in a large saucepan over medium heat. Add the onion and garlic and cook, stirring occasionally, until softened and lightly browned, 6 to 8 minutes. Stir in the red pepper flakes, diced tomatoes (with their juices), 1 teaspoon salt, and ½ teaspoon black pepper, bring to a simmer, and cook, stirring occasionally, until the juices are slightly thickened, 15 to 20 minutes.

Stir the tuna, capers, and lemon zest into the sauce. Add the drained spaghetti, along with a generous drizzle of olive oil, and toss well to combine. Taste and add more salt, black pepper, and/or red pepper flakes, if desired.

Serve the spaghetti hot, sprinkled with parsley and, if desired, Parmesan.

JEWISH-STYLE PASTA AMATRICIANA

Pasta Amatriciana alla Giudia

SERVES 4 TO 6

Bucatini all'Amatriciana, which is traditionally prepared with cured pork cheek (guanciale) and grated Pecorino Romano, is hardly kosher-friendly fare. But since it is a classic Roman dish (by way of Amatrice, where it originated), it is no surprise that Roman Jews have found a way to adapt it. In the Jewish version, which can be found on the menus of several restaurants in the Ghetto neighborhood, the guanciale is replaced with cubes of carne secca—beef cured with salt and pepper. (Carne secca is difficult to source outside of Rome, but beef bacon or cubed pastrami also work well in this dish.) Finding a good substitute for the cheese is harder, but the sauce is already vibrant with flavor without it. I knew this dish was a winner when my husband, Yoshie, who puts hot sauce on absolutely everything, tasted it and said, "This doesn't need a thing."

Kosher salt

¾ pound (340 g) bucatini or spaghetti

2 tablespoons extra-virgin olive oil

6 ounces (170 g) Roman-style carne secca, *cubed,* or pastrami or beef bacon, *chopped*

1 large yellow onion, *finely chopped*

3 medium garlic cloves, *finely chopped*

½ teaspoon red pepper flakes

One 28-ounce (795 g) can whole peeled tomatoes

Bring a large pot of generously salted water to a boil. Add the pasta, give it a stir, and cook until just shy of al dente (about 1 minute less than the timing on the package). Drain the pasta, reserving 1 cup (240 ml) of the cooking water.

Meanwhile, heat the oil in a large deep frying pan over medium heat. Add the carne secca and cook, stirring occasionally, until browned, about 5 minutes.

Pour off and discard all but about 2 tablespoons of the rendered fat from the pan, then add the onion and cook, stirring occasionally, until softened, 6 to 8 minutes. Add the garlic and red pepper flakes and cook, stirring, until fragrant, about 1 minute.

Pour the tomatoes and their juices into a medium bowl and carefully squeeze the tomatoes to break them up. Add the squashed tomatoes, their juices, and ½ teaspoon salt to the pan, reduce the heat to medium-low, and cook, stirring occasionally, until the sauce thickens a bit, 15 to 20 minutes.

Add the drained pasta and about ½ cup (120 ml) of the reserved cooking water to the frying pan, turn the heat up to medium-high, and vigorously toss the pasta and sauce together until the pasta is fully al dente and coated with sauce, 2 to 3 minutes. If the sauce looks dry, add a little more of the reserved pasta water (you probably won't need all of it). Taste and add more salt if needed. Serve hot.

Challah in Rome

F*ROM PASTA AND* pizza to freshly baked bread, there is no shortage of incredible carbs in Rome. But challah—the braided loaves traditionally served on Shabbat and many Jewish holidays—is another story. When Yoshie and I honeymooned there in our mid-twenties, I remember pulling him excitedly toward the bakery in the Ghetto neighborhood one Friday morning, expecting to see bronzed loaves lining the display window. We saw piles of cookies and pastries, but challah was not on the menu. Only later did it occur to me that the braided challah I grew up with, which is German and Austrian in origin, would be decidedly out of context at a Roman Jewish bakery.

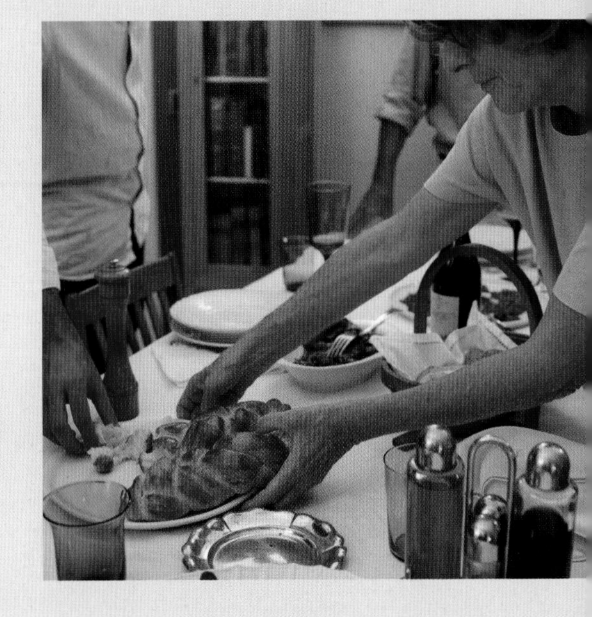

"I never had challah until I grew up," said Roberta Nahum, the former president of Rome's chapter of ADEI WIZO (Italy's Jewish Women's Association). "We celebrated Shabbat with our normal, everyday bread." By the 1990s, though, Nahum told me, some Roman Jews who had tasted Ashkenazi-style challah elsewhere—in Israel, the United States, or other parts of Europe—began to bake it at home for Shabbat. "Now it is more en vogue," she said. And indeed, if you know where to look—in certain kosher food stores, at Rome's Chabad-Lubavitch headquarters, or at a Shabbat dinner table in someone's home if you are lucky—you can find challah in Rome today.

STUFFED TOMATOES WITH RICE

Pomodori con Riso

SERVES 4 TO 6

There's something about the alchemy of soft, basil-scented rice encased in tomatoes that have been roasted to the point of collapse that is completely captivating. The layer of potatoes in the bottom of the baking dish, which turn creamy in the oven and soak up ample tomato flavor, simply gilds the lily. Pomodori con riso is traditionally served on Passover, since it is customary for Italian Jews to eat rice during the holiday. I like to make them for alfresco dinners and lazy weekend picnics in the summer, when the tomatoes in the market taste like distilled sunshine.

½ cup (100 g) Arborio or Carnaroli rice

8 medium ripe tomatoes (2½ to 3 pounds / 1.1 to 1.3 kg)

¼ cup (60 ml) extra-virgin olive oil, *plus more for drizzling*

3 medium garlic cloves, *finely chopped*

2 tablespoons *finely chopped* fresh basil, *plus more for serving*

Kosher salt and freshly ground black pepper

2 medium Yukon Gold potatoes (about 1 pound / 454 g), *peeled, halved lengthwise, and cut into ¼-inch- (6 mm) thick wedges*

Freshly grated Parmesan *for serving (optional)*

Bring a small saucepan half filled with water to a boil over high heat. Stir in the rice, reduce the heat to medium-high, and cook, stirring occasionally, until the rice is partly softened, 5 to 7 minutes. Drain and let cool slightly.

Preheat the oven to 375°F (190°C).

Cut the top ½ inch (1.25 cm) off each tomato and reserve. Use a sturdy spoon to carefully hollow out the tomatoes, leaving about ¼ inch (6 mm) of flesh intact all around. Transfer the tomato pulp and seeds to a food processor and process until well chopped but still a little chunky. (Or chop the pulp by hand.)

Transfer 1½ cups (355 ml) of the chopped tomato pulp and juice to a bowl (discard the rest or reserve for another use) and stir in the partly cooked rice, olive oil, garlic, basil, 1 teaspoon salt, and ½ teaspoon pepper.

Place the potato wedges in a 9 × 13-inch (23 × 33 cm) baking dish. Drizzle generously with olive oil, season with salt and pepper, and toss to combine, then spread the potatoes evenly over the bottom of the pan.

Generously season the insides of the tomatoes with salt and pepper. Fill the tomatoes with the rice mixture, place the reserved caps on top, and arrange them on top of the potatoes, filled side up.

Cover the baking dish with aluminum foil and bake until tomatoes are very tender and the rice has plumped, about 1 hour. Uncover the dish and continue baking until the tomatoes are beginning to collapse and the potatoes are creamy in texture, 10 to 20 minutes. Remove from the oven and let cool for at least 30 minutes before serving.

Serve the tomatoes warm or at room temperature, showered with basil and, if desired, Parmesan.

RISOTTO WITH PEAS

Risotto coi Piselli

SERVES 6

Roman Jews serve this creamy tomato sauce–enriched risotto on Passover, but if it is not your custom to eat rice or legumes during the holiday, it is equally satisfying year-round. This recipe makes an abundant amount of risotto. I like to use any leftovers to make Supplì al Telefono, mozzarella-stuffed rice fritters (page 140).

4 cups (1 l) vegetable broth, *store-bought or homemade (page 109)*

4 cups (1 l) water

Kosher salt

¼ cup (60 ml) extra-virgin olive oil

1 large yellow onion, *finely chopped*

¼ teaspoon freshly ground black pepper, *plus more if needed*

1½ cups (300 g) Arborio or Carnaroli rice

½ cup (120 ml) dry white wine

1 cup (250 g) tomato puree (passata)

1 tablespoon tomato paste

1 cup (120 g) shelled fresh peas or frozen peas

½ cup (10 g) fresh flat-leaf parsley leaves, *finely chopped, plus more for serving*

¾ cup (45 g) freshly grated Parmesan (*optional*)

NOTE: *If starting with fresh peas in the pod, you will need approximately 1 pound/454 g.*

Combine the vegetable broth and water in a large saucepan, and bring to a simmer over medium heat. Stir in 1 teaspoon salt, then turn the heat down to medium-low to keep the mixture at a bare simmer.

Meanwhile, heat the olive oil in a large deep frying pan or Dutch oven over medium-low heat. Add the onion, 1 teaspoon salt, and the pepper and cook until the onion is softened but not browned, 10 to 12 minutes. Add the rice and cook, stirring, until well coated, about 2 minutes.

Add the wine, raise the heat to medium, and cook, stirring frequently, until most of the liquid has evaporated, 2 to 3 minutes. Add the tomato puree and tomato paste and cook, stirring often, until reduced and thickened, about 2 minutes.

Add about ½ cup (120 ml) of the simmering broth mixture and cook, stirring constantly, until all of the liquid has been absorbed. Add another ½ cup (120 ml) of the broth mixture and stir until it has been absorbed, then repeat the process. Once you've added about half of the broth mixture, stir in the fresh peas; if using frozen peas, hold off until about three-quarters of the liquid has been incorporated. Continue to gradually add the broth mixture until the rice is creamy and tender but slightly al dente, 25 to 30 minutes total. (You may not need all of the liquid.) The risotto should look somewhat soupy because it will tighten off the heat, so add a final splash of broth if necessary.

Taste and add a little more salt and/or pepper, if desired. (If you used unsalted or low-salt broth, you might need to add quite a bit more salt.) Stir in the chopped parsley and the Parmesan, if using.

Serve immediately, sprinkled with a little chopped parsley. Store leftovers, covered, in the fridge. Reheat over medium heat, adding a splash of broth or water.

TOMATO RICE PIE

Tortino di Riso

SERVES 6 TO 8

I have eaten several versions of this decadent tomato rice dish (locally it is referred to as a "pie," but it is actually closer to a scoopable casserole) while in Rome and enjoyed them all, but the standout was at Casalino Osteria Kosher—a restaurant in the Ghetto neighborhood that serves top-quality versions of traditional Roman Jewish fare. The restaurant's matriarch, Letizia Della Seta, visits almost every day to make sure the dishes come out just so. In the case of this dish, that means using a generous amount of rich tomato sauce and an ample glug of olive oil so the rice gets slick and saturated with flavor.

1½ cups (300g) Carnaroli or other medium-grain white rice

One 24.5-ounce (700 g) bottle or can tomato puree (passata)

3 tablespoons tomato paste

½ cup (120 ml) water

5 small garlic cloves, *smashed and peeled, halved lengthwise if large*

¼ cup (5 g) fresh basil leaves, *finely chopped, plus more for serving*

2 teaspoons kosher salt

⅔ cup (160 ml) extra-virgin olive oil

Bring a medium saucepan half filled with water to a boil over high heat. Stir in the rice, reduce the heat to medium-high, and cook, stirring occasionally, until the rice is halfway softened, 5 to 7 minutes. Drain and let cool slightly.

Preheat the oven to 375°F (190°C).

Add the tomato pureée, tomato paste, water, garlic, basil, salt, and olive oil to a large bowl and whisk to fully combine. Add the parboiled rice and stir to coat.

Transfer the mixture to a 9 × 13-inch (23 × 33 cm) baking dish, spreading it out evenly, and bake, uncovered, until well browned around the edges and firm but still saucy on top, 40 to 45 minutes. Remove from the oven and let cool slightly.

Scoop the rice onto serving plates and serve warm, sprinkled with chopped basil.

MAIN DISHES

Secondi

Stuffed Zucchini, 242

Micaela Pavoncello: Rome's Unparalleled Tour Guide

THE *FIRST TIME* I met Micaela Pavoncello was in 2009, when I took her walking tour of Rome's Jewish Ghetto. In a city brimming with tour guides, Micaela stood out for her engaging style, her deep personal connection to her subject (she was born and raised in Rome by a Libyan Jewish mother and a father whose Roman Jewish heritage dates back to the time of Caesar), and her encyclopedic knowledge of the neighborhood and its history.

After the tour, which began in the basement of Rome's Tempio Maggiore (Great Synagogue) and ended with slices of sour cherry and ricotta pie, Micaela hopped on her Vespa and sped away to meet her boyfriend (now husband), Angelo Sonnino, leaving me and my husband, Yoshie, in a cloud of breathless admiration. Here, I realized, was a kindred spirit—someone who recognized the deep beauty in Jewish history, tradition, and culture, and who wanted to make it come alive for other people.

Over the years, Micaela and I have kept in touch. We have gotten a little older (though no less glamorous, she likes to remind me!), had babies (I have Max and Beatrice, she has Gabriel, Nathan, and Isaac), and matured into our respective careers. When I began thinking about writing a Roman Jewish cookbook, Micaela was the first person I reached out to—both because I had a feeling she would be a font of knowledge and a great connector with people to interview (she was both) and because I wanted to ask for her blessing. She has been an invaluable collaborator along the way.

On a recent trip back to Rome in the fall of 2021, I took Micaela's tour again. Like everyone in the hospitality and tourism industry, her business took a hit during the pandemic—so it was a joy to see her back where she shines brightest.

As the tour was ending, we followed her out onto Via del Portico d'Ottavia, where we ran into an older man with a vibrant smile named Emanuele di Porto. He grew up in the Ghetto neighborhood and was just a boy when Nazi guards took his mother (and more than 1,000 other members of the community) away to Auschwitz. He lives on an upper floor of the same walkup building where he grew up. The day we met him was his ninetieth birthday, so Micaela (who knows every "*zio*" and "*zia*" on the block) stopped him, shared his story, and had our tour group sing Happy Birthday in both Italian and Hebrew. His kind eyes shone and I started to cry at this beautiful person who, thanks to Micaela's gifts, felt for a moment like family.

ONION FRITTATA

Frittata di Cipolle

SERVES 2 TO 4

Yes, this frittata only has four ingredients (five, if you include the bread to serve it with). But here's the thing: it's fantastic. On one visit to Rome, during the holiday of Sukkot, I tagged along with Roman Jewish tour guide Miacela Pavoncello (see page 184) as she dashed into a bakery, post-tour and before picking up her three boys from soccer practice, to buy ingredients for dinner in her synagogue's sukkah that night.

Back at her apartment, within a matter of minutes (big thanks to the family's nanny, who helped cook), we were packing up the Tortino di Riso (page 179) Micaela had made earlier that day and fitting slices of Frittata di Cipolle into squares of Pizza Bianca (page 190). The softened onions are thinly sliced rather than chopped, which lends texture to the frittata. Micaela said some versions also include sautéed tomatoes, and you could certainly kick up the flavor with chopped herbs or grated Parmesan. But that evening in the sukkah, it was the no-frills onion frittata I kept reaching for—a star all on its own.

3 tablespoons extra-virgin olive oil

2 medium yellow onions, *halved through the root and thinly sliced crosswise*

Kosher salt

7 large eggs, *lightly beaten*

Pizza Bianca (page 190) *for serving (optional)*

Preheat the oven to 375°F (180°C).

Heat the oil a medium nonstick, ovenproof frying pan over medium-low heat. Add the onions with a pinch of salt and cook, stirring occasionally, until softened and golden brown, 10 to 15 minutes.

Meanwhile, vigorously whisk the eggs and ½ teaspoon salt together in a bowl until no white streaks remain.

Pour the egg mixture over the onions and stir gently to distribute the ingredients evenly in the pan. Transfer the pan to the oven and bake until the top is just set, 10 to 15 minutes. Remove the frittata from the oven and allow to cool for 10 minutes to let it set.

Gently run a rubber spatula around the edges of the pan, then carefully transfer the frittata to a serving plate or cutting board. Serve warm or at room temperature, tucked into slices of pizza bianca, if desired.

ARTICHOKE FRITTATA

Frittata di Carciofi

SERVES 4

In her handwritten cookbook, *Dal 1880 ad Oggi* (see page 152), Donatella Limentani Pavoncello includes an artichoke-studded frittata as part of her Passover menu. In my riff on it, a sprinkling of fresh herbs adds a touch of springtime to the light-but-filling frittata. It makes a lovely main dish for lunch or dinner during the week of Passover (or anytime). For a decidedly untraditional (but so tasty!) cross-cultural flavor kick, try drizzling on the Libyan Jewish garlic and chile sauce, Filfel Chuma (page 88), just before serving.

NOTE: *You can also make this frittata with fresh artichokes. Clean 2 large artichokes according to the instructions on page 58, then quarter and slice them. Add them to the pan along with a splash of water, and cover the pan for a few minutes to help soften them, then proceed with the recipe as directed.*

3 tablespoons extra-virgin olive oil

1 medium yellow onion, *finely chopped*

Kosher salt and freshly ground black pepper

One 14-ounce (400 g) can artichoke quarters, *drained*

2 medium garlic cloves, *finely chopped*

8 large eggs

2 tablespoons *finely chopped* fresh basil, *plus more for serving*

2 tablespoons *finely chopped* fresh flat-leaf parsley, *plus more for serving*

½ cup (35 g) freshly grated Parmesan or Pecorino Romano (*optional*)

Preheat the oven to 375°F (180°C).

Heat the oil in a medium nonstick, ovenproof frying pan over medium heat. Add the onion with a generous pinch of salt, cover the pan, and cook, stirring occasionally, until softened and lightly browned, 6 to 8 minutes.

Add the artichokes, raise the heat to medium-high, and cook, stirring occasionally, until lightly browned, 6 to 8 minutes. Add the garlic and cook, stirring, until fragrant, about 1 minute.

While the artichokes are cooking, whisk the eggs, basil, parsley, about two thirds of the cheese, if using, ½ teaspoon salt, and a generous amount of black pepper together in a bowl. Pour the egg mixture over the artichokes and stir gently to distribute the artichokes evenly in the pan.

Sprinkle the remaining cheese, if using, over the top of the frittata, then transfer the pan to the oven. Bake until the top is set and lightly golden, 10 to 15 minutes. Remove from the oven and allow to cool for 10 minutes to let the frittata set.

Gently run a rubber spatula around the edges of the pan, then carefully transfer the frittata to a serving plate or cutting board. Serve warm or at room temperature, sprinkled with fresh herbs.

Gerusalemme Città della Pace
ROMA ANTICA
ROMA SPARITA NEGLI ACQUARELLI DI ETTORE ROESLER FRANZ
Roma scomparsa nelle fotografie di Ettore Roesler Franz
Roma scomparsa
CONVERSATIONS
CONVERSATIONS
I GIOIELLI DI ROMA
De Marchi
Le Fontanelle
Leo Rosten
oy
oy
oy!

ROMAN FLATBREAD

Pizza Bianca

SERVES 6 TO 8

Pizza bianca is similar to focaccia, but it's made with a basic dough, rather than one enriched with olive oil. And whereas focaccia is typically tall and fluffy, pizza bianca is relatively thin, with a crunchy golden top and satisfying chew. The flatbread is widely available in Rome's bakeries, where it is sold in rectangles that can be split open and stuffed with various fillings. Roman Jews queue up to buy their pizza bianca at Antico Forno Urbani, a nearly 100-year old bakery in the Jewish Ghetto neighborhood that turns out kosher breads and pizza from its storied ovens. A square of its flatbread makes the perfect home for a wedge of frittata or any number of Roman Jewish vegetable dishes, like Roasted Tomato Halves (page 65) or Silky Marinated Zucchini (page 44).

3½ cups (490 g) all-purpose flour, *plus more for the baking sheet*

1¼ teaspoons kosher salt

1 teaspoon active dry yeast

1½ cups (355 ml) lukewarm water

Extra-virgin olive oil *for brushing*

Coarse sea salt *for topping*

Add the flour, salt, and yeast to the bowl of a stand mixer fitted with the paddle attachment and mix briefly on low to combine. Switch to the dough hook, add the water, and mix on medium speed for 5 minutes. The dough will be relatively wet, but resist the urge to add more flour.

Remove the bowl from the mixer stand and use a rubber spatula to scrape any dough off the sides and down into the bottom. Cover the bowl with plastic wrap and let rise in a warm place until the dough doubles, about 3 hours. (The lengthy rise time helps develop the dough's flavor.)

Line a large rimmed baking sheet with parchment paper, leaving an overhang at either end, and sprinkle the parchment with flour. Pour the dough onto the center of the baking sheet, using a spatula as needed to coax it out of the bowl. Using lightly floured hands, and working from the middle of the dough outward, gently pat and stretch it into a very large rectangle approximately ¼ inch (6 mm) thick. Take care to make the dough evenly thick. Cover loosely with a clean dish towel and let rise at room temperature for 1 hour.

Preheat the oven to 500°F (260°C).

Uncover the dough and press your fingertips evenly across the surface to dimple it. Lightly brush or drizzle the top of the dough with a little olive oil (1 to 2 tablespoons should be plenty), then sprinkle evenly with sea salt.

Bake until the pizza bianca is golden brown and cooked through, 12 to 15 minutes, rotating the baking sheet back to front halfway through baking. Remove from the oven and use the overhanging parchment to slide the pizza bianca onto a large cutting board. Let cool for 5 to 10 minutes.

Serve warm or at room temperature, sliced into rectangles. Leftovers can be revived in an oven or toaster oven.

PUMPKIN FRITTATA

Frittata di Zucca

SERVES 4

Rome's Sephardi Jews eat pumpkin on Rosh Hashanah as a symbolic food intended to ward off evil decrees. The connection is linguistic—the word for squash in Aramaic, *qara*, sounds similar to the Hebrew verb for "to rip or tear," so pumpkins and squash are eaten in the hopes that any harsh decrees will be "torn up" in the year ahead. Here the autumnal gourd is softened in olive oil and folded into a rustic frittata equally worthy of brunch or dinner. A dash of cinnamon adds unexpected warmth.

3 tablespoons extra-virgin olive oil

1 medium yellow onion, *finely chopped*

Kosher salt and freshly ground black pepper

One 1-pound (454 g) sugar pumpkin or butternut squash, *peeled, halved, seeded, and cut into ½-inch (1.25 cm) cubes (about 3 cups)*

½ teaspoon ground cinnamon

8 large eggs

Preheat the oven to 375°F (180°C).

Heat the oil in a medium nonstick, ovenproof frying pan over medium heat. Add the onion with a generous pinch of salt, cover the pan, and cook, stirring occasionally, until softened and lightly browned, 6 to 8 minutes.

Add the pumpkin, cover the pan, and cook, stirring occasionally, until softened and lightly browned, about 10 minutes. Stir in the cinnamon.

While the pumpkin is cooking, whisk the eggs, ½ teaspoon salt, and a generous amount of black pepper together in a bowl.

Pour the egg mixture over the pumpkin, stir gently to distribute the pumpkin evenly in the pan, and transfer the pan to the oven. Bake until the top of the frittata is set, 10 to 15 minutes. Remove from the oven and allow to cool for 10 minutes to let the frittata set.

Gently run a rubber spatula around the edges of the pan, then carefully transfer the frittata to a serving plate or cutting board. Serve warm or at room temperature.

American Chefs Embrace Roman Jewish Cuisine

R*OMAN JEWISH CUISINE* does not have the same name recognition in America as other types of Jewish cuisine. (At least not yet!) However, across the country, chefs have drawn inspiration from the kitchens of the Roman Jewish Ghetto. In San Francisco, chef David Nayfeld riffs on Roman Jewish dishes—and the Jewish cuisines of other Italian cities—at his celebrated restaurant Che Fico. Nayfeld's parents were Jewish refugees from the former Soviet Union (Belarus) who stopped in Rome as part of the asylum-seeking process. "Those months in Rome were the first moments that felt like freedom to them," Nayfeld said.

After starting his career working at some of the country's best fine-dining establishments (including Eleven Madison Park in New York City), Nayfeld traveled to Italy to stage (apprentice) in family-run restaurants, apprentice at butcher shops, and eat in every trattoria he could find. He ended up tapping into a passion for regional Italian cuisine. "The culture spoke to me, but more than that, I kept discovering all of these Jewish historical sites that felt like coming into contact with my own identity," he said. Today the menu at Che Fico honors his link to cucina Ebraica, marking Jewish-inspired dishes on the menu with a small Jewish star. "I want to teach our diners that Jewish food is more than they may think it is," he said.

In Los Angeles, chef Steve Samson of Rossoblu has also pulled inspiration from the Roman Jewish kitchen. An LA native, he grew up with an Ashkenazi-American Jewish father and a Catholic mother from Bologna, and in Italy, he found connections between his two lineages in the Jewish kitchens of Venice and Rome. "I had these two food and family-based cultures and was excited to explore them," he said. Rossoblu's menu is not explicitly Jewish, but over the years, Samson has featured special Italian Jewish menus in the lead-up to Rosh Hashanah and Passover as a way of honoring his dual heritage.

Across the country, in Philadelphia, the James Beard Award–winning chef Marc Vetri has also found ways to pay homage to Italian Jewish cuisine. Vetri, who has both Ashkenazi Jewish and Sicilian lineage, discovered Roman Jewish cuisine early in his career, and he said it helped him embrace both sides of his own family more fully. In the late 1990s, he was approached by the James Beard Foundation about hosting an Easter dinner at the James Beard House in New York City. "I said, 'What about a Passover dinner? I'm Jewish!'"

For the Passover dinner, he researched Roman Jewish cuisine and created a feast that included wood-fired matzo, honey-soaked matzo fritters, whole roasted lamb, red mullet served over white polenta, and a frittata flavored with the classic Roman Jewish pairing of spinach, raisins, and pine nuts. It was, not surprisingly, a hit with guests. "Leave it to the Italians to make Jewish food taste so good!" he said.

SPINACH FRITTATA WITH RAISINS AND PINE NUTS

SERVES 4

This frittata was inspired by a dish that the Philadelphia-based chef Marc Vetri included on an Italian Jewish–themed Passover menu he served at the James Beard House in New York City in the late 1990s. (See page 195 for more about the menu.) The meal included a frittata inspired by the classic Roman Jewish combination of spinach with pine nuts and raisins. Some families also serve spinach frittatas (without the raisins and pine nuts) for Rosh Hashanah. My interpretation of Vetri's frittata adds lemon zest and creamy mascarpone for an egg dish that is anything but ordinary.

For the Topping

1 teaspoon extra-virgin olive oil

3 tablespoons pine nuts

3 tablespoons golden raisins

1 teaspoon chopped fresh oregano

1 packed teaspoon grated lemon zest *(from about 1 medium lemon)*

Kosher salt

For the Frittata

2 tablespoons extra-virgin olive oil

1 medium yellow onion, *finely chopped*

5 ounces (140 g) baby spinach (about 4½ cups)

1 medium garlic clove, *minced, grated, or pushed through a press*

8 large eggs

⅓ cup (50 g) freshly grated Parmesan

1½ teaspoons chopped fresh oregano

½ teaspoon kosher salt

¼ teaspoon freshly ground black pepper

⅓ cup (80 g) mascarpone

Finely chopped fresh flat-leaf parsley *for sprinkling*

CONTINUES

PREPARE THE TOPPING

Heat the oil in a small frying pan over medium heat. Add the pine nuts and cook, stirring occasionally, until golden and fragrant, 2 to 3 minutes. Add the raisins and cook, stirring often, for about 1 minute, then stir in the oregano, lemon zest, and a small sprinkling of salt. Remove from the heat and set aside.

PREPARE THE FRITTATA

Preheat the oven to 375°F (180°C).

Heat the oil in a medium nonstick, ovenproof frying pan over medium heat. Add the onion and cook, stirring occasionally, until softened and lightly browned, 6 to 8 minutes. Add the spinach, raise the heat to medium-high, and cook, stirring often, until the spinach wilts and any water it releases evaporates, 5 to 7 minutes. Add the garlic and cook, stirring, until fragrant, about 1 minute.

While the onion and spinach are cooking, whisk the eggs, Parmesan, oregano, salt, and pepper together in a bowl.

Pour the egg mixture over the onions and spinach and stir gently to distribute the ingredients evenly in the pan. Dollop the top of the frittata with the mascarpone, then transfer the pan to the oven.

Bake the frittata until the top is set and lightly golden, 10 to 15 minutes. Remove from the oven and allow to cool for 10 minutes to let the frittata set.

Serve directly from the pan, or gently run a rubber spatula around the edges, then carefully slide the frittata onto a serving plate or cutting board. Serve warm or at room temperature, generously sprinkled with parsley and the pine nut and raisin topping.

EGGPLANT PARMESAN

Parmigiana di Melanzane

SERVES 4 TO 6

On my most recent trip to Rome, I tasted and then utterly devoured the eggplant Parmesan at Casalino Osteria Kosher in the Jewish Ghetto. Their version combined a tangle of silky, olive oil–infused eggplant with an abundance of garlicky tomato sauce and melted cheese. I am more familiar with American-style eggplant Parmesan, which coats the eggplant pieces in flour or bread crumbs before frying them, but Casalino's iteration of the dish was the best I have ever had. Until I get back to Rome again, my version aims to bring a bit of that decadence home. Like their non-Jewish neighbors (and Americans too!), Roman Jews eat eggplant Parmesan as an everyday dish. But it is also commonly served on Shavuot, when dairy dishes are traditional.

3 medium eggplants (about 3 pounds / 1.4 kg), *not peeled, stems removed and sliced lengthwise into ¼-inch- (6 mm) thick planks*

Kosher salt

2 tablespoons extra-virgin olive oil

1 large yellow onion, *finely chopped*

4 medium garlic cloves, *finely chopped*

½ teaspoon freshly ground black pepper

One 24.5-ounce (700 g) bottle or can tomato puree (passata)

½ cup (120 ml) water

Vegetable oil (such as sunflower or grapeseed) *for frying*

½ cup (10 g) fresh basil leaves, *roughly torn*

1 pound (454 g) mozzarella, *cut into ¼-inch (6 mm) cubes*

2 cups (140 g) freshly grated Parmesan

CONTINUES

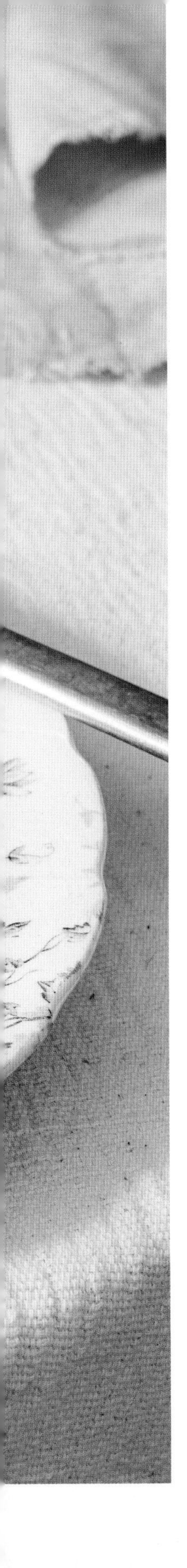

Line two large baking sheets with clean dish towels or several layers of paper towels. Layer the eggplant planks on top (it's okay if they overlap a little) and sprinkle generously with salt. Allow to rest for 1 hour to draw out some moisture, then firmly pat the eggplant dry with paper towels.

Meanwhile, heat the olive oil in a large saucepan over medium heat. Add the onion and cook, stirring occasionally, until softened and lightly browned, 6 to 8 minutes. Add the garlic, 1 teaspoon salt, and the black pepper and cook, stirring, until fragrant, about 1 minute.

Stir in the tomato puree and water, partially cover the pan, and cook, stirring occasionally, until the sauce thickens, 15 to 20 minutes. Set aside.

Line a large plate or baking sheet with paper towels and set nearby. Heat ¼ inch (6 mm) of vegetable oil in a large frying pan over medium heat until shimmering. Add a single layer of eggplant planks to the hot oil and fry, flipping once, until lightly golden and tender, about 3 minutes per side. Transfer the fried eggplant to the prepared plate and continue frying the remaining eggplant in batches, adding more oil to the pan as necessary.

Preheat the oven to 400°F (200°C).

Spread about one third of the tomato sauce in the bottom of a 9 × 13-inch (23 × 33 cm) baking dish. Layer about half of the eggplant slices over the sauce (overlapping is okay), then top with another one third of the sauce and about half of the basil, mozzarella, and Parmesan. Layer the remaining eggplant slices over the top, followed by the remaining sauce, basil, and both cheeses.

Bake, uncovered, until the eggplant mixture is bubbling and lightly browned, 30 to 35 minutes. Remove from the oven and let rest for 10 to 15 minutes before serving. It should be quite saucy and scoopable, rather than sliceable.

SPICY TOMATO-POACHED EGGS

Shakshuka

SERVES 2 OR 3

Libyan versions of this popular North African tomato-poached egg dish tend to be richly sauced, abundantly spiced, and heavy on the garlic. They do not typically include bell pepper, so the red pepper I added to this recipe is optional but recommended, especially if you are more familiar with Israeli versions, which tend to be heavier on vegetables. Serve the shakshuka straight from the pan with good bread for mopping up the sauce.

¼ cup (60 ml) extra-virgin olive oil, *plus more for serving*

1 medium yellow onion, *very finely chopped*

1 red bell pepper, *seeded and finely chopped (optional)*

8 medium garlic cloves, *thinly sliced*

1 fresh red chile pepper, *halved, seeded, if desired, and thinly sliced*

¼ cup (60 g) tomato paste

1½ teaspoons hot paprika

1 teaspoon ground cumin

½ teaspoon caraway seeds, *coarsely ground (optional)*

1 teaspoon kosher salt, *plus more if needed*

¼ teaspoon freshly ground black pepper

One 28-ounce (795 g) can crushed tomatoes

4 to 6 large eggs

Chopped fresh basil *for topping*

Spicy Garlic and Chile Sauce (page 88) *for topping (optional)*

Preheat the oven to 375°F (190°C).

Heat the oil in a large ovenproof frying pan over medium heat. Add the onion, bell pepper, if using, garlic, and chile pepper and cook, stirring occasionally, until softened and lightly browned, 8 to 10 minutes. Add the tomato paste, paprika, cumin, caraway, if using, salt, and pepper and cook, stirring, until fragrant, 1 to 2 minutes.

Stir in the crushed tomatoes and bring to a simmer. Reduce the heat to medium-low and cook, stirring occasionally, until the sauce thickens, about 15 minutes. Taste and add additional salt, if desired.

Using the back of a spoon, create shallow wells in the sauce for the eggs. Carefully break one egg into each well. Transfer the pan to the oven and bake until the egg whites are opaque but the yolks are still jiggly, 8 to 12 minutes. (Err on the side of slightly undercooked eggs, as they will continue to set after the shakshuka is removed from the oven.)

Serve hot, drizzled with a little more olive oil, sprinkled with basil, and topped with a few dollops of chile sauce, if desired.

VEGETABLE STEW FOR COUSCOUS

Zuppa per Couscous

SERVES 8

This comforting, flavorful stew, which is served spooned over steamed couscous, is the epitome of everyday home cooking for Rome's Libyan Jews. It is packed with vegetables (other versions of the dish include turnips, kohlrabi, and/or cabbage) and can be simmered with browned chicken pieces or left vegetarian, as it is here. The cinnamon is not typically added, but the sweet spice perfectly complements the turmeric's earthy flavor. For an extra hit of heat, drizzle a little Spicy Garlic and Chile Sauce (page 88) over the top before serving.

¼ cup (60 ml) extra-virgin olive oil

2 medium yellow onions, *halved through the root and cut into ½-inch-(1.25 cm) thick wedges*

4 medium garlic cloves, *thinly sliced*

3 medium carrots, *peeled, halved lengthwise if thick, and cut into 2-inch (5 cm) pieces*

2 celery stalks, *cut into 2-inch (5 cm) pieces*

1½ teaspoons kosher salt, *plus more if needed*

¼ teaspoon freshly ground black pepper, *plus more if needed*

¾ teaspoon ground turmeric

½ teaspoon ground cinnamon

¼ to ½ teaspoon red pepper flakes, *plus more if needed*

3 tablespoons tomato paste

Two 15-ounce (425 g) cans chickpeas, *rinsed and drained*

1 small butternut squash (about 1½ pounds / 680 g), *peeled, halved, seeded, and cut into 2-inch (5 cm) chunks*

2 medium Yukon Gold potatoes (about 1 pound / 454 g), *peeled and quartered lengthwise*

2 small zucchini (about ½ pound / 227 g), *cut into 1-inch (2.5 cm) thick rounds*

2 medium plum tomatoes (about ½ pound / 227 g), *quartered and seeds removed*

2 quarts (2 l) vegetable broth, *store-bought or homemade (page 109)*

Steamed couscous *for serving*

Roughly chopped fresh flat-leaf parsley *for serving*

CONTINUES

DA GIGGETTO
CUCINA ROMANA

Heat the oil in a large pot over medium heat. Add the onions, garlic, carrots, and celery and cook, stirring occasionally, until they begin to soften and turn lightly golden, 10 to 12 minutes. Add the salt, black pepper, turmeric, cinnamon, the desired amount of red pepper flakes, and the tomato paste and cook, stirring, until fragrant, 1 to 2 minutes.

Add the chickpeas, squash, potatoes, zucchini, and tomatoes, then pour in the vegetable broth, raise the heat to high, and bring to a boil. Lower the heat to medium, partially cover the pot, and cook, stirring occasionally, until the vegetables are tender, 40 to 45 minutes.

Taste and add additional salt, black pepper, and/or red pepper flakes, if desired. (You may need to add quite a bit more salt if you used unsalted or reduced-salt vegetable broth.)

To serve, spoon the couscous into a large wide bowl. Use a slotted spoon to arrange the vegetables on top of the couscous, then spoon or ladle some of the broth over the top. Serve hot or warm, generously sprinkled with parsley.

SOLE WITH LEMON AND HERBS

Sogliole al Limone e Erbetta

SERVES 4 TO 6

A version of this light, lemony fish dish is included in Donatella Limentani Pavoncello's classic cookbook, *Dal 1880 ad Oggi* (see page 152). My take expands on hers slightly, adding onions, garlic, and lemon zest for additional oomph, along with a splash of white wine to tie everything together. It's quite simple to prepare, but the bright, citrus-forward flavor sets it apart. Serve the fish with Spaghetti with Artichokes and Bottarga (page 162) for an enticing weeknight meal.

2 pounds (907 g) sole fillets (or other firm white fish fillets), *skin removed*

Kosher salt and freshly ground black pepper

3 tablespoons extra-virgin olive oil

2 small yellow onions, *halved through the root and thinly sliced*

2 medium garlic cloves, *thinly sliced*

1 cup (240 ml) dry white wine

½ packed teaspoon grated lemon zest

2 teaspoons fresh lemon juice

Chopped fresh flat-leaf parsley *for serving*

Preheat the oven to 400°F (200°C). Lightly grease a 9 × 13-inch (23 by 33 cm) baking dish.

Season the fillets with salt and pepper and arrange them in the baking dish (it is okay if they overlap). Set aside.

Heat the oil in a medium frying pan over medium heat. Add the onions and garlic and cook, stirring occasionally, until softened and lightly browned, 8 to 10 minutes. Add the wine, lemon zest, lemon juice, and ½ teaspoon salt to the pan, raise the heat to medium-high, and bring to a boil. Carefully pour the mixture around the fillets.

Cover the baking dish with foil and bake until the fish is opaque and flakes easily with a fork, 8 to 10 minutes (or longer, if your fillets are thick). Use a fish spatula to transfer the fish and onions to a serving plate.

Pour the liquid from the baking dish back into the frying pan and set over high heat. Bring the cooking liquid to a boil and cook, stirring often, until thickened and glossy, 3 to 5 minutes. Taste and add more salt and/or pepper if needed.

Spoon the sauce over the fish and serve hot or warm, sprinkled with chopped parsley.

TOMATO-POACHED COD

Merluzzo alla Romana

SERVES 4 TO 6

Silvia Nacamulli, a Roman Jewish chef and cooking instructor based in London, taught me how to make this tomato-poached cod dish over a video chat. She prefers to use fresh cod (merluzzo), but it is also traditionally made with salt cod (baccalà). Some versions of the recipe incorporate pine nuts and raisins, but Silvia swears by a hint of ground cinnamon and fresh basil to perfume the tomato sauce.

Tomato-Poached Salt Cod (Baccalà alla Romana)

Follow the recipe as above, replacing the cod fillets with deboned salt cod (baccalà). Before cooking, soak the dried cod fillets, refrigerated, in water for at least 24 hours (ideally, closer to 48 hours), changing the water several times, until most of the salt is rinsed away and the fish is soft and pliable. Drain, pat dry with paper towels, and cut into serving-sized pieces.

One 28-ounce (795 g) can whole peeled tomatoes

1 cup (250 g) tomato puree (passata)

¼ cup (60 ml) extra-virgin olive oil

2 yellow onions, *halved through the root and thinly sliced*

3 medium garlic cloves, *thinly sliced*

1½ teaspoons ground cinnamon

Kosher salt and freshly ground black pepper

¼ cup (60 ml) dry white wine

2 pounds (907 g) cod fillets, *skin removed*

½ cup (10 g) fresh basil leaves, *roughly torn if large, plus more for finishing*

Put the whole tomatoes, with their juices, in a large bowl and gently squeeze them to break them up into small pieces. Stir in the tomato puree and set aside.

Heat the oil in a large wide saucepan over medium-low heat. Add the onions and cook, stirring occasionally, until softened and golden, 10 to 15 minutes.

Add the garlic, cinnamon, 1¼ teaspoons salt, and ½ teaspoon black pepper and cook, stirring, until fragrant, 1 to 2 minutes. Stir in the wine, followed by the tomato mixture. Raise the heat to medium-high and bring to a low boil, then reduce the heat to medium-low, partially cover the pan, and cook, stirring often, until the sauce thickens a bit, 15 to 20 minutes.

Meanwhile, sprinkle the cod fillets on both sides with salt and pepper. Add the fillets to the sauce (it is okay if they overlap), along with the basil leaves, and spoon some of the sauce on top of the fillets. Cover the pan, raise the heat to medium, and cook, undisturbed, until the fish is cooked through and flakes easily with a fork, 7 to 10 minutes (or longer for thicker fillets).

Serve hot, straight from the pan, topped with basil leaves.

WHOLE ROASTED FISH WITH RAISINS AND PINE NUTS

Triglie con Pinoli e Passerine

SERVES 4 TO 6

Roman Jews serve this beautiful whole roasted fish dish to break the Yom Kippur fast. It is traditionally made with red mullet, a Mediterranean fish that has been revered in Rome since ancient times. If you cannot find it, other whole fish like red snapper or branzino make fine substitutes. You can also use fish fillets, if you prefer, adjusting the cooking time accordingly. The raisins and pine nuts in the sweet and tangy sauce point to the Sephardi influence on Roman Jewish cuisine.

¼ cup (60 ml) plus 2 teaspoons extra-virgin olive oil

¼ cup (30 g) pine nuts

Kosher salt and freshly ground black pepper

Two 1-pound (454 g) whole fish (such as mullet, red snapper, or branzino), *cleaned and scaled*

1 large yellow onion, *halved through the root and thinly sliced*

⅓ cup (45 g) golden raisins, *soaked in warm water for 5 minutes and drained*

¼ cup (60 ml) white or red wine vinegar

¼ cup (60 ml) water

1½ teaspoons granulated sugar

1 packed teaspoon grated lemon zest *(from about 1 medium lemon)*

Chopped fresh flat-leaf parsley *for sprinkling (optional)*

Preheat the oven to 375°F (190°C).

Heat the 2 teaspoons oil in a large ovenproof frying pan over medium heat. Add the pine nuts and cook, stirring frequently, until fragrant and golden, 3 to 5 minutes. Transfer the pine nuts to a plate, season lightly with salt and pepper, and set aside.

Season the fish inside and out with salt and pepper, and set aside.

Heat the remaining ¼ cup (60 ml) oil in the same frying pan over medium heat. Add the onion, ½ teaspoon salt, and ¼ teaspoon pepper and cook, stirring occasionally, until the onion is softened and lightly golden, 6 to 8 minutes. Add the raisins, vinegar, water, and sugar and bring the mixture to a simmer.

Nestle the fish into the pan, spoon a little of the pan juices over the top, and scatter with the lemon zest. Cover the pan, transfer to the oven, and roast for 10 minutes. Uncover the pan and sprinkle the toasted pine nuts over the fish. Continue roasting, uncovered, until the fish is fully cooked through, 5 to 10 minutes.

Transfer the fish to a serving platter and spoon the sauce over the top. Serve hot or warm, sprinkled with parsley, if desired.

SPICY TOMATO-POACHED FISH

Haraimi

SERVES 4 TO 6

Variations of this iconic tomato-poached fish dish, which is served on Shabbat and holidays, can be found throughout North Africa. The Libyan version is distinctive for its abundant use of spices and thick, concentrated sauce. As the restaurateur Daniela Gean told me, "The fish should not be swimming in sauce." When I watched Ghily Guetta, a Roman-born Libyan Jew, make haraimi in her kitchen, she used a food processor to chop the onion into an almost creamy paste so it would melt imperceptibly into the dish. So naturally I now do that too. Guetta also poached a whole, cut up fish in the sauce instead of steaks, so feel free to make that swap at home. Serve with steamed couscous or plenty of good bread.

¼ cup (60 ml) extra-virgin olive oil

1 large yellow onion, *very finely chopped (see headnote)*

6 medium garlic cloves, *minced, grated, or pushed through a press*

1 fresh red chile pepper, *seeds removed, if desired, and thinly sliced*

2 tablespoons sweet paprika

2½ teaspoons ground cumin

2 teaspoons hot paprika, *plus more if desired*

½ teaspoon caraway seeds, *coarsely ground*

½ teaspoon granulated sugar

Kosher salt and freshly ground black pepper

⅓ cup (80 g) tomato paste

1¾ cups (430 g) tomato puree (passata)

¾ cup (180 ml) water

2 pounds (907 g) firm white fish steaks or fillets (such as sea bass, snapper, or halibut), *skin removed, if desired*

Roughly chopped fresh flat-leaf parsley *for serving*

Lemon wedges *for serving*

Heat the oil in a large deep frying pan over medium heat until shimmering. Add the onion and cook, stirring occasionally, until softened and lightly browned, 6 to 8 minutes. Add the garlic and chile pepper and cook until fragrant, 1 to 2 minutes. Add the sweet paprika, cumin, hot paprika, caraway seeds, sugar, 1 teaspoon salt, and ½ teaspoon black pepper and cook, stirring, until fragrant, about 1 minute.

Stir in the tomato paste, tomato puree, and water, bring to a simmer, and cook, stirring occasionally, until the sauce thickens a bit, 10 to 12 minutes. Taste and add additional salt and/or hot paprika, if desired.

Season the fish steaks on both sides with salt and pepper. Nestle the steaks in the pan, spooning some of the sauce over the top. Cover the pan and cook, undisturbed, until the fish is cooked through and flakes easily with a fork, 7 to 10 minutes (longer for thicker pieces of fish).

Serve hot, garnished with chopped parsley and with lemon wedges alongside for squeezing.

Libyan Cuisine in Rome

W*HEN I FIRST* started researching this cookbook, I felt torn about whether or not to include recipes from Rome's Libyan Jewish community. Roman Jewish history goes back more than two thousand years, and the traditional dishes that emerged from the Roman Jewish Ghetto have countless stories to tell, all on their own. I worried that widening the scope would dilute my focus.

Then I spoke with Laura Ravaioli, a Rome-based chef and television personality. "There are two spirits to Jewish Roman food, Roman and Libyan," she told me. "Both sides have learned to create something beautiful out of nothing." Her words touched me because they helped me realize that while Rome's Libyan Jewish community is young—the majority arrived in or around 1967 (see page 28 for more)—their story of resilience and of finding joy amidst hardship echoes the story of all Roman Jews.

Libyan dishes differ from classic Roman dishes in significant ways. The cuisine tends to be more strongly flavored and spicier than Roman cuisine—redolent of cumin, caraway, hot paprika, and a heavy hand with garlic. And, rather than homemade pastas, Libyan meals are not complete without fluffy steamed couscous. But a through-line of Jewish ritual, family, and, as Ravaioli put it, an ability to make something from nothing binds the disparate cuisines together.

In only five decades, Libyan Jews have become an integral part of Rome's Jewish community. Several of the restaurants lining Via del Portico d'Ottavia in the Ghetto neighborhood are owned and operated by Libyan

Jews—including many that serve traditional Roman Jewish dishes. So it is not at all surprising to find deep-fried artichokes and crispy potato burik on the same menu. In my own travels to Rome, I remember sipping Libyan mint tea with roasted peanuts alongside Rome's honey-sweetened matzo fritters. (They make a lovely duo; see the recipes on pages 314 and 149.)

The two cuisines have begun to mingle in people's homes as well. "If you go to a Shabbat dinner in Rome today, it can be so mixed," said Daniela Gean, a restaurateur who moved with her family from Libya to Rome when she was a baby. "You might find artichokes followed by spicy Libyan fish, or see people serving stracotto di manzo [Roman Jewish beef stew, page 235] over couscous instead of rigatoni."

I am so grateful to that conversation with Ravaioli for clarifying that, without hesitation, Libyan Jews are not separate from Rome's Jewish community. Their families, and the meals they share, are just a newer thread in an ancient tapestry. So while this cookbook does not capture the entirety of Libyan Jewish cuisine, I hope it honors the community's contributions to Rome's historic but also evolving culinary landscape.

FRIED FISH WITH VINEGAR AND ONIONS

Pesce Aceto e Cipolla

SERVES 4 TO 6

There are two methods for making this classic Libyan Jewish dish. The first poaches the fish steaks directly in the sweet and tangy sauce. But I prefer the second way, which briefly fries the fish in oil to crisp it up just a bit before adding it to the sauce. Serve the fish (the dish's Libyan name is hoc bel hal) with hearty bread alongside for swiping up the extra sauce. And for an additional kick of spice, drizzle a little Spicy Garlic and Chile Sauce (page 88) over the top at the table.

¼ cup (60 ml) extra-virgin olive oil

2 large yellow onions, *very finely chopped*

Vegetable oil (such as sunflower or grapeseed) *for frying*

All-purpose flour *for coating*

6 firm fish steaks or fillets (such as sea bass, sea bream, or red snapper), *about 6 ounces (170 g) each, patted dry*

Kosher salt and freshly ground black pepper

3 medium garlic cloves, *minced, grated, or pushed through a press*

2 tablespoons tomato paste

2 teaspoons granulated sugar

1 teaspoon hot paprika

1¼ cups (296 ml) water

¼ cup (60 ml) red wine vinegar

Heat the olive oil in a large frying pan over medium heat. Add the onions, cover the pan, and cook, stirring occasionally, until softened and beginning to brown, about 10 minutes. Reduce the heat to medium-low, uncover the pan, and continue cooking, stirring often, until the onions are tender and golden, 15 to 20 minutes.

Meanwhile, heat ¼ inch (6 mm) of vegetable oil in a second large frying pan over medium heat until shimmering. Spread a little flour on a plate, and line a second plate with paper towels.

Working in batches, season the fish steaks with salt and pepper and dip them in the flour, turning to coat both sides and shaking off the excess. Add the fish to the hot oil and fry, turning once, until lightly golden, 2 to 3 minutes per side. Transfer to the paper towel–lined plate and set aside.

Add the garlic, tomato paste, sugar, paprika, 1 teaspoon salt, and ¼ teaspoon black pepper to the caramelized onions and cook, stirring, until fragrant, about 1 minute. Stir in the water and vinegar, raise the heat to medium-high, and cook until the sauce thickens slightly, about 5 minutes.

Nestle the fried fish into the sauce and simmer, basting the fish with the sauce occasionally, until the sauce has thickened and the fish is cooked through, 3 to 5 minutes (thicker fillets may take longer). Taste and add more salt if needed.

Serve hot, with the sauce spooned over the fish.

ROAST CHICKEN WITH ROSEMARY, GARLIC, AND POTATOES

Pollo Arrosto

SERVES 4 TO 6

On an early research deep dive for this cookbook, I stumbled across a *New York Times* article from 1986 that described Lattanzi, an Italian restaurant located in Manhattan's theater district with a menu that included Roman Jewish dishes. "As children we lived near the Ghetto," said executive chef Paolo Lattanzi in the article, which also included mention of this classic roasted chicken dish. "We didn't know then that we were eating Jewish food. It was Italian, Roman, the food of my city, and it was very good." Lattanzi is still thriving today from its perch on New York City's historic Restaurant Row. Perfumed with garlic and rosemary and sitting atop potatoes that turn creamy and flavorful in the oven, this dish is similarly timeless.

¼ cup (60 ml) extra-virgin olive oil

10 medium garlic cloves, *2 minced, grated, or pushed through a press, 8 smashed and peeled*

1½ tablespoons *finely chopped* fresh rosemary, *plus 4 rosemary sprigs*

1 packed teaspoon grated lemon zest *(from about 1 medium lemon)*

1¼ teaspoons kosher salt

½ teaspoon freshly ground black pepper

3 medium Yukon Gold potatoes (about 1½ pounds / 680 g), *peeled, halved, and cut into ¼-inch- (6 mm) thick wedges*

4 pounds (1.8 kg) bone-in, skin-on chicken thighs and legs, *excess fat trimmed*

½ cup (120 ml) dry white wine or chicken broth

Chopped fresh flat-leaf parsley *for serving (optional)*

Preheat the oven to 400°F (200°C).

Whisk together the olive oil, minced garlic, chopped rosemary, lemon zest, salt, and pepper in a medium bowl.

Arrange the potatoes, the whole garlic cloves, and the rosemary sprigs in the bottom of a large roasting pan. Drizzle with about half of the olive oil–rosemary mixture and toss well with tongs or your hands to coat.

Arrange the chicken pieces on top of the potatoes. Brush the chicken evenly with the remaining olive oil mixture, then add the wine to the baking dish, taking care to pour it around the chicken, not over the top.

Roast the chicken for 30 minutes. Spoon some of the pan juices over the top, gently stir the potatoes (lifting up the chicken pieces as necessary) to facilitate even cooking, and continue roasting until the potatoes are tender and chicken is well browned and cooked through, another 20 to 25 minutes. Remove from the oven and let rest for about 10 minutes before serving.

Serve hot, sprinkled with parsley, if desired.

CHICKEN WITH PEPPERS

Pollo con Peperoni

SERVES 4 TO 6

Chicken braised with silky roasted bell peppers and tomatoes is a classic Roman dish, and for good reason. Made with just a handful of ingredients, it captures the essence of summer's bounty. Roman Jews love the dish as much as their neighbors—in Donatella Limentani Pavoncello's beautiful cookbook, *Dal 1880 ad Oggi* (see page 152), she includes a variation of the dish made with morsels of cut-up chicken breast. She calls it Chicken Delights with Peppers, which I love, because the dish is, indeed, delightful. Serve it with lots of crusty bread for sopping up the vibrant, flavorful sauce.

4 medium yellow or orange bell peppers, *washed and dried (stems on is fine)*

3 tablespoons extra-virgin olive oil, *plus more if needed*

4 pounds (1.8 kg) bone-in, skin-on chicken thighs and legs, *excess fat trimmed*

Kosher salt and freshly ground black pepper

4 medium garlic cloves, *thinly sliced*

¼ teaspoon red pepper flakes (*optional*)

½ cup (120 ml) dry white wine

One 14.5-ounce (411 g) can whole peeled tomatoes

Chopped fresh basil *for serving*

ROAST AND PEEL THE PEPPERS
Preheat the broiler and arrange the peppers on a baking sheet. Broil the peppers, turning every 5 minutes or so with tongs, until they are blistered all over and collapsing on themselves, 15 to 20 minutes. Remove the peppers from the broiler, cover with foil or paper towels, and let cool slightly.

Once the peppers are cool enough to handle, remove and discard the skins and seeds and slice them into strips. Set aside. (*This step can be completed up to 2 days in advance. Store the peppers, covered, in the fridge.*)

PREPARE THE CHICKEN
Heat the oil in a Dutch oven or other large pot over medium-high heat until shimmering. Season the chicken pieces with salt and pepper and, working in batches, add the chicken, skin side down, to the pot. Sear, turning once, until golden brown on both sides, 10 to 12 minutes per batch; transfer the browned chicken to a plate. Set aside.

CONTINUES

Turn the heat down to medium and add a drizzle of oil if the Dutch oven looks dry. Add half of the roasted pepper strips, the garlic, and red pepper flakes, if using, and cook, stirring occasionally, until the garlic is tender and fragrant, about 2 minutes. Stir in the wine and let cook down by about half, 1 to 2 minutes.

Meanwhile, put the tomatoes, with their juices, in a medium bowl and gently squeeze them to break them up into small pieces. Add the tomatoes and their juices to the Dutch oven, along with ¾ teaspoon salt and a generous amount of black pepper.

Nestle the chicken pieces in the sauce, spooning some of it over the top. Turn the heat up to medium-high and bring to a boil, then reduce the heat to medium-low, cover, and cook, stirring occasionally, until the chicken is tender, about 45 minutes.

Uncover, turn the heat back to medium-high, and cook, stirring often, until the sauce thickens a bit, about 10 minutes. Stir in the remaining roasted pepper strips, taste, and add more salt, if desired. Serve hot, generously sprinkled with chopped basil.

NOTE: *You can substitute jarred roasted bell peppers to save the time of roasting the peppers yourself. The flavor of the final dish will not be quite as delicate, but it will still be very tasty.*

E.4.00KG
€3,00 KG

CHICKEN AND VEAL MEATBALLS IN TOMATO-CELERY SAUCE

Polpette di Pollo con Sedani / Ngozzamoddi

SERVES 4 TO 6

When I first tried this dish, I was struck by the prominent use of celery. Unlike many recipes, in which celery is so finely chopped that it disappears into the mix, this dish featured distinctive batons of celery bobbing unapologetically in the tomato sauce. I liked that brazen celery almost as much as I liked the tender chicken and veal meatballs swimming alongside it.

The recipe's more colloquial name, ngozzamoddi, is curious, since it stems from the Hebrew word *azmot*, meaning "bones," and there are no bones in it. But in the past, when Roman Jews were forced to survive on desperately meager means, home cooks sometimes added finely pulverized bones to the meat mixture to stretch it. Circumstances have changed, fortunately, but I give credit to those enterprising home cooks for finding ways to feed their families during hard times.

For the Sauce

¼ cup (60 ml) extra-virgin olive oil

1 medium yellow onion, *finely chopped*

6 large celery stalks, *halved lengthwise (or into thirds, if thick) and cut into 2-inch-(5 cm) batons*

4 medium garlic cloves, *thinly sliced*

¼ teaspoon red pepper flakes, *plus more if needed*

One 24.5-ounce (700 g) bottle or can tomato puree (passata)

½ cup (120 ml) water

1¼ teaspoons kosher salt, *plus more if needed*

1 teaspoon granulated sugar

¼ teaspoon freshly ground black pepper

For the Meatballs

1 pound (454 g) ground chicken (ideally dark meat)

1 pound (454 g) ground veal

1 medium yellow onion, *grated on the large holes of a box grater*

1 large egg, *lightly beaten*

⅓ cup (30 g) unseasoned bread crumbs

¾ teaspoon kosher salt

½ teaspoon ground cinnamon

½ teaspoon freshly ground black pepper

Chopped fresh flat-leaf parsley *for serving (optional)*

MAKE THE SAUCE

Heat the oil in a large saucepan over medium heat. Add the onion, celery, and garlic and cook, stirring occasionally, until the celery begins to soften, about 10 minutes. Add the red pepper flakes and cook, stirring, until fragrant, 1 minute.

Add the tomato puree, water, salt, sugar, and black pepper and bring the liquid to a simmer, then reduce the heat to medium-low and cook, stirring occasionally, until the sauce thickens slightly, 5 to 7 minutes. Remove from the heat and set aside.

MAKE THE MEATBALLS

Add the ground chicken, ground veal, grated onion, egg, bread crumbs, salt, cinnamon, and black pepper to a large bowl and mix well to combine. Scoop out ¼ cup (60 g) of the meatball mixture and, using wet hands, form into an oval about 3 inches (7.5 cm) long. It is okay if the mixture feels quite delicate at this stage, but if it is too delicate to form into meatballs, refrigerate for about 15 minutes. Place the meatball on a large plate and continue with the remaining mixture.

Place the sauce back over medium heat and bring to a simmer. Carefully arrange the meatballs in the sauce (it is okay if they are not all submerged in the sauce). Cover the pan, turn the heat to medium-low, and simmer the meatballs, gently shaking the pan and basting the meatballs with the sauce once or twice, until cooked through, 30 to 35 minutes.

Uncover the pan, raise the heat to medium-high, and cook until the sauce thickens slightly, about 5 minutes. Taste and add more salt and/or red pepper flakes, if desired.

Serve the meatballs hot, with the sauce spooned over top and sprinkled with parsley, if desired.

NOTES: *For the most tender batons of celery, use a vegetable peeler to remove the fibrous outer layer of the stalks.*

You can make the meatballs with all chicken instead of a mix of chicken and veal, but since a lot of the sauce's flavor comes from the meatballs, it will not be as savory or rich that way. If you do choose to go all chicken, use ground dark meat rather than white.

CHICKEN AND VEAL LOAF WITH ROSEMARY

Polpettone

SERVES 4 TO 6

Not all meatloaves are created equal, and this one is a knockout. A mix of ground dark-meat chicken and veal gives it the perfect balance of lightness and juicy texture. The rustic loaf is perfumed with rosemary and garlic and seared before it goes in the oven, which creates a lovely golden crust.

On a recent visit to Rome, I was delighted to see a half dozen pre-prepped polpettoni in the display case at the modern kosher butcher shop, Pascarella (see page 230). If you can't hop over to Rome to pick some up, this recipe will take you straight there. The meat mixture does require an extended chilling time, so be sure to plan ahead.

¼ pound (113 g) rustic white bread, *crust removed and torn into 1-inch (2.5 cm) pieces (about 2 cups)*

1 pound (454 g) ground chicken *(dark meat)*

1 pound (454 g) ground veal

2 large eggs, *lightly beaten*

1 small yellow onion, *grated on the large holes of a box grater and lightly squeezed to remove excess liquid*

5 medium garlic cloves, *2 minced, grated, or pushed through a press, 3 smashed and peeled*

1½ teaspoons *finely chopped* fresh rosemary, *plus 2 large rosemary sprigs*

½ cup (10 g) *finely chopped* fresh flat-leaf parsley

1½ teaspoons kosher salt

½ teaspoon freshly ground black pepper

1 cup (60 g) unseasoned bread crumbs

⅓ cup (80 ml) extra-virgin olive oil, *plus more if needed*

¾ cup (180 ml) dry white wine

Place the torn bread in a bowl, cover with water, and let the bread soak until thoroughly softened, 10 to 15 minutes.

Meanwhile, combine the chicken, veal, eggs, grated onion, minced garlic, chopped rosemary, parsley, salt, and black pepper in a large bowl. Squeeze out as much water as you can from the soaked bread and add it to the bowl, crumbling it as you do so. Use your hands to mix the ingredients together until thoroughly combined. Cover and refrigerate until firm enough to handle, at least 2 hours, and up to overnight.

Preheat the oven to 350°F (180°C).

Place a large piece of parchment paper on a work surface (or on a large baking sheet, to catch any spills) and sprinkle about half of the bread crumbs onto the parchment. Place the chilled meat mixture on top and use your hands and the parchment to pat and roll it into a thick log roughly 8 × 4 inches (20 by 10 cm). Spread the remaining bread crumbs over the top and sides of the loaf, evenly coating it.

Heat the olive oil in a large ovenproof frying pan over medium heat until shimmering. Using a large sturdy spatula, carefully transfer the meatloaf to the frying pan. (This step will feel a little awkward because the meat is still relatively soft, just do your best and act decisively). Sear until deeply golden brown on the first side, 3 to 5 minutes. Using two sturdy spatulas, carefully flip the loaf over and brown on the second side. If the pan starts to look dry, drizzle in a little more oil as needed. (If there are excess bread crumbs in the oil, use a spoon or a paper towel to wipe them out and discard.) Continue flipping and searing the loaf until it is browned on all sides, then add the whole garlic cloves and the rosemary sprigs to the pan.

Pour the wine into the pan and bring to a boil, then baste the loaf generously with the pan juices.

Loosely cover the pan with foil and transfer to the oven to finish cooking through, 30 to 40 minutes. When it is done, a thermometer inserted into the thickest part of the loaf should read 160°F (71°C).

Remove from the oven and let the loaf rest for about 10 minutes before slicing. Store leftovers, covered, in the fridge for up to 3 days.

NOTE: *Some versions of this meatloaf are served chilled for Shabbat lunch. I personally find it most flavorful and succulent when it is warm, but sliced leftovers from the fridge make great sandwiches.*

Pascarella: Rome's Next-Gen Kosher Butcher

B*UTCHER SHOPS ARE* rarely joyful places to visit. But when you walk into Pascarella Carni Kasher, a sunny, brightly tiled storefront in Rome's Trastevere neighborhood, a feeling of cheerful conviviality is immediately apparent. The craftsmanship is obvious too, from the deli cases lined like a museum display with glistening bresaola, veal salami, and salt-and-pepper-cured carne secca, to the immaculate meat counter, behind which stylishly coiffed, white-coated men do a brisk business in high-end steaks, stew meat, and lamb chops.

Pascarella was founded in 2001 by Graziano Spizzichino, a veteran of the business who started working as a cleaner in a butcher shop in the 1960s at the age of nine. After years of partnering with his brother Rubino and opening several butcher shops around Rome, he put down roots in his first kosher-certified store—first along with his wife, and later bringing his children, Angelo and Emanuela, onboard.

Today, Pascarella is a true family-run business, and the Spizzichinos work together to infuse a sense of contemporary flair into the ancient practice of kosher butchering. But make no mistake: only Graziano's white butcher coat has the word "Boss" embroidered on the back!

כשר
PASCARELLA
CARNI KASHER

BRAISED CHICKEN AND CHICKPEA STEW

Tbeha con Ceci

SERVES 6 TO 8

Just before the Yom Kippur fast begins, Libyan Jews serve this hearty, nourishing stew to help fortify themselves for the journey ahead. Some families follow the custom of smashing some of the chickpeas in the dish to represent how, on the eve of the Day of Atonement, human beings are imperfect vessels awaiting divine judgment and striving to mend life's broken places. The saucy mix of chicken, chickpeas, potatoes, and zucchini relies on plenty of hot paprika for a spicy kick, so adjust that up or down to your own preference. Serve it with couscous or bread, and rejoice when it comes time to heat up the leftovers—like most stews, this one tastes even better the second day.

4 pounds (1.8 kg) bone-in, skin-on chicken thighs and legs, *excess fat trimmed*

Kosher salt and freshly ground black pepper

2 tablespoons extra-virgin olive oil

2 large yellow onions, *halved through the root and thinly sliced*

4 medium garlic cloves, *thinly sliced*

2 tablespoons hot paprika, *plus more if needed*

1½ tablespoons sweet paprika

1 teaspoon ground cinnamon

½ cup (110 g) tomato paste

1 cup (250 g) tomato puree (passata)

6 cups (1.4 l) chicken broth, *store-bought or homemade*

2 medium Yukon Gold potatoes (about 1 pound / 454 g), *peeled and quartered lengthwise*

2 medium zucchini (about 1 pound / 454 g), *halved lengthwise and cut into 2-inch (5 cm) pieces*

Two 15-ounce (425 g) cans chickpeas, *rinsed and drained*

Roughly chopped fresh flat-leaf parsley *for serving*

Pat the chicken dry with paper towels and season on both sides with salt and pepper.

Heat the oil in a Dutch oven or soup pot over medium-high heat until shimmering. Working in batches, add the chicken pieces, skin side down, and sear, turning once, until golden brown on both sides, 10 to 12 minutes per batch. Transfer the browned chicken to a plate as it is done. Set aside.

Add the onions and garlic to the Dutch oven, lower the heat to medium, and cook, stirring occasionally, until softened and golden brown, 8 to 10 minutes. Add the hot paprika, sweet paprika, cinnamon, 1 teaspoon salt, and ½ teaspoon black pepper and cook, stirring, until fragrant, about 1 minute.

Stir in the tomato paste, tomato puree, and chicken broth. Nestle the browned chicken and the potatoes into the liquid. Raise the heat to high and bring to a bubble, then reduce the heat to medium-low, cover the Dutch oven, and cook, stirring once or twice, for 40 minutes.

Add the zucchini and drained chickpeas to the pot, cover, and continue cooking until the chicken and vegetables are very tender, another 30 to 40 minutes. Uncover, raise the heat to high, and cook until the liquid thickens slightly, about 5 minutes.

Taste and add more salt and/or hot paprika, if desired. (If you started with unsalted or reduced-salt chicken broth, you may need to add a good bit more salt.) Serve hot, sprinkled with chopped parsley and more hot paprika, if desired.

SLOW-BRAISED BEEF STEW

Stracotto di Manzo

SERVES 6 TO 8

When Yoshie and I visited Rome after getting married, we scored a fortuitous invite to Shabbat dinner at Giovanni Terracina's apartment. Giovanni runs the kosher catering company Le Bon Ton, and his home cooking did not disappoint. One small complication: I was a longtime vegetarian, and the meal Giovanni served was a veritable feast of meat dishes, including stracotto di manzo (literally, "overcooked beef")—an iconic Roman Jewish stew traditionally served for Shabbat and holidays. Scanning the glorious table in front of me, I took a deep breath, turned to Yoshie, and quietly said, "If the phrase 'When in Rome' ever applies, it's tonight." And what a meal it was. (That dinner does not mark the official moment I stopped identifying as a vegetarian, but I think it is fair to say it played a role!)

Stracotto is typically served as two courses. First, the ample sauce is spooned over rigatoni and enjoyed as a primi. The meat is then served as part of the main course. Not all stracotto recipes include wine, but the version Giovanni shared with me does. And since his wonderful stracotto was my first taste of the dish, it will always be my gold standard.

2 tablespoons extra-virgin olive oil, *plus more if needed*

3 pounds (1.4 kg) boneless beef chuck, *cut into 2-inch (5 cm) pieces*

2 medium yellow onions, *finely chopped*

2 celery stalks, *finely chopped*

4 medium garlic cloves, *finely chopped*

1 cup (236 ml) dry red wine

Two 24.5-ounce (700 g) bottles or cans tomato puree (passata)

2 teaspoons kosher salt, *plus more if needed*

½ teaspoon freshly ground black pepper

Heat the oil in a large Dutch oven over medium-high heat. Working in batches, add the beef and cook, stirring occasionally, until lightly browned on all sides, 3 to 5 minutes per batch; transfer the beef to a large plate as it is browend. Add a drizzle more oil if the pot begins to look dry. Set the beef aside.

Add the onions, celery, and garlic to the pot, reduce the heat to medium, and cook, stirring occasionally, until softened and lightly browned, 8 to 10 minutes. Stir in the wine, raise the heat to medium-high, and bring to a boil.

Add the tomato puree and browned beef (along with any juices that have accumulated on the plate) to the Dutch oven, and bring to a boil. Reduce the heat to low, cover, and cook, stirring occasionally, until the beef is very tender and the sauce is creamy and thick, 2½ to 3 hours.

Stir in the salt and pepper. Taste and add more salt, if desired. Serve hot.

BEEF BRISKET STRACOTTO

SERVES 6

In 2018, chef Steve Samson offered a special Italian Jewish-inspired Rosh Hashanah menu at his acclaimed LA restaurant, Rossoblu. His brisket recipe, which I have adapted here, takes the classic Ashkenazi main and weaves in the flavors of Rome. While not a traditional Roman Jewish dish, it tastes like a love letter from a chef to the city that inspires him.

1 tablespoon *finely chopped* fresh rosemary, *plus 2 small rosemary sprigs*

2 teaspoons *finely chopped* fresh sage

Kosher salt and freshly ground black pepper

One 4- to 5-pound (1.8 to 2.3 kg) brisket

2 tablespoons vegetable oil (such as sunflower or grapeseed), *plus more if needed*

1 large yellow onion, *halved through the root and thinly sliced*

2 large carrots, *peeled, halved lengthwise if thick, cut into 1-inch (2.5 cm) pieces*

2 celery stalks, *halved lengthwise if thick, cut into 1-inch (2.5 cm) pieces*

8 medium garlic cloves, *thinly sliced*

2 tablespoons tomato paste

1¼ cups (295 ml) dry red wine

2½ cups (590 ml) beef broth

2 bay leaves

Mix together the chopped rosemary, sage, 1 teaspoon salt, and ¼ teaspoon pepper in a small bowl. Pat the brisket dry with paper towels, then rub the salt and spice mixture evenly on both sides of the meat.

Preheat the oven to 325°F (160°C).

Heat the oil in a large frying pan over medium-high heat. Add the brisket and sear, turning once, until browned on both sides, 8 to 10 minutes. Transfer the meat to a baking dish that is large enough to comfortably accommodate it and set aside.

If there is a lot of rendered fat in the frying pan, pour off and discard all but about 2 tablespoons. Or, if the pan looks dry, add a drizzle of oil. Add the onion, carrots, celery, garlic, and rosemary sprigs to the pan and cook, stirring occasionally, until the onions begin to soften, about 5 minutes. Add the tomato paste and cook, stirring, for about 1 minute. Pour in the red wine and cook, stirring often, until the liquid cooks down a bit, 2 to 3 minutes. Add the broth, bay leaves, 1 teaspoon salt, and a generous amount of black pepper and bring the mixture to a boil, stirring often.

Gently pour the vegetable and broth mixture over the brisket. Cover the baking dish snugly with aluminum foil, transfer to the oven, and braise for 2 hours.

Remove the brisket from the oven and flip the meat over. Re-cover the baking dish and continue cooking until the meat is fork-tender, 1½ to 2 hours longer. Remove the brisket from the oven and let cool slightly before slicing.

Serve hot, with the juices and vegetables spooned over the meat.

BRISKET FRITTATA

Frittata di Carne

SERVES 2 TO 4

This frittata answers the question, "What should I do with my leftover brisket—or, more accurately for this cookbook, my leftover Stracatto di Manzo (page 235)?" The traditional recipe includes little more than eggs, shredded meat (typically slow-cooked beef shin), salt, and pepper. It's already full-flavored that way, but I like it even more with softened onions and garlic, along with an herbaceous hit of chopped fresh oregano. I typically serve this frittata for a quick dinner with a green salad and a glass of wine.

2 tablespoons extra-virgin olive oil

1 medium yellow onion, *finely chopped*

Kosher salt and freshly ground black pepper

1½ cups (150 g) shredded meat from Stracotto di Manzo *(page 235) or* shredded cooked flanken

2 small garlic cloves, *finely chopped*

1½ teaspoons finely chopped fresh oregano *(or ¾ teaspoon dried)*

7 large eggs, *lightly beaten*

Preheat the oven to 375°F (180°C).

Heat the oil in a medium nonstick, ovenproof frying pan over medium heat. Add the onion and a generous pinch of salt, cover the pan, and cook, stirring occasionally, until the onion is softened and lightly browned, 6 to 8 minutes. Add the shredded meat, garlic, and oregano and cook, stirring, until fragrant, about 2 minutes.

Whisk the eggs, 1/4 teaspoon salt, and a generous amount of black pepper together in a bowl. Pour the egg mixture over the meat and onions and gently stir to distribute the ingredients evenly in the pan.

Transfer the pan to the oven and bake until the top is just set, 10 to 15 minutes. Remove from the oven and allow to cool for 10 minutes to let the fritatta set.

Gently run a rubber spatula around the edges of the pan, then carefully transfer the frittata to a serving plate or cutting board. Serve warm or at room temperature.

HERBED VEAL ROLLS

Involtini di Vitello

SERVES 6

This recipe was inspired by one I came across in Giuliano Malizia's pocket-sized cookbook *La Cucina Ebraico-Romanesca*. To make it, you (or your butcher) pound veal cutlets very thin, roll them up around a savory filling, and simmer them in wine and broth until tender and flavorful. Most Roman recipes fill the rolls with pork prosciutto, but Malizia's version suggests substituting prosciutto made from goose. For those of us who do not have access to that, beef bacon works well as a substitute.

¼ cup (35 g) unseasoned bread crumbs

1 cup (240 ml) chicken broth, *plus more for soaking the bread crumbs*

6 ounces (170 g) goose prosciutto or beef bacon, *chopped*

¼ cup (5 g) fresh flat-leaf parsley leaves, *finely chopped, plus more for serving*

6 veal cutlets (about ¼ pound / 113 g each), *pounded to a ¼-inch (6 mm) thickness*

Kosher salt and freshly ground black pepper

3 tablespoons extra-virgin olive oil

¼ cup (60 ml) dry white wine

Put the bread crumbs in a medium bowl and add enough broth to cover. Let stand for 5 minutes, then drain in a fine-mesh sieve set over a bowl, pressing with the back of a spoon to remove as much liquid as possible, and return the bread crumbs to the medium bowl; discard the broth.

Add the proscuitto or bacon and parsley to the bowl and mix well to combine.

Lay the veal cutlets out on a work surface and lightly season with salt and pepper. Divide the beef bacon mixture among the cutlets, spreading it into a thin layer. Starting at one of the short ends, roll each cutlet up around the filling and secure the seams with a toothpick. (You can also tie the bundles with kitchen twine.)

Heat the olive oil in a large frying pan over medium-high heat. Add the veal bundles and sear, turning once, until browned on both sides, 2 to 3 minutes per side. Add the wine and cook until it mostly evaporates. Add the 1 cup (240 ml) broth and bring to a simmer, then cover the pan, turn the heat down to medium-low, and cook until the rolls are tender, about 20 minutes.

Transfer the rolls to a serving platter and carefully remove the toothpicks (or twine). Turn the heat under the pan up to high and cook, stirring occasionally, until the sauce thickens a bit, about 5 minutes.

Spoon the sauce over the rolls and serve hot, sprinkled generously with chopped parsley.

STAUB
STAUB

Clockwise from bottom left: *Jewish-Style Fried Artichokes, 128; Slow-Braised Beef Stew, 235; Silky Marinated Zucchini, 44; Chicken with Peppers, 222; Sautéed Dandelion Greens, 76*

STUFFED ZUCCHINI

Zucchine Romanesche Ripiene di Carne

SERVES 4 TO 6

Also called *zucchine ripene alla romana*, or Roman-style stuffed zucchini, this classic saucy dish (pictured on page 182) is loved equally by Roman Jews and their non-Jewish neighbors. (The primary difference is that the Jewish versions typically do not include Parmesan or other cheese in the filling.) It is traditionally made with zucchine romanesche, a thin, light green version of the vegetable that has distinctive vertical ridges. If you cannot find it, standard zucchini works as a substitute—just be sure to look for relatively small, firm ones.

1 pound (454 g) ground beef

⅓ cup (30 g) unseasoned bread crumbs

1 large egg, *lightly beaten*

3 tablespoons warm water

½ cup (10 g) fresh flat-leaf parsley leaves, *finely chopped, plus more for serving*

½ cup (10 g) fresh basil leaves, *finely chopped, plus more for serving*

6 medium garlic cloves, *2 minced, grated, or pushed through a press, 4 chopped*

Kosher salt and freshly ground black pepper

6 small zucchini (about 1½ pounds / 680 g), *ends trimmed and cut into 2-inch (5 cm) lengths*

One 28-ounce (795 g) can whole peeled tomatoes

1½ cups (370 g) tomato puree (passata)

1 teaspoon granulated sugar

¼ cup (60 ml) extra-virgin olive oil, *plus more for serving*

¼ to ½ teaspoon red pepper flakes

Put the ground beef in a medium bowl and add the bread crumbs, egg, warm water, parsley, basil, minced garlic, 1 teaspoon salt, and ¼ teaspoon black pepper. Mix with your hands until thoroughly combined; set aside.

Use a zucchini or apple corer to carefully remove the cores of the zucchini pieces, leaving a roughly ¼-inch (6 mm) shell. Set aside.

Put the tomatoes, with their juices, in a medium bowl and gently squeeze them to break them up into small pieces. Stir in the tomato puree, sugar, 1 teaspoon salt, and a generous amount of pepper. Set aside.

Heat the olive oil in a large wide saucepan over medium heat. Add the chopped garlic and the desired amount of red pepper flakes and cook, stirring, until fragrant, about 1 minute. Add the tomato mixture and bring to a boil, then turn the heat down to medium-low, partially cover the pan, and cook, stirring occasionally, until the sauce thickens slightly, 5 to 10 minutes.

Meanwhile, stuff the hollowed-out zucchini pieces with the meat mixture.

Carefully add the zucchini to the simmering sauce (it is okay if the pieces are not completely covered by the sauce). Form any leftover filling into 1-inch (2.5 cm) meatballs and tuck them into the sauce as well. Cover the pan and cook, occasionally basting the top of the zucchini with the sauce, until it is tender and the meat is cooked through, about 30 minutes.

Raise the heat to medium, partially cover the saucepan, and continue cooking, stirring and basting occasionally, until the sauce thickens a bit more, 10 to 15 minutes. Remove from the heat and let rest for 10 to 15 minutes.

Transfer the zucchini, any meatballs, and sauce to a serving platter and serve warm, drizzled with a little olive oil and sprinkled with parsley and basil.

NOTE: *Zucchini corers are inexpensive and readily available at kitchen shops and online. If you plan to make this dish, it is worth investing in one. The zucchini "cores" can be chopped and added to soups, or sautéed and added to frittatas or pasta dishes.*

The "Fifth Quarter" (Quinto Quarto)

W*HEN AN ANIMAL* is butchered, it is often quartered before being broken down into smaller cuts. The leftover scraps—the pancreas, spleen, brain, heart, lungs, and tripe—account for nearly a quarter of the animal's total weight. In Rome, these innards are called the quinto quarto, or "fifth quarter," and have been incorporated into many iconic dishes.

Some historians say that Rome's fifth-quarter cuisine dates back to the late nineteenth century, when workers at the slaughterhouse in the city's Testaccio neighborhood were partially compensated with the offal of the animals they had butchered. Those workers and their families are certainly an important part of the story, but many of the classic dishes predate the slaughterhouse's opening and, in fact, likely originated in the Roman Jewish Ghetto.

With extremely limited resources at their disposal, and countless restrictions placed upon them during the Ghetto period, "Jews had a monopoly on the fifth quarter," said Roman Jewish historian and tour guide Micaela Pavoncello (see page 184). For centuries, dishes like fried brains and sweetbreads, stewed tripe, braised oxtail, and calf intestines that still contained milk from the animal's mother (called pajata) could be found in Roman Jewish kitchens. (The partially digested milk inside the intestines was not classified as true "dairy," and therefore did not break the kosher prohibition against mixing milk and meat.)

Today, fifth-quarter dishes are still served in both homes and restaurants, but they are less common than they once were. For many, tastes have changed as Romans have gained access to a wider array of ingredients that render the fifth quarter less important. The mad cow disease scare of the late twentieth century also made certain cuts that were linked with the disease (particularly veal brains and intestines) very difficult to source.

For Jewish cooks, kashrut adds an additional barrier. Some Roman Jewish families still prepare braised oxtail, but you have to have an in with your butcher to locate a kosher cut. Tripe with kosher certification is also now virtually impossible to find. Case in point: La Taverna del Ghetto, which was the first kosher restaurant in the Jewish Ghetto neighborhood to celebrate Roman Jewish cuisine, gave up its own kosher certification so it could continue serving the community's ancient dishes.

One dish that remains fairly common, though, is coratella con carciofi—a mixture of sautéed onion, artichokes, and lamb entrails (often the heart, lungs, and trachea, and sometimes the liver, kidneys, or spleen). Originating in Rome's Jewish kitchens, it was adopted by Romans across the city and is still served in some restaurants, including Ba'Ghetto and BellaCarne in the Ghetto neighborhood. The entrails' intense, mineral flavor is offset by that of the delicate spring artichokes. And despite the dish's humble origins, today it is considered a delicacy by those who love it. When in Rome, it is worth seeking out!

BRAISED OXTAIL STEW

Coda alla Vaccinara

SERVES 6

This rich, saucy beef stew is one of the stars of Rome's "fifth quarter" cuisine (see page 244). Translated as "oxtail cooked in the butcher's style," it takes a less desirable cut of beef and transforms it into a deeply flavorful, feast-worthy dish. Roman Jews love coda alla vaccinara just as much as their neighbors, but finding kosher-certified oxtail can be a challenge. (The cow's sciatic nerve runs directly through the flesh of the oxtail and, according to kosher law, has to be carefully removed in order to be deemed fit.) If you keep kosher and can't find oxtail, an equal amount of meaty short ribs makes a delicious substitute.

2 tablespoons extra-virgin olive oil, *plus more if needed*

3 pounds oxtails, *cut into approximately 3-inch (7.5-cm) pieces*

Kosher salt and freshly ground black pepper

1 medium yellow onion, *finely chopped*

1 large carrot, *peeled and finely chopped*

2 tablespoons tomato paste

1 cup (250 g) tomato puree (passata)

1 cup (240 ml) dry white wine

½ teaspoon ground cinnamon

One 28-ounce (795 g) can peeled whole tomatoes

3 celery stalks, *halved lengthwise (or into thirds if thick) and cut into 2-inch (5 cm) pieces*

¼ cup (30 g) pine nuts

¼ cup (35 g) dark raisins

Preheat the oven to 325°F (160°C).

Heat the oil in a Dutch oven or other large ovenproof pot over medium heat. Season the oxtail pieces on all sides with salt and pepper. Working in batches, add the oxtails to the Dutch oven and sear, turning once, until browned on both sides, 8 to 10 minutes per batch. Remove the browned oxtails to a plate.

If there is a lot of rendered fat in the Dutch oven, pour off and discard all but 2 tablespoons. Or, if it looks dry, add a drizzle of oil. Add the onion and carrot to the pot and cook, stirring occasionally, until beginning to soften and brown, 6 to 8 minutes.

Stir in the tomato paste, followed by the tomato puree and wine. Raise the heat to medium-high and bring the mixture to a boil. Stir in the cinnamon, ½ teaspoon salt, and a generous amount of black pepper, then add the whole tomatoes and their juices, squeezing the tomatoes between your fingers to break them up as you add them.

Return the browned oxtails to the Dutch oven and add the celery. Bring the mixture to a boil, then cover and transfer to the oven. Cook, turning the oxtails with tongs once or twice, for 1½ hours.

Remove the pot from the oven and stir in the pine nuts and raisins, then cover, return to the oven, and continue cooking until the meat is falling off the bone, 30 to 60 minutes. Remove from the oven and let stand, covered, for 15 minutes.

Taste the sauce and add more salt and/or pepper as needed. Serve hot.

GARLIC AND ROSEMARY ROASTED LAMB

Abbacchio alla Giudia

SERVES 6 TO 8

This juicy rosemary-and-garlic-scented roasted lamb is equally cherished on Easter and Passover tables in Rome. When I spoke with Roberta Nahum, the former president of Rome's chapter of ADEI WIZO (Italy's Jewish Women's Association), she cited the dish as a testament to Jews' ability to both absorb and contribute to their local culinary environment. Indeed, the dish is referred to interchangeably as "*alla Giudia,* Jewish-style, and *alla Romana*, Roman-style. (On the subject of names, the Italian word for lamb is *agnello*, but here the word *abbacchio* refers to a tender, delicately flavored breed of milk-fed lamb native to the Lazio region.) A Roman Jewish seder would not feel complete without this springtime dish. But if it is not your family's custom to eat roasted lamb on Passover (see page 252), it makes an equally sensational centerpiece anytime you serve it.

5 medium Yukon Gold potatoes (about 2½ pounds / 1.1 kg), *halved lengthwise and cut into ¾-inch- (2 cm) thick wedges*

12 medium garlic cloves, *10 smashed and peeled; 2 minced, grated, or pushed through a press*

6 large rosemary sprigs, plus 2 tablespoons *finely chopped* fresh rosemary

¼ cup (60 ml) extra-virgin olive oil

Kosher salt and freshly ground black pepper

1 boneless lamb shoulder (about 4 pounds / 1.8 kg), *tied with kitchen twine (see Note)*

⅓ cup (80 ml) dry white wine

Preheat the oven to 450°F (230°C).

Spread the potato wedges over the bottom of a large roasting pan. Tuck the whole garlic cloves and 4 of the rosemary sprigs in between the potatoes.

Stir together the olive oil, minced garlic, and chopped rosemary in a small bowl. Drizzle half of the mixture over the potatoes, sprinkle with ½ teaspoon salt and ¼ teaspoon black pepper, and toss well to coat.

Place the lamb shoulder on top of the potatoes and top with the remaining 2 rosemary sprigs. Drizzle the remaining olive oil mixture over the top, sprinkle with 3/4 teaspoon salt and ¼ teaspoon pepper, and rub evenly over the top of the meat.

Add the wine to the roasting pan, pouring it around the potatoes and being careful not to pour it directly over the lamb. Roast for 40 minutes, then gently shake the roasting pan and baste the lamb with any pan juices.

CONTINUES

Carefully lift up the lamb and stir the potatoes to facilitate even browning, then replace the lamb. Continue roasting until the potatoes and lamb are deeply browned and an instant-read thermometer stuck into the thickest part of the meat registers 145°F (63°C), another 25 to 35 minutes. Remove the roasting pan from the oven and let the dish rest for 15 minutes.

Transfer the lamb to a cutting board, and transfer the potatoes and garlic cloves to a serving platter. Remove and discard the twine and slice the lamb, then layer the lamb over the potatoes. Serve hot, with the pan juices spooned over the top, if desired.

NOTE: *Tying a boneless lamb shoulder with string helps facilitate even cooking. Many butchers sell boneless lamb shoulders pretied or will tie them for you. If you are starting with an untied lamb shoulder, first trim off any excess fat (leaving a generous fat cap on top). Then roll up the lamb and tie it several times crosswise and once or twice lengthwise with kitchen twine.*

dopo
Notte Italiana
2019
EXTRA DRY

Lamb, Flour, Rice, and Peas: Passover in Rome

I *GREW UP IN* an Ashkenazi Jewish home, where my family followed certain rules on Passover, even though we were not otherwise religiously observant. Anything made with wheat, rye, barley, spelt, or oats (chametz) was off the table during the week-long holiday. We also avoided ingredients like corn, rice, and legumes that fell into the murkier kitniyot category. (Kitniyot includes anything deemed to closely resemble the prohibited grains.)

Roman Jews follow the Sephardi custom of eating kitniyot, which means that along with matzo (called azzima in Italy), rice, fava beans, and green peas feature heavily on their holiday menus. More surprisingly, one of the women I interviewed—Ghila Ottolenghi Sanders, a Roman Jew who now lives in Atlanta, Georgia—told me that many families end their seder meals with ciambellette, sweet ring-shaped cookies (page 266).

"Oh, you must make them with matzo meal for Passover, right?" I asked. But Ghila assured me they were made with wheat flour, and had been for countless generations. The flour her family, like most families, used was checked to make sure it had not come into any contact with water. And, as with making matzo, the cookies had to be prepared on a sparklingly clean surface and baked within 18 minutes to ensure no leavening occurred, which would render them chametz.

In 2013, at the behest of Israel's chief rabbinate, the Rabbinical Association of Italy banned making the cookies at home during Passover. Naturally the decision was met with outrage from community members who felt like their centuries-long tradition was being ripped away. So a compromise was found: a few Jewish institutions in Rome set up public baking days where families could reserve a time slot in a kosher kitchen and bake their cookies under supervision. Ghila told me families now come together every year to bake in the days leading up to Passover—a moment of innovation and community-building born out of restriction.

Another obvious contrast between Roman seder tables and other seder tables is the presence of roasted lamb. Ashkenazi and many Sephardi families eschew roasted lamb for the seder meal, but it is by far the most common main dish for Roman Jews. Before the destruction of the Second Temple in Jerusalem in 70 CE, the Israelites practiced the custom of sacrificing lambs on the eve of Passover. After the Temple fell and Jewish ritual was severed from the Temple's altar, the practice died away.

In commemoration of the collective pain brought on by the Temple's destruction, most Jewish communities scrupulously avoid lamb for the seder. (The one exception is the symbolic roasted shankbone that sits on the seder plate, but it is not eaten.) However, the Roman Jewish community and its traditions are so ancient that they predate the Temple's destruction. So the community's custom of eating roasted lamb for the holiday is a testament to their exceptionally long history in Rome.

BRAISED LAMB CHOPS WITH ARTICHOKES AND FAVA BEANS

Agnello alla Giudia

SERVES 6

This recipe is my interpretation of the classic Roman Passover combination of lamb, spring artichokes, and verdant fava beans braised in a bright but richly flavored broth. I use lamb shoulder chops to give the dish its decadent, showstopping appeal, but you could also use about 4 pounds (1.8 kg) of bone-in lamb shoulder, cut into 2-inch (5 cm) pieces (ask your butcher to do this). If it is not your custom to serve lamb or fava beans on Passover (see page 252), this dish is equally wonderful served for another special spring meal.

3 tablespoons extra-virgin olive oil, *plus more if needed*

6 lamb shoulder chops (about ¾ pound / 340 g each), *trimmed of excess fat and patted dry*

Kosher salt and freshly ground black pepper

1 large yellow onion, *finely chopped*

6 medium garlic cloves, *finely chopped*

½ cup (120 ml) dry white wine

2 cups (475 ml) chicken broth, *store-bought or homemade*

2 tablespoons fresh lemon juice

4 large artichokes, *cleaned according to the instructions on page 58,* or 2 cups (200 g) thawed frozen artichoke quarters

1¼ cups (125 g) frozen peeled fava beans, *thawed*

1 packed teaspoon grated lemon zest *(from about 1 medium lemon)*

Finely chopped fresh flat-leaf parsley *for serving*

Heat the olive oil in a large Dutch oven over medium-high heat. Season the lamb chops with salt and pepper on both sides. Working in batches, add the lamb chops to the hot oil and sear, flipping once, until browned on both sides, 6 to 8 minutes per batch. Transfer the seared chops to a large plate as they are done, then set aside.

If there is a lot of rendered fat in the bottom of the Dutch oven, pour off all but 2 tablespoons. Or, if the pot looks dry, add another tablespoon of olive oil. Add the onion and garlic and cook, stirring often, until softened and lightly golden, 6 to 8 minutes. Add the wine and cook, stirring to release any browned bits at the bottom of the pot, until slightly reduced, 1 to 2 minutes.

Add the chicken broth, lemon juice, ½ teaspoon salt, and ½ teaspoon pepper to the pot. Nestle the browned chops into the liquid (it is okay if they aren't all submerged), and pour any juices that have accumulated on the plate over the top. Raise the heat to high and bring the liquid to a boil. Cover, reduce the heat to medium-low, and cook, stirring and turning the chops occasionally, until the meat is tender, about 1 hour.

Meanwhile, if you are using fresh artichokes, halve the cleaned artichokes lengthwise and slice them into ¼-inch- (6 mm) thick slices.

Stir the artichokes (fresh or frozen) into the cooking liquid, partially cover the Dutch oven, and cook until the artichokes are tender, 15 to 20 minutes; a few minutes before the dish is done, add the fava beans with the lemon zest, and cook until the beans are tender but still bright green.

Arrange the lamb chops, artichokes, and fava beans on a large serving platter. Turn the heat under the Dutch oven to high and cook, stirring occasionally, until the liquid reduces by half, 8 to 10 minutes. Taste and add more salt and pepper if needed.

Spoon a generous amount of the braising liquid over the lamb chops and serve hot, sprinkled with fresh parsley. (If desired, you can make the dish in advance, allow it to cool, and refrigerate it overnight. Scoop off and discard the layer of fat that has congealed on top of the sauce, then gently reheat on the stovetop or in the oven to serve.)

SAUCY STUFFED VEGETABLES

Mafrum

SERVES 6

Libyan Jews serve this majestic stuffed vegetable dish for Shabbat and holidays. The meat-filled vegetables are individually coated in flour and egg and panfried before being simmered in the flavorful sauce. They are decidedly worth the effort for a special-occasion meal. You can choose to stuff just one type of vegetable (potatoes and eggplants are common), or follow the lead of many Libyan home cooks and mix and match whatever vegetables you have on hand.

For the Sauce

¼ cup (60 ml) extra-virgin olive oil

1 large yellow onion, *finely chopped*

4 medium garlic cloves, *thinly sliced*

1 teaspoon kosher salt, *plus more if needed*

½ teaspoon freshly ground black pepper

1 teaspoon sweet paprika

1 teaspoon hot paprika

2 tablespoons tomato paste

1 cup (250 g) tomato puree (passata)

2 cups (480 ml) chicken broth or vegetable broth, *store-bought or homemade (page 109)*

For the Filling

2 ounces (57 g) rustic white bread, *torn into 1-inch (2.5-cm) pieces (about 1 cup)*

1 pound (454 g) ground beef

1 teaspoon kosher salt

½ teaspoon freshly ground black pepper

½ teaspoon ground cinnamon

1 large egg

1 small yellow onion, *grated on the large holes of a box grater*

2 medium garlic cloves, *minced, grated, or pushed through a press*

½ cup (10 g) fresh flat-leaf parsley leaves, *finely chopped*

For the Vegetables and Frying

2½ pounds (1.1 kg) vegetables, *such as potatoes, eggplants, zucchini, onions, and/or small bell peppers, prepared according to the following instructions (page 258)*

Vegetable oil (such as sunflower or grapeseed) *for frying*

1 cup (140 g) all-purpose flour

3 large eggs

CONTINUES

Preparing Vegetables for Mafrum

Potatoes and Eggplants

Peel and slice into 1/2-inch- (1.25 cm) thick rounds. Using a sharp knife, make a horizontal slit into each round, stopping a little beyond halfway through. (Take care not to go all the way through to the other side.) You should end up with round vegetable slices that can be opened like clams.

Zucchini

Trim off the ends and cut into 2-inch (5 cm) lengths. Use a zucchini or apple corer to carefully remove the zucchini "cores," leaving a shell roughly ¼ inch (6 mm) thick.

Onions

Slice off both ends of each onion. Make a vertical slit down one side of the onion, cutting through to the center. Transfer to a saucepan, cover with water, and bring to a boil over high heat. Reduce the heat to medium and simmer, partially covered, until the onions soften and begin to come apart, 20 to 30 minutes. Drain and let cool slightly, then separate the individual onion layers, which will be rolled around the filling.

Bell Peppers

Halve lengthwise (quarter if larger) and remove the stems and seeds.

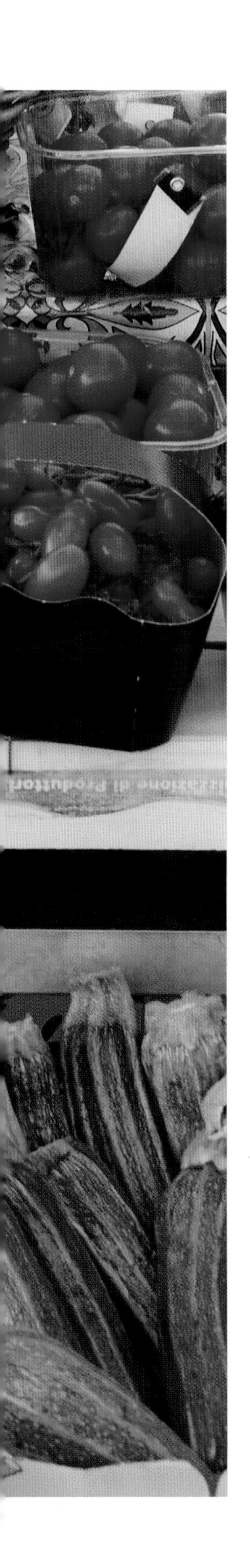

MAKE THE SAUCE
Heat the olive oil in a large Dutch oven over medium heat until shimmering. Add the onion and garlic and sauté until softened and lightly golden, 6 to 8 minutes. Add the salt, pepper, sweet paprika, and hot paprika and cook, stirring, until fragrant, about 1 minute.

Add the tomato paste, tomato puree, and broth to the pot and stir to combine. Bring to a boil, then lower the heat to a simmer and cook until the flavors have had a chance to meld, about 15 minutes. Taste and add additional salt if needed. Remove from the heat and set aside. (*The sauce can be made up to 2 days in advance and stored, covered, in the fridge.*)

MAKE THE FILLING
Place the torn bread in a bowl and cover with warm water. Let the bread soak until it is thoroughly softened, 10 to 15 minutes.

Combine the ground beef, salt, pepper, cinnamon, egg, onion, garlic, and parsley in a large bowl. Squeeze out as much water as you can from the soaked bread and add it to the bowl, crumbling the bread as you do so. Use your hands to mix the meat mixture until thoroughly combined.

FILL AND FRY THE VEGETABLES
Scoop up rounded tablespoons of the filling and gently press them into the prepared vegetables.

Heat about ½ inch (1.25 cm) of oil in a large frying pan over medium heat until shimmering. Meanwhile, spread the flour in a shallow bowl; beat the eggs in another bowl.

Working in batches, dip the stuffed vegetables in the flour, flipping to coat both sides and shaking off any excess, then dip in the egg, allowing any excess to drip off. Gently slip the prepared vegetables into the hot oil and fry, flipping once, until golden brown on both sides, about 3 minutes per side. Transfer to a large plate and add additional oil to the pan as needed while you fry the remaining vegetables.

Set the Dutch oven holding the sauce back over medium heat and bring to a simmer. Nestle the fried vegetables into the sauce. (They will overlap considerably; the potatoes should be submerged as much as possible, since they cook more quickly and evenly under liquid.) Reduce the heat to low, cover, and cook, occasionally basting the vegetables with the sauce, until they are tender, about 1 hour. Serve hot, with the sauce spooned over top.

SWEETS

Dolci

Twisted Sweet Bread with Dried Fruit, 300

CHEWY ALMOND COOKIES

Amaretti / Abambar

MAKES ABOUT 20 COOKIES

The moment my plane lands in Rome, I make a beeline to Pasticceria il Boccione, the 200-year old kosher bakery located in the heart of the Jewish Ghetto neighborhood (see page 276). If I'm lucky, they are still stocked with amaretti—sweet, almondy dough piped into chubby swirls and baked until crisped on top and chewy within. Rome's Libyan Jews fancy a similar cookie, abambar, which is made from essentially the same ingredients but rolled and pressed into rounds and topped with almonds, rather than piped. Both versions have become go-to Passover desserts for my family, as well as year-round additions to our cookie jar.

2 large egg whites

1½ cups (185 g) confectioners' sugar, *sifted*

1 teaspoon almond extract

¼ teaspoon kosher salt

2½ cups (250 g) blanched almond flour

About 20 whole or sliced unsalted almonds *for decoration*

Preheat the oven to 325°F (160°C). Line two baking sheets with parchment paper.

Combine the egg whites, sugar, almond extract, and salt in the bowl of a stand mixer fitted with the paddle attachment. (Or use a handheld electric mixer and a large bowl.) Beat on medium speed until the sugar dissolves. Beat in the almond flour in two stages, scraping down the sides of the bowl as necessary, until a dough the texture of soft almond paste forms.

Using lightly moistened or oiled hands, scoop out rounded tablespoons of the dough, roll them into balls, and place them on the baking sheets, about 1 inch (2.5 cm) apart. Using the tip of your finger, gently press the center of each cookie, flattening it slightly and leaving an indentation. Gently press an almond into each indentation.

Bake, rotating the baking sheets back to front and top to bottom halfway through baking, for 15 to 20 minutes, until the cookies are lightly golden on top. (The bottoms will be a few shades darker.) Transfer the cookies to wire racks to cool. The cookies will continue to firm up as they cool.

The cookies can be stored in an airtight container in the fridge for up to 1 week, or in the freezer for up to 3 months.

Variation: Swirled Amaretti

Follow the recipe through the second paragraph, adding 1 additional egg white to the dough. Transfer the dough to a pastry piping bag fit with a star tip and pipe into 1-inch- (2.5 cm) wide swirled mounds on the baking sheets. Omit the decorative almonds. Bake as directed.

SWEET CITRUS RING COOKIES

Ciambellette

MAKES ABOUT 2 DOZEN COOKIES

The recipe for these crisp, sweet ring-shaped cookies was adapted from one shared with me by Ghila Ottolenghi Sanders, a Roman Jew who is now the director of an arts organization in Atlanta, Georgia. "My mother's mother was an exceptional cook and handwrote a recipe booklet she gave to her three children," Ghila told me. "The recipes have no quantities or instructions on temperature. It's all very approximate, but it's about bringing in all of your senses to the kitchen."

Although the dough is made with flour, Roman Jews traditionally make ciambellette (the name translates as "little doughnuts") for Passover, hastily preparing the cookies on a sparkling-clean surface to avoid any accidental contact between flour and liquid that could lead to leavening. (Read more about this unique custom on pages 252–53.) They are a delightful cookie: snappy, full of citrusy flavor, and a perfect match for a cup of espresso.

2¼ cups (315 g) all-purpose flour, *plus more if needed*

½ teaspoon kosher salt

½ cup (120 ml) extra-virgin or light olive oil

1 cup (200 g) granulated sugar, *plus more for rolling*

2 large eggs

1 teaspoon vanilla extract

2 packed teaspoons grated lemon zest *(from about 2 medium lemons)*

1½ packed teaspoons grated orange zest *(from about 1 medium orange)*

Preheat the oven to 350°F (180°C). Line two baking sheets with parchment paper.

Whisk together the flour and salt in a medium bowl; set aside.

Whisk the olive oil, sugar, eggs, vanilla, lemon zest, and orange zest together in a large bowl until fully combined and glossy. Add the flour mixture in two stages, stirring with a sturdy spoon until you have a thick, slightly tacky dough. If the dough is too soft or sticky to roll with floured hands, add a little more flour, 1 tablespoon at a time, until you reach the desired consistency.

Sprinkle a generous layer of sugar onto a large plate. Using lightly floured hands, pinch off rounded tablespoons of the dough and roll between your palms into ropes that are about 4 inches (10 cm) long and ½ inch (1.25 cm) thick. Gently roll each rope in the sugar to coat on all sides, then place on the prepared baking sheets, bringing the ends together into a ring shape and lightly pinching them to seal. (The dough will feel delicate, but it will firm up during baking.)

Bake, rotating the baking sheets top to bottom and back to front once halfway through baking, for 20 to 25 minutes. The tops of the cookies should be just barely golden and the bottoms lightly golden and crisp. Transfer the cookies to a wire rack to cool.

The cookies can be stored in an airtight container in the fridge for up to 1 week, or in the freezer for up to 3 months.

CINNAMON ALMOND COOKIES

Biscottini con le Mandorle

MAKES ABOUT 30 COOKIES

These almond-studded cinnamon cookies might just be the perfect after-dinner nibble. Inspired by the biscottini I always buy at the kosher bakery, Pasticceria il Boccione, in the Jewish Ghetto neighborhood (see page 276), they are crisp on the outside and a little chewy within. A bit of cocoa powder accentuates their mellow sweetness without overpowering the cinnamon flavor. Serve them alongside espresso or tea.

1½ cups (210 g) all-purpose flour, *plus more for rolling*

2½ tablespoons unsweetened cocoa powder

1½ teaspoons ground cinnamon

¼ teaspoon kosher salt

2 large eggs

1 cup (200 g) granulated sugar

¾ cup (105 g) unsalted roasted almonds

Preheat the oven to 350°F (180°C). Line a large baking sheet with parchment paper.

Whisk together the flour, cocoa powder, cinnamon, and salt in a medium bowl.

Beat together the eggs and sugar in a large bowl with a sturdy spoon until well combined. Add the dry ingredients to the wet in two stages, stirring until a firm but pliable dough forms. Add the almonds and stir well to combine. It will seem like a lot of almonds for the amount of dough. If necessary, use lightly floured hands to knead them into the dough.

Turn the dough out onto a lightly floured surface and divide it into 2 equal pieces. Use lightly floured hands to roll each piece into a log that is about 1 inch (2.5 cm) thick and 8 inches (20 cm) long. If the dough is sticking, sprinkle a little more flour over the top. Place both logs on the baking sheet, leaving a few inches between them.

Bake, rotating the baking sheet back to front halfway through baking, until the dough is dry and firm to the touch, about 30 minutes. Remove from the oven and let the logs cool and firm up for 10 minutes.

Set the logs on a cutting board and use a serrated knife to slice them into ½-inch- (1.25 cm) thick rounds. Transfer the cookies to a wire rack to cool completely. They will continue to firm up as they cool but should remain chewy at the center.

The cookies can be stored in an airtight container in the fridge for up to 1 week, or in the freezer for up to 3 months.

Left to right: *Chewy Almond Cookies, 265; Cinnamon Almond Cookies, 268; Lemony Almond Cake, 286; Chocolate and Almond Cake, 284; Mint Tea with Roasted Peanuts, 314*

DRIED FRUIT AND NUT BAR COOKIES

Pizza Ebraica

MAKES ABOUT 10 LARGE BAR COOKIES (OR 2 DOZEN SMALLER COOKIES)

The Roman Jewish Ghetto's most famous "pizza" has nothing to do with sauce or cheese. Instead, pizza Ebraica are crispy-edged, soft-centered, absolutely addictive bar cookies. Their exact origins are unclear, but they were likely brought to Rome by Sephardi Jews fleeing the Spanish Inquisition. The cookies (the name roughly translates as "Jewish-style pie") are also sometimes called *pizza dolce* ("sweet pie") or *pizza de beridde* ("bris pie")—the latter because they are traditionally served at circumcisions.

Locals and tourists alike form long lines outside Pasticceria il Boccione (see page 276) to buy the 200-year old kosher pastry shop's beloved pizza Ebraica. Most famously, in 2008, Pope Benedict XVI declared Boccione's take on the cookies to be his favorite dessert in all of Rome.

The bakery's pizza Ebraica are at least an inch thick, and emerge from the oven with the charred patina that has become Boccione's trademark. They are perfect, full stop, but a challenge to re-create at home. I have the best luck when I pat the dough a bit thinner, and take the cookies out of the oven when they are well browned rather than fully singed. I do follow Boccione's impressive ratio of dough to nuts and dried fruit, however, making sure every bite is brimming with crunchy almonds, buttery pine nuts, and sweet-tart raisins and cherries.

⅔ cup (160 ml) vegetable oil (such as sunflower)

⅓ cup (80 ml) dry white wine

1½ cups (210 g) all-purpose flour, *plus more for shaping*

1 cup (100 g) almond flour

1 cup (200 g) granulated sugar

½ teaspoon kosher salt

½ cup (70 g) unsalted roasted almonds, *left whole or very roughly chopped*

¼ cup (30 g) pine nuts

½ cup (70 g) dark raisins, *soaked in warm water for 5 minutes and drained well*

½ cup (75 g) candied cherries, *roughly chopped, or dried cherries, soaked in water for 5 minutes, drained, and roughly chopped*

⅓ cup (40 g) candied citron or candied orange peel, *roughly chopped*

CONTINUES

Preheat the oven to 375°F (190°C). Line two large baking sheets with parchment paper.

Whisk together the vegetable oil and wine in a large bowl, until combined.

Whisk together the all-purpose flour, almond flour, sugar, and salt in a medium bowl. Add the dry ingredients to the oil mixture in a few stages, stirring until a soft dough forms. Add the almonds, pine nuts, raisins, cherries, and candied citron and, using clean hands, knead them into the dough. It will look like too many mix-ins for the amount of dough, but keep kneading until mostly incorporated. It's okay if a few of the mix-ins are still falling out of the dough.

Turn the dough out, divide into 2 equal portions, and place one portion in the center of each prepared baking sheet. Lightly flour your hands, then pat and press the dough into rectangles about 8 × 4 inches (20 × 10 cm) and ¾ inch (1.9 cm) thick. Using a floured bench scraper or knife, slice each rectangle crosswise into 5 brick-shaped pieces. (It can be tricky to cut through whole almonds, just do your best and pat the pieces back together as necessary.) Gently nudge the pieces away from one another on the baking sheet, leaving about ½ inch (1.25 cm) space between the cookies.

Bake, rotating the pans back to front and bottom to top halfway through baking, for 20 to 25 minutes, until the cookies are a few shades darker on top and quite browned (almost burnt) around the edges. The cookies will still feel soft on top, but they will firm up as they cool.

Remove the baking sheets from the oven and set on wire racks to cool for about 10 minutes, then transfer the cookies to the racks to cool completely.

Serve the bars as is or break into smaller pieces, if desired. The cookies can be stored, in an airtight container, in the fridge for up to 1 week, or in the freezer for up to 3 months.

Yotvata
70

Rome's Oldest Kosher Bakery

N*EARLY EVERY NEIGHBORHOOD* in Rome has a beloved antico forno (literally, "ancient oven"), and in the Ghetto neighborhood, that esteemed title belongs to Pasticceria il Boccione. The kosher bakery, which has been located on the corner of Via del Portico d'Ottavia for nearly 200 years, sits inside a tiny storefront with an arched doorway, a burnt-sienna exterior distressed by centuries of age, and absolutely no signage to indicate you have reached the right place.

And yet somehow people find their way—drawn in by the heady scent of almonds and caramelized sugar. (The line of tourists and locals snaking out of the door each morning also serves as an effective marker.) Inside, multiple generations of the Limentani family attend to the constant stream of customers with brisk, no-nonsense efficiency. I distinctly remember the momentary panic I felt the first time I made it to the front of the line and did not yet know my order. I ended up randomly pointing at things and fumbling my way through payment. Every sugary bite after that experience felt well earned.

The throngs are there to try the shop's cinnamon biscottini, rich ricotta tarts layered with sour cherry jam, chewy amaretti, and the signature pizza Ebraica ("Jewish-style pizza"), which isn't a pizza at all, but rather a mile-high bar cookie studded with almonds, raisins, pine nuts, and candied cherries. Never mind that nearly everything Pasticceria il Boccione bakes comes out of their hardworking ovens a bit singed and blistered. That is part of the charm. Their cookies and cakes may not be elegant, but each bite serves as a reminder that true beauty often comes from within.

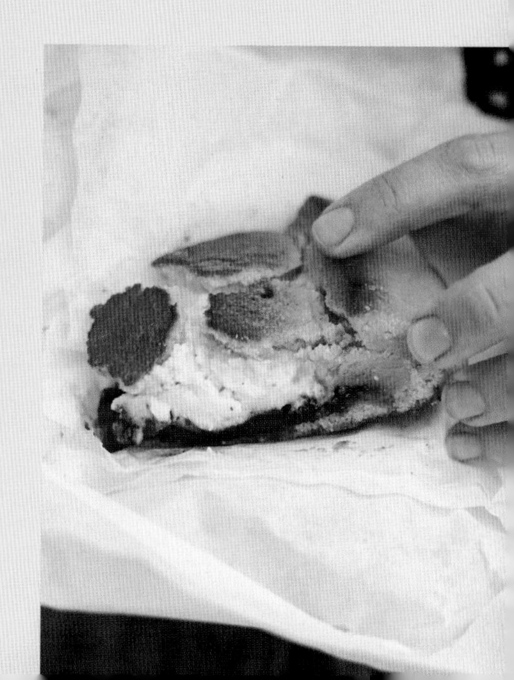

CRUNCHY CHOCOLATE ORANGE COOKIES

MAKES ABOUT 30 COOKIES

In 2010, pastry chef Laura Raccah opened Mondo di Laura, a Roman bakery specializing in American-style cookies with Italian flair. Today her distinctively crisp and full-flavored cookies can be spotted in oversized glass jars in food shops throughout the Jewish Ghetto neighborhood and packaged in supermarkets across the city. While her cookies are not traditionally Jewish, she is a Libyan Jew who was raised in Rome, and it is important to her that everything she bakes is pareve and kosher certified. These crunchy chocolate and orange cookies are inspired by one of my favorite Raccah creations: a biscuit she named Ghilty. The deep chocolate flavor is perfectly offset by the citrus.

1½ cups (210 g) all-purpose flour

⅓ cup (25 g) unsweetened cocoa powder

½ teaspoon baking soda

¼ teaspoon kosher salt

⅓ cup (80 ml) vegetable oil (such as sunflower)

1 cup (200 g) granulated sugar

⅓ cup (40 g) confectioners' sugar

2 large egg whites

2 teaspoons vanilla extract

1 packed teaspoon grated orange zest *(from about 1 small orange)*

2 ounces (57 g) bittersweet chocolate, *melted and slightly cooled*

¼ cup (40 g) *finely chopped* candied orange peel or crystallized ginger

Preheat the oven to 350°F (180°C). Line two large baking sheets with parchment paper.

Whisk together the flour, cocoa powder, baking soda, and salt in a medium bowl.

Add the oil, granulated sugar, confectioners' sugar, egg whites, vanilla extract, and orange zest to the bowl of a stand mixer fitted with the paddle attachment (or use a large bowl and a handheld electric mixer) and beat on medium speed until well combined. Add the melted chocolate and beat to combine. Add the flour mixture to the wet mixture in two stages, beating on medium speed and scraping down the sides of the bowl as needed, until you have a thick batter. Add the chopped orange peel and beat to combine.

Pinch off tablespoons of the dough, roll into balls, and place on the prepared cookie sheets, leaving about 1 inch (2.5 cm) of space between the cookies. Use your fingertips to press each cookie to flatten it slightly.

Bake, rotating the baking sheets back to front and top to bottom halfway through baking, for 14 to 16 minutes, until the cookies are dry and cracked on top. Remove the cookies from the oven and transfer to wire racks to cool. They will continue to firm and crisp up as they cool but will still have a bit of chew at the center.

The cookies can be stored in an airtight container in the fridge for up to 1 week, or in the freezer for up to 3 months.

TEATIME SHORTBREAD

Greiba

MAKES ABOUT 2 DOZEN COOKIES

These Libyan Jewish shortbread cookies are a study in contrasts—sweet but mellow, sandy-textured yet also creamy, light but deeply satisfying. Most Libyan greiba recipes are made with butter, but according to Hamos Guetta, who lovingly chronicles his community's cuisine via YouTube (see page 78), the Jewish version of the cookie must be made with oil, which keeps them pareve. Or, as he emphatically wrote to me, "No butter, never." Greiba are lovely plain, but you can also play around with the flavor profile by adding a couple drops of orange blossom water or rose water, some grated citrus zest, or cinnamon. Serve them alongside Libyan Mint Tea with Roasted Peanuts (page 314).

3 cups (420 g) all-purpose flour

1 cup (120 g) confectioners' sugar

¼ teaspoon kosher salt

1½ teaspoons baking powder

1 cup (240 ml) vegetable oil (such as sunflower)

About 24 blanched whole almonds *for decorating*

Preheat the oven to 325°F (180°C). Line two large baking sheets with parchment paper.

Whisk together the flour, sugar, salt, and baking powder in a large bowl. Make a well in the center of the mixture and add the oil. Using a sturdy spoon, gradually incorporate the oil into the flour mixture until a soft dough forms. If the dough is still crumbly, use your hands to gently knead it together in the bowl until all of the flour is incorporated. Cover the bowl with a tea towel and let the dough rest at room temperature for 15 minutes to allow the flour to hydrate further.

Scoop out rounded tablespoons of the dough, gently roll and press into balls, and place on the prepared baking sheets, about 1 inch (2.5 cm) apart. (Lightly moisten or oil your hands if the dough is sticking.) Use your index finger to flatten the cookies slightly, then gently press an almond into each indentation.

Bake for 10 to 12 minutes, until the cookies are just dry; they should take on almost no color and leave a bit of powdery residue on your finger when you touch the top. They will be quite fragile straight from the oven but will continue to set as they cool. Remove from the oven and let the cookies cool for 10 minutes on the baking sheets, then transfer to wire racks to cool completely.

The cookies can be stored in an airtight container in the fridge for up to 1 week, or in the freezer for up to 3 months.

RICOTTA CHEESECAKE

Cassola

SERVES 6 TO 8

Ricotta-based cheesecakes were most likely introduced to Rome by Sephardi Jews who fled Sicily during the Spanish Inquisition. The cakes were originally cooked in a pan set on the stovetop, like an oversized pancake. Over time, an oven-baked version (also called *channà*) emerged and became a favorite of both Jewish and non-Jewish Romans. Today cassola is a popular Christmas dessert in the city's Catholic community. Roman Jews, meanwhile, serve it on Shavuot, when dairy dishes are commonly eaten. On a visit to Rome, I enjoyed a memorably light and delicately sweet wedge of cassola at the kosher restaurant Yotvata (see page 103), located just beyond the Jewish Ghetto neighborhood. My version is inspired by that tasty memory.

Unsalted butter and unseasoned bread crumbs *for the pan*

3 cups (720 g) whole-milk ricotta, *drained in a sieve for 30 minutes*

¾ cup (150 g) granulated sugar

3 large eggs

1 tablespoon cornstarch or potato starch

1½ teaspoons vanilla extract

1 teaspoon ground cinnamon

¼ teaspoon kosher salt

⅓ cup (45 g) dark raisins (*optional*)

Confectioners' sugar *for dusting*

Preheat the oven to 350°F (180°C). Generously grease an 8-inch (20 cm) round cake pan with butter. Add a small handful of bread crumbs to the pan and tilt it in all directions to lightly coat the bottom and sides, then pour out and discard the excess crumbs. Set the pan aside.

Add the ricotta, sugar, eggs, cornstarch, vanilla, cinnamon, and salt to the bowl of a stand mixer fitted with the paddle attachment (or use a large bowl and a handheld electric mixer) and beat at medium speed until fully combined and smooth (there will still be some texture from the ricotta), about 1 minute. Stir in the raisins, if using.

Transfer the batter to the prepared cake pan and bake until puffed and golden on top and set at the center, with just a hint of jiggle, 50 to 60 minutes. Place the cake pan on a wire rack to cool completely. (Do not cut the cassola while it is still hot.)

When ready to serve, dust the cake with confectioners' sugar and cut into wedges. Store leftovers, covered, in the fridge for up to 3 days.

CHOCOLATE AND ALMOND CAKE

Torta di Mandorle e Cioccolata

SERVES 8

Flourless chocolate cakes are like the "little black dress" of the dessert world—a classic and elegant fit for nearly any occasion. And this one, which was inspired by a recipe in Claudia Roden's *The Book of Jewish Food,* is a knockout. It has a rich and fudgy center and an unexpected (but wonderful!) nubby texture from the finely ground almonds—a hint to this Roman Jewish cake's Sephardi roots. It shines on the Shabbat or Passover table but is also easy enough to make as a casual snacking cake. Serve it as is or dolloped with freshly whipped cream.

2 cups (275 g) blanched whole almonds

6 ounces (170 g) bittersweet chocolate, *chopped*

1 cup (200 g) granulated sugar

1 teaspoon vanilla extract

⅛ teaspoon kosher salt

8 large egg whites

Confectioners' sugar *for dusting* (*optional*)

Preheat the oven to 350°F (180°C). Lightly grease a 9-inch springform or regular round cake pan. Line the bottom of the pan with parchment paper.

Add the almonds and chocolate to the bowl of a food processor and pulse, scraping down the sides of the bowl as needed, until very finely ground. Add the sugar, vanilla, and salt and pulse until thoroughly combined. (The texture should resemble barely damp sand.) Transfer the mixture to a large bowl.

Put the egg whites in the bowl of a stand mixer fitted with the whisk attachment (or use a large bowl and a handheld electric mixer) and beat on medium-high speed until stiff peaks form, 2 to 4 minutes. (The egg whites are ready if when you lift up the whisk, they stand straight up, holding their shape.)

Add a generous scoop of the egg whites to the almond-chocolate mixture and gently fold in with a rubber spatula. Add the rest of the whites and fold just until no white streaks or clumps remain. Transfer the batter to the prepared cake pan and smooth the top.

Bake until the center of the cake is just set; a tester inserted into the center should come out clean, 25 to 30 minutes. (Be careful not to overbake—err on the side of very slightly underbaked.) Place the cake pan on a wire rack to cool.

Run a butter knife around the edges of the pan, then gently unmold the cake and transfer to a serving plate. Serve warm or at room temperature, dusted with confectioners' sugar, if desired.

LEMONY ALMOND CAKE

Bocca di Dama

SERVES 8

I am obsessed with this sunny dream of an almond cake. The cake's name, which translates as "mouth of a woman," lyrically hints at its beguiling, cloud-like texture and decadent almond flavor. This recipe was adapted from one taught to me by Silvia Nacamulli, a Roman Jewish cooking instructor who lives in London. She told me that the cake is beloved by Roman Jews and Libyan Jews alike, with different variations typically served for Passover and to break the fast after Yom Kippur. The Libyan version of the cake is spread with a glossy, meringue-like icing, but I prefer it the way Nacamulli showed me—topped simply with sliced almonds and a dusting of confectioners' sugar. The cake pairs well with Caramelized Fruit (page 313).

2 cups (200 g) blanched almond flour, *plus more for the pan*

6 large eggs, *separated*

¾ cup (150 g) superfine sugar

⅛ teaspoon kosher salt

1 packed teaspoon grated lemon zest *(from about 1 medium lemon)*

3 tablespoons fresh lemon juice

½ teaspoon almond extract

Sliced almonds *for topping*

Confectioners' sugar *for sprinkling*

Preheat the oven to 375°F (190°C). Lightly grease the bottom and sides of a 9-inch (23 cm) springform cake pan. Fit a round of parchment paper into the bottom of the pan, then lightly grease the parchment. Add a small handful of almond flour to the pan and tilt it in all directions to lightly coat the bottom and sides. Pour out and discard the excess almond flour and set the pan aside.

In the bowl of a stand mixer fitted with the paddle attachment (or use a large bowl and a handheld electric mixer), beat together the egg yolks and superfine sugar at medium-high speed until light and billowy, 2 to 3 minutes. Beat in the almond flour and salt until fully combined, scraping down the sides of the bowl as necessary. (The batter will be thick at this stage.) Add the lemon zest, lemon juice, and almond extract and beat to combine. Transfer the batter to a large bowl.

Wash the mixer bowl with cold water, dry completely, and fit the mixer with the whisk attachment. Add the egg whites to the bowl and beat at medium-high speed until stiff peaks form, 2 to 4 minutes.

Add a generous scoop of the egg whites to the batter and gently fold in with a rubber spatula. Add the rest of the whites and fold just until no white streaks remain. Transfer the batter to the prepared cake pan, gently smooth the top, and sprinkle evenly (lightly or more generously, as desired) with sliced almonds.

Bake until the cake is golden brown and a tester inserted into the center comes out clean, 20 to 25 minutes. Place the cake pan on a wire rack to cool completely.

Run a butter knife around the edges of the pan to release the cake, then gently remove the springform ring and transfer the cake to a cake plate. Just before serving, dust the top of the cake with confectioners' sugar.

SYRUPY SEMOLINA CAKE

Safra

SERVES 6 TO 8

Semolina-based cakes are a hallmark of Middle Eastern and North African cooking. The Libyan Jewish version, called *safra* (which means "yellow" in Arabic), is golden in color, tender, lightly syrupy, and dotted with raisins. (You can leave them out if raisins in baked goods aren't your thing.) Safra is enjoyed for many holidays and occasions, including Purim and to help break the Yom Kippur fast, when the cake is traditionally served with coffee, tea, and homemade sweetened almond milk. Like all semolina-based cakes, this one becomes increasingly moist and flavorful the longer it sits, so plan to make it a day or two before you want to serve it. It is a treat all on its own, and even better dolloped with yogurt, mascarpone, or whipped cream.

For the Cake

1¾ cups (300 grams) fine semolina

1 cup (200 g) granulated sugar

2 teaspoons baking powder

¼ teaspoon kosher salt

⅓ cup (45 g) dark raisins (*optional*)

¾ cup (180 ml) fresh orange juice

½ cup (120 ml) light olive oil or vegetable oil (such as sunflower)

1 large egg

Blanched whole almonds and sesame seeds *for decoration*

For the Syrup

1½ cups (355 ml) water

1 cup (150 g) granulated sugar

2 tablespoons mild honey

2 packed teaspoons grated orange zest *(from about 2 small oranges)*

CONTINUES

MAKE THE CAKE

Preheat the oven to 350°F (180°C). Line an 8 × 8-inch (20 × 20 cm) square baking pan with parchment paper.

Whisk together the semolina, sugar, baking powder, salt, and raisins, if using, in a medium bowl. Add the orange juice, oil, and egg and whisk to combine. Let the batter stand for about 15 minutes to hydrate the semolina.

Pour the batter into the prepared pan and smooth the top, making sure to spread the batter into the corners of the pan. Bake until the top is just barely set, 15 minutes.

Remove the pan from the oven and, using a sharp knife, score the cake into squares or diamonds. Top each square or diamond with an almond (gently press the almonds into the cake if necessary), then sprinkle with sesame seeds.

Place the cake back in the oven and bake until the top is golden brown, 20 to 25 minutes longer.

MEANWHILE, MAKE THE SYRUP

Stir together the water and sugar in a small saucepan and bring to a boil over high heat, then lower the heat to medium and simmer, stirring often, until slightly reduced and thickened, 2 to 3 minutes. Remove from the heat and whisk in the honey and orange zest.

When the cake is done, take it out of the oven and place the pan on a wire rack. Use a sharp knife to retrace the lines already scored into the cake. Slowly and evenly pour the hot syrup over the hot cake (it will look like a lot of syrup at first, but the cake will absorb it as it cools). Let cool completely before serving. Store leftovers, covered, in the fridge for up to 4 days.

SOUR CHERRY RICOTTA PIE

Crostata di Ricotta e Visciole

MAKES ONE 9-INCH / 23 CM PIE

Many Italian tarts and pies are either baked without a top crust or topped with a lattice, but this sour cherry and ricotta pie is double-crusted. An eighteenth-century papal decree forbade Jews from selling bread, meat, or dairy products to Christians, as a way to further curtail their already very limited opportunities for making a living. According to local lore, Jewish bakers covered their ricotta pies with a layer of pasta frolla (short-crust pastry) to conceal the contents and evade the cruel prohibition.

Today the Jewish Ghetto's storied kosher bakery, Pasticceria il Boccione (see page 276), makes a stellar version of the pie, sandwiching the cherry jam and sweetened ricotta between layers of a thick cookie-like crust. While nothing can beat biting into the creamy confection at the source, the recipe below comes pretty close to "the real thing." If you, like some Roman Jewish home cooks, would prefer a butter-based crust for your crostata, swap in the dough recipe from the Chocolate-Speckled Ricotta Pie on page 294.

For the Dough

½ cup (80 ml) vegetable oil (such as sunflower)

1 cup (200 g) granulated sugar

2 large eggs

2 to 3 tablespoons warm water

1 packed teaspoon grated lemon zest *(from about 1 medium lemon)*

3 cups (420 g) all-purpose flour, *plus more if needed*

½ teaspoon baking powder

½ teaspoon kosher salt

For the Filling

2 cups (480 g) whole-milk ricotta, *drained in a sieve for 30 minutes*

¾ cup (90 g) confectioners' sugar, *sifted*

1 teaspoon vanilla extract (*optional*)

⅛ teaspoon kosher salt

¾ cup (225 g) good-quality sour cherry jam or preserves

For the Egg Wash

1 large egg yolk *beaten with* ½ teaspoon water

CONTINUES

MAKE THE DOUGH

Add the vegetable oil, sugar, eggs, 2 tablespoons warm water, and the lemon zest to a large bowl and whisk to thoroughly combine.

Whisk together the flour, baking powder, and salt in a medium bowl and add to the wet mixture in two stages, stirring with a sturdy spoon until a thick dough forms. If the dough is too dry, stir in up to another 1 tablespoon water, a little at a time. Or, if it feels too sticky, stir in a little more flour, 1 tablespoon at a time, until the desired consistency is reached. Cover and set aside.

Preheat the oven to 350°F (180°C). Set out a 9-inch (23 cm) metal or ceramic pie plate.

MAKE THE FILLING

Thoroughly whisk together the drained ricotta, confectioners' sugar, vanilla, if using, and salt in a medium bowl.

Divide the dough into 2 equal pieces and knead gently to form each into a disk. On a floured surface, using a floured rolling pin, roll out one of the dough disks into a 12-inch (30 cm) circle. Carefully transfer the dough to the pie plate, fitting it into the bottom and up the sides of the pan, and trim off the overhang. Prick the bottom of the pie shell in several places with a fork.

Spread the cherry jam evenly over the bottom of the pie shell, then top with the ricotta mixture, smoothing the top with a spatula.

Roll out the remaining dough into a 10-inch (25 cm) circle and drape it over the top of the pie. Trim off any overhanging dough, then roll the dough under itself all around the perimeter to seal the top and bottom crusts together. Make a few small slits in the top crust to allow steam to escape during baking, then brush the entire top of the pie with egg wash. (You will not use all of it.)

Bake until the pie is slightly puffed and the crust is golden brown, 35 to 45 minutes. Set the pie on a wire rack and allow it to fully cool before slicing, at least 2 hours. (Do not try to slice it while it is still hot, or you will end up with a soggy, ricotta-flooded mess!)

CHOCOLATE-SPECKLED RICOTTA PIE

Crostata di Ricotta e Cioccolato

MAKES ONE 9-INCH / 23 CM PIE

This decadent pie is a variation on Rome's more famous Sour Cherry Ricotta Pie (page 291). The sweet ricotta filling is threaded through with irregular shards of chopped chocolate, giving it the speckled appearance and appeal of stracciatella gelato. You can use the butter-based dough included here, or make a cookie-like oil-based dough that mimics the one used at Rome's historic kosher bakery, Pasticceria il Boccione, following the recipe on page 291.

For the Dough

2 cups (280 g) all-purpose flour

3 tablespoons granulated sugar

½ teaspoon kosher salt

½ teaspoon baking powder

1 packed teaspoon grated lemon zest *(from about 1 lemon)*

12 tablespoons (1½ sticks /170 g) cold unsalted butter, *cut into small pieces*

2 large egg yolks, *lightly beaten*

¼ cup (60 ml) cold water, *plus more if needed*

For the Filling

2 cups (480 g) whole-milk ricotta, *drained in a sieve for 30 minutes*

¾ cup (90 g) confectioners' sugar, *sifted*

1 teaspoon vanilla extract

⅛ teaspoon kosher salt

1/4 pound (113 g) bittersweet or semisweet chocolate, *chopped*

For the Egg Wash

1 large egg yolk *beaten with ½* teaspoon water

MAKE THE DOUGH
Whisk together the flour, sugar, salt, baking powder, and lemon zest in a large bowl. Add the butter pieces and use a pastry cutter or your fingertips to press and mix the ingredients together until the butter is the size of small peas.

Whisk together the egg yolks and cold water in a small bowl until smooth. Sprinkle the egg yolk mixture over the flour mixture and stir to combine; clumps of dough should form. If they do not, stir in more cold water 1 tablespoon at a time until the desired consistency is reached. Gently knead the dough in the bowl to bring it together into a single mass.

Turn the dough out, divide it into 2 equal pieces, and form each one into a disk. Wrap the disks snugly in plastic wrap or parchment paper and refrigerate for at least 2 hours, and up to 2 days.

Preheat the oven to 350°F (180°C). Set out a 9-inch (23 cm) metal or ceramic pie plate.

On a lightly floured surface, using a lightly floured rolling pin, roll out one of the dough disks into a 12-inch (30 cm) circle. Carefully transfer the dough to the pie plate, fitting it into the bottom and up the sides (do not trim the overhanging dough yet). Prick the bottom of the pie shell in several places with a fork and refrigerate for about 15 minutes.

MEANWHILE, MAKE THE FILLING
Beat together the drained ricotta, confectioners' sugar, vanilla, and salt in a medium bowl until smooth. Fold in the chopped chocolate.

Remove the pie plate from the fridge and spread the ricotta mixture into the pie shell, smoothing the top. Roll out the remaining dough disk into a 10-inch (25 cm) circle and drape it over the top of the pie. (It may seem like there is not enough filling, but it will puff up in the oven.) Use a sharp knife to trim off the overhanging dough, then roll the dough under itself all around the perimeter to seal the top and bottom crusts together. Make a few small slits in the top crust to allow steam to escape during baking, then brush the entire top of the pie with egg wash. (You will not use all of it.)

Bake until the pie is slightly puffed and the crust is golden brown, 35 to 45 minutes. Set the pie on a wire rack and allow it to fully cool before slicing, at least 2 hours. (Do not try to slice the pie while it is still hot, or you will end up with a soggy, ricotta-flooded mess!)

JAM TART

Crostata di Marmellata

MAKES ONE 9-INCH / 23 CM TART

Jam tarts are everywhere in Rome (and throughout Italy), their glistening centers peeking out through golden lattice crusts. Sour cherry jam is the typical Roman Jewish filling, but I also like to play around with other thick jams like fig preserves, or a swirl of apricot and raspberry. Some recipes sprinkle the tart with sliced almonds, and at the kosher restaurant Renato al Ghetto, co-proprietor Giorgia Renato tops some of her crostate with pine nuts. The sweet jam in this tart would be perfectly offset by cool, billowy dollops of whipped cream.

NOTE: *Baking powder is not always used in pasta frolla (short-crust pastry), but it gives the crust a more tender texture.*

For the Dough

2 cups (280 g) all-purpose flour

3 tablespoons granulated sugar

1 teaspoon baking powder

½ teaspoon kosher salt

12 tablespoons (1½ sticks / 170 g) cold unsalted butter or margarine, *cut into small pieces*

2 large egg yolks, *lightly beaten*

¼ cup cold water, *plus more if needed*

For the Filling and Finishing

1 to 1½ cups (300 to 450 g) good-quality sour cherry jam *(or other thick jam)*

1 large egg yolk *beaten with ½* teaspoon water, *for egg wash*

MAKE THE DOUGH

Add the flour, sugar, baking powder, and salt to the bowl of a food processor and pulse a few times to combine. Add the butter pieces and pulse until the mixture is the texture of coarse sand.

Whisk together the egg yolks and cold water in a small bowl until the yolks dissolve. Sprinkle the mixture over the flour mixture and pulse to combine; clumps of dough should form. If they do not, pulse in more water, 1 tablespoon at a time, until the desired consistency is reached.

Turn the dough out onto a work surface and gently knead to bring it together into a single mass. Divide the dough into 2 equal pieces and form each one into a disk. Wrap the disks snugly in plastic wrap or parchment paper and refrigerate for at least 2 hours, and up to 2 days.

Preheat the oven to 350°F (180°C). Set out a 9-inch (23 cm) metal or ceramic pie plate.

On a lightly floured surface, using a lightly floured rolling pin, roll out one of the dough disks into a 12-inch (30 cm) circle. Carefully transfer the dough to the pie plate, fitting it into the bottom and up the sides (do not trim the overhanging dough yet). Prick the bottom of the pie shell in several places with a fork and refrigerate for about 15 minutes.

Remove the pie plate from the fridge and spread the desired amount of jam (use the larger amount for a thicker pie) evenly over the bottom of the pie shell. Roll out the remaining dough disk into a 10-inch (25 cm) circle. Cut the dough into ¾-inch- (2 cm) wide strips and arrange them in a lattice pattern on top of the pie. Trim the excess dough around the edges, then fold the edges over the ends of the lattice strips. (The scraps of dough can be rerolled and used to make thumbprint jam cookies, or something similar, if desired.)

Brush the top of the pie with the egg wash. (You will not use all of it.) Bake until the crust is slightly puffed and golden brown, 30 to 45 minutes. Set the pie on a wire rack and allow it to fully cool before slicing.

71

Ristorante Pizzeria Sheva

TWISTED SWEET BREAD WITH DRIED FRUIT

La Treccia

MAKES 2 LOAVES

These sweet twisted loaves (pictured on page 262), filled with dried and candied fruit, can usually be seen in the window of Pasticceria il Boccione, the Roman Ghetto neighborhood's ancient kosher bakery (see page 276). Passersby sometimes mistake them for challah—and there is definitely a resemblance—but they are closer to a cross between panettone and babka. Loaves of la treccia (which translates as "the braid") are commonly served at celebratory occasions like circumcisions, bar mitzvahs, or weddings. I like to bake them for brunch and serve up toasted slices slathered with butter.

½ cup (70 g) dark raisins

½ cup (70 g) golden raisins

1 package (2¼ teaspoons / 7 g) active dry yeast

½ cup (100 g) plus 1 teaspoon granulated sugar

¾ cup (180 ml) warm water

4 to 4½ cups (560 to 630 g) cups all-purpose flour, *plus more for rolling*

½ teaspoon kosher salt

3 large eggs

⅓ cup (80 ml) vegetable oil (such as sunflower), *plus more for the bowl*

1½ teaspoons vanilla extract

1 packed teaspoon grated lemon zest *(from about 1 medium lemon)*

1½ cups (210 g) mixed candied or dried fruit (such as cherries, orange peel, and citron), *chopped if large*

Confectioners' sugar *for dusting*

Put the raisins in a small bowl and cover with warm water. Let sit for about 5 minutes, then drain well and set aside.

Stir together the yeast, the 1 teaspoon granulated sugar, and the warm water in a large bowl. Let sit until foaming and bubbly, about 5 minutes.

Meanwhile, whisk together 4 cups (560 g) flour, the remaining ½ cup (100 g) granulated sugar, and the salt in a medium bowl.

Add 2 of the eggs, the vegetable oil, vanilla extract, and lemon zest to the yeast mixture and mix to combine. Add the flour mixture and the drained raisins and stir until a shaggy dough comes together. Turn the dough out onto a lightly floured surface and knead well, adding up to ½ cup (70 g) additional flour as needed, until you have a supple, elastic dough; you likely will not need all of the flour. (The kneading can also be done in the bowl of a stand mixer fitted with a dough hook, 5 to 7 minutes)

Add about 1 teaspoon oil to a large bowl, add the dough, and turn to coat. Cover the bowl and let sit in a warm place until the dough is almost doubled in size, about 2 hours.

Line two 8½ x 4½-inch (22 × 10 cm) loaf pans with parchment paper, leaving an overhang on two opposite sides of the pan, and set aside. Gently deflate the dough and divide it into 2 equal pieces.

Roll out one piece of the dough into a large rectangle about ¼ inch (6 mm) thick. Sprinkle half of the mixed fruits over the dough (this will not be enough to fully cover it, but do your best to distribute them evenly). Starting with one of the long sides, roll the dough up tightly like a jelly roll. Fold the roll over on itself to make a closed horseshoe shape, then twist two or three times, as if you were wringing out a towel. (Aim for an equal thickness down the whole loaf.) Tuck the twisted roll into one of the loaf pans. Repeat with the remaining dough and mixed fruits. Loosely cover the loaf pans with a clean dish towel and let rise until puffed, about 1 hour.

Preheat the oven to 350°F (180°C).

Beat the remaining egg in a small bowl, then brush an even layer of egg over the top of each loaf. (You will not use all of the egg.) Bake the loaves until deep golden brown, 35 to 40 minutes. Transfer the loaf pans to a wire rack to cool for about 10 minutes, then use the overhanging parchment to lift out the loaves and transfer them to the rack to cool for at least 1 hour.

Just before slicing, dust the tops of the loaves generously with confectioners' sugar.

HAMAN'S EARS

Orecchie d'Aman

MAKES ABOUT 50 FRITTERS

The Jewish holiday of Purim celebrates the triumph of Queen Esther of ancient Persia over Haman, the cruel-hearted advisor to the Persian king Ahasuerus. Esther managed to thwart Haman's plot to kill all of the Jews in the Persian Empire, showing immense bravery and resilience in the face of grave danger. In honor of her courage, Ashkenazi Jews make hamantaschen, which are meant to evoke Haman's pockets or hat and allow the sweet revenge of symbolically "demolishing" the enemy. Roman Jews, however, make orecchie d'Aman. The fried pastries are intended to resemble a different attribute of Haman—namely, his ears—but the intention behind them is the same. In her cookbook *Dal 1880 ad Oggi* (see page 152), Donatella Limentani Pavoncello sprinkles her orecchie d'Aman with vanilla sugar, but I prefer a snowy dusting of confectioners' sugar.

2 cups (280 g) all-purpose flour

½ teaspoon baking powder

¼ teaspoon kosher salt

2 large eggs

3 tablespoons granulated sugar

¼ cup (60 ml) vegetable oil (such as sunflower), *plus more for deep-frying*

1½ teaspoons vanilla extract

2 to 3 tablespoons water

Confectioners' sugar or Vanilla Sugar (page 150) *for dusting*

Add the flour, baking powder, and salt to the bowl of a food processor and pulse a few times to combine. Lightly beat together the eggs, sugar, oil, vanilla, and 2 tablespoons water in a small bowl, add to the flour mixture, and pulse, scraping down the sides of the bowl as necessary, until a firm but pliable dough begins to come together. If the dough seems crumbly or dry, add up to 1 more tablespoon of water, a little at a time, until the desired consistency is reached.

Transfer the dough to a work surface and knead a few times to bring it together, then form it into a ball. Transfer to a bowl, cover with a tea towel, and let rest for 30 minutes.

When ready to fry, heat about 2 inches (5 cm) of oil in a small deep saucepan over medium heat until it reaches 350°F (180°C) on a deep-fry thermometer. Line a baking sheet with paper towels and set nearby.

While the oil heats, divide the dough in half and leave one half covered. On a floured surface, using a floured rolling pin, roll out the piece of dough into a large rectangle as thin as possible (or use a pasta machine). Use a sharp knife to cut the dough into 2 × 3-inch (5 × 7.5 cm) rectangles. Fold the two corners of one of the longer sides of each rectangle over and down toward the opposite long side to make a sailboat shape. Use a fork to crimp and seal the edges. Repeat with the remaining portion of dough.

Using a fork, carefully transfer one fritter to the hot oil and hold it together with the fork under the oil until it holds its shape, 10 to 15 seconds. (If it opens a little, don't worry; it will still taste great.) Fry, flipping once, until lightly golden and puffed, 1 to 2 minutes total. Use a slotted spoon or tongs to transfer the fritter to the paper towel–lined baking sheet and continue to fry the remaining fritters, adding more oil to the saucepan as necessary. The process can be a bit tricky at first, but as you get used to it, you will be able to have more than one fritter frying at a time.

Dust the fritters generously with confectioners' sugar, or, if using vanilla sugar, fill a bowl with the sugar and dip the fritters into it while they are still warm. Serve warm or at room temperature.

NOTE: *This recipe makes quite a few fritters, but it can easily be halved if you are serving a smaller crowd.*

SYRUPY FRIED PASTRY ROSES

Debla

MAKES ABOUT 30 PASTRIES

Variations of thinly rolled pastry fried to resemble roses are popular throughout North Africa. Libyan Jews make debla to celebrate the holiday of Purim and serve them alongside a variety of other cookies and confections, with glasses of hot tea. The roses emerge from the oil airy and crisp, and are then coated in a sweet, sticky syrup and sprinkled with toasted sesame seeds. The pastries take some time to prepare and a bit of practice to master, but they are well worth the effort.

For the Pastry Roses

2 cups (280 g) all-purpose flour

½ teaspoon baking powder

¼ teaspoon kosher salt

2 large eggs

¼ cup (60 ml) vegetable oil (such as sunflower), *plus more for deep-frying*

1½ teaspoons vanilla extract

2 to 3 tablespoons water

For the Syrup and Finishing

1¼ cups (250 g) granulated sugar

1 cup (240 ml) water

1½ tablespoons fresh lemon juice

Toasted sesame seeds *for sprinkling*

MAKE THE FRITTERS
Add the flour, baking powder, and salt to the bowl of a food processor and pulse a few times to combine. Lightly beat together the eggs, oil, vanilla, and 2 tablespoons water in a small bowl, add to the flour mixture, and pulse, scraping down the sides of the bowl as necessary, until a firm but pliable dough begins to come together. If the dough seems crumbly or dry, add up to 1 more tablespoon of water, a little at a time, until the desired consistency is reached.

Transfer the dough to a work surface and knead a few times to bring it together, then form it into a ball. Transfer to a bowl, cover with a tea towel, and let rest for 30 minutes.

When ready to fry, heat about 2 inches (5 cm) of oil in a small deep saucepan over medium heat until it reaches 350°F (180°C) on a deep-fry thermometer. Line a baking sheet with paper towels and set nearby.

While the oil heats, divide the dough in half and keep one half covered. On a floured surface, using a floured rolling pin, roll the dough into a large rectangle that is as thin as possible (or use a pasta machine). Use a sharp knife to cut the rectangle into long 1-inch- (2.5 cm) wide strips.

Pick up one strip and wrap it loosely around your fingers—first around two fingers, then three, then four, creating a coiled rose shape. Gently slip the coil off your fingers and onto the tines of a fork, making sure the fork is holding the loose end of the dough closed. Dip the fork into the hot oil, swirling the pastry a bit as it begins to blister and puff. Once the rose holds its shape, carefully remove the fork and fry, flipping once, until it is crisp and golden, about 2 minutes. Use a slotted spoon or tongs to transfer the fried dough to the paper towel–lined baking sheet and continue the process with the remaining dough, adding more oil to the saucepan as necessary. The process can be a bit tricky at first, but as you get used to it, you will be able to have more than one rose frying at a time.

MAKE THE SYRUP

Add the sugar and water to a small saucepan over medium-high heat and bring to a boil. Reduce the heat to medium and cook until the syrup thickens a bit, 3 to 5 minutes. Remove from the heat and stir in the lemon juice.

Working in small batches, add the fried roses to the syrup, turning them gently with tongs to coat them thoroughly, then sprinkle with sesame seeds. Serve at room temperature.

Ristorante
Spirito DiVino
verisure
DIVIETO
DI SOSTA
32

ATTENZIONE!

CHOCOLATE MARZIPAN

Marzapane al Cioccolato

MAKES ABOUT 16 MARZIPAN BALLS

Reading through Donatella Limentani Pavoncello's beautiful cookbook, *Dal 1880 ad Oggi* (see page 152), I came across a recipe for chocolate marzipan in her Purim menu and immediately wanted to try it. This riff on her recipe makes a soft, pliable dough, more similar to almond paste in texture, that is rolled into small truffle-like balls. I like to coat the truffles in sugar and top them with sliced almonds for a more elegant presentation. The marzipan has a luscious chocolate flavor, offset by a heady perfume of almond extract. These make a great gift, and they have become a staple of my family's Purim celebration.

1½ cups (150 g) blanched almond flour

1 cup (120 g) confectioners' sugar

¼ cup (20 g) unsweetened cocoa powder

⅛ teaspoon kosher salt

1 teaspoon almond extract

2 to 3 tablespoons cold water

Granulated sugar *for rolling*

Sliced almonds for decoration (*optional*)

Add the almond flour, confectioners' sugar, cocoa powder, and salt to the bowl of a food processor and pulse to combine, scraping down the sides of the bowl as necessary. Add the almond extract and 2 tablespoons water and pulse until the mixture begins to form a large clump. If the mixture is too dry, add up to 1 more tablespoon of water, a little at a time, as needed. Transfer the mixture to a bowl.

Pinch off tablespoons of the mixture and roll into balls. (Wash and dry your hands if the mixture is sticking.) Spread a little granulated sugar on a plate and roll the marzipan balls in sugar to coat on all sides. Top each ball with a sliced almond, if desired. The marzipan can be stored, covered, in the fridge for up to 2 weeks.

ROMAN-STYLE HAROSET

MAKES ABOUT 2 CUPS (400 G)

Every Roman Jewish family has its own recipe for haroset—the nut and fruit-based mixture served at the Passover seder to symbolize the mortar used by the Israelites when they were enslaved in ancient Egypt. Some are as straightforward as finely ground almonds mixed with sugar, grated apple, and sweet wine. Others, like this one, are more elaborate, blending an array of nuts and fruits into a sweet paste that is perfect for spreading on matzo.

1 cup (100 g) walnut halves

½ cup (70 g) unsalted unroasted almonds

¼ cup (30 g) hazelnuts *(skin-on is fine)*

1 small apple, *peeled, halved, cored, and roughly chopped*

1 small ripe banana, *peeled and cut into chunks*

1 small orange, *peeled and roughly chopped, any seeds removed*

4 medium dried Medjool dates, *pitted and chopped*

4 dried figs (such as Calimyrna), *stems removed and chopped*

1½ teaspoons ground cinnamon, *plus more for sprinkling*

2 tablespoons sweet red wine (such as Manischewitz) or grape juice

TOAST THE NUTS
Preheat the oven to 350°F (180°C).

Spread the walnuts, almonds, and hazelnuts on a baking sheet. Bake, stirring the nuts or shaking the baking sheet once or twice, until they are a few shades darker and toasty smelling, 5 to 8 minutes. Remove from the oven and transfer to a plate to cool.

Transfer the cooled nuts to a food processor and add the apple, banana, orange, dates, figs, and cinnamon. Process, scraping down the sides of the bowl as necessary, until a textured paste forms. Add the wine and pulse to combine.

Transfer the haroset to a serving bowl, cover, and refrigerate for at least 1 hour, and up to 1 day, to allow the flavors to deepen. Just before serving, sprinkle the haroset with a little cinnamon.

LIBYAN-STYLE HAROSET

Lalek

MAKES ABOUT TWENTY 1-INCH (2.5 CM) BALLS

The Libyan Jewish take on Passover haroset combines a panoply of nuts, fruits, and spices. Like other North African harosets, the mixture is typically rolled into balls that can be served as is or gently smashed onto a piece of matzo. My recipe draws inspiration from two sources—a video on Hamos Guetta's YouTube channel devoted to Libyan and Roman Jewish cooking (see page 78) and a recipe from Linda Guetta Hassan's cookbook *La Cucina Ebraica Tripolina*.

1 cup (100 g) walnut halves

½ cup (70 g) unsalted unroasted almonds

¼ cup (30 g) hazelnuts *(skin-on is fine)*

1 cup (190 g) dried Medjool dates (8 to 10), *pitted and chopped*

1 cup (140 g) dark raisins

1 small apple, *peeled and grated on the large holes of a box grater*

1 teaspoon ground cinnamon

½ teaspoon ground ginger

⅛ teaspoon ground nutmeg

¼ teaspoon kosher salt

TOAST THE NUTS
Preheat the oven to 350°F (180°C).

Spread the walnuts, almonds, and hazelnuts on a baking sheet. Bake, stirring the nuts or shaking the baking sheet once or twice, until they are a few shades darker and toasty smelling, 5 to 8 minutes. Remove from the oven and transfer to a plate to cool.

Transfer the cooled nuts to a food processor and pulse until roughly chopped. Add the dates, raisins, grated apple (don't squeeze it dry), cinnamon, ginger, nutmeg, and salt and pulse, scraping down the sides of the bowl as necessary, until the mixture forms a thick paste. If you pinch it between your fingers, it should hold together. Transfer the mixture to a bowl.

Scoop out a rounded tablespoon of the haroset mixture and gently squeeze and roll it into a ball. Place on a large plate and continue making balls with the remaining mixture. Serve at room temperature or chilled. The haroset can be stored, covered, in the fridge for up to 1 week.

SPICED APPLE PRESERVES

Mele Marmellata

MAKES ABOUT 1½ CUPS (400 G)

Some Libyan Jewish families serve chunky preserves made from apples or quinces on Rosh Hashanah as a symbol of the sweet year ahead. In this version, which is flavored with cinnamon and star anise, the apples are cut into relatively large pieces, so you end up with soft, sticky-sweet bites of apple rather than a smooth jam. Serve it with cheese, spooned onto toast or challah, or as a topping for yogurt—or as a sweet bite to celebrate the Jewish New Year.

5 medium baking apples (about 2 pounds / 907 g), *washed and patted dry*

1½ cups (300 g) granulated sugar

½ cup (120 ml) water

2 cinnamon sticks

1 star anise (*optional*)

2 teaspoons fresh lemon juice

Peel the apples, quarter, and core them. Cut each quarter lengthwise in half (or into thirds, if the apples are larger), then slice crosswise into roughly ¾-inch (2 cm) pieces. Set aside.

Stir together the sugar and water in a wide saucepan and bring to a boil over medium-high heat. Add the apple pieces to the boiling sugar syrup and stir. Tuck the cinnamon sticks and star anise, if using, into the apples, drizzle the lemon juice over the top, and cook, stirring occasionally, until all but a few tablespoons of the liquid has cooked off and the liquid is thick and syrupy, 30 to 35 minutes.

Remove from the heat and discard the cinnamon sticks and star anise. Transfer the mixture to a glass container and let cool. The apples will shrink and the liquid will continue to thicken as it cools.

Store the preserves, covered, in the fridge for up to 1 month.

CARAMELIZED FRUIT

Frutta Caramellata

SERVES 4 TO 6

Frutta caramellata is the Roman Jews' equivalent to Eastern Europe's fruit compotes—something light and sweet to enjoy after a decadent meal. Keep things simple by working with just one kind of stone fruit, or play around with different combinations. True to its name, the caramelized fruit is quite sweet, so it pairs particularly well with a dollop of tangy yogurt or mascarpone. It also makes a dreamy accompaniment to Chewy Almond Cookies (page 265) and Lemony Almond Cake (page 286).

6 fresh figs, *stems trimmed*

4 to 6 apricots, peaches, or nectarines (or a mix), depending on size, *skin left on, quartered lengthwise and pitted*

3 wide strips lemon peel *(see Note)*

¾ cup (150 g) granulated sugar

1¼ cups (295 ml) water

1 tablespoon fresh lemon juice, *plus more as needed*

Arrange the figs stem end up and stone fruit cut side down in a medium deep frying pan; it is okay if the fruits overlap a little. Tuck the lemon peel into the pan.

Whisk together the sugar, water, and lemon juice in a medium bowl until the sugar begins to dissolve. Pour the mixture evenly over the fruit and bring the liquid to a boil over medium-high heat. Reduce the heat to medium-low and simmer, occasionally spooning the liquid over the fruit and carefully flipping the fruit halfway through cooking, until the fruit is tender and the liquid has reduced to a syrup, 35 to 40 minutes.

Remove the pan from the heat, transfer the fruit and syrup to a bowl, and let cool completely.

If the figs are on the larger side, cut them lengthwise in half, if desired. Taste the syrup and add more lemon juice as needed. Cover and refrigerate until chilled before serving. The fruit can be stored, covered, in the fridge for up to 2 weeks.

NOTE: *Give your lemons a good scrub, then use a vegetable peeler to remove wide, thick strips of peel.*

MINT TEA WITH ROASTED PEANUTS

Shai Cacauia

SERVES 4 TO 6

On my nightstand, I keep a framed picture of Yoshie and me in our mid-twenties—newly married, baby-faced, and toasting the camera with gold-rimmed glasses of mint tea. The photo was taken at a Jewish food and wine festival in Rome. The tea was shai cacauia, a Libyan tea that is often steeped with fresh mint.

Traditional versions of the tea are very strong and are served in three courses alongside trays of sweets. The first two glasses are aerated by pouring the tea back and forth between two vessels until a layer of foam forms. The third is served a bit lighter and topped with boiled or roasted peanuts or almonds. This nutty layer might seem unusual, but the combination of savory crunch and sweet, minty tea is lovely. Yoshie and I are a little older now and not quite as fresh-faced. But the photo reminds me that a toast to good times is only a glass of tea away.

½ cup (70 g) unsalted unroasted peanuts

4 cups (1 l) water

2 tablespoons loose black tea leaves (such as Ceylon or Darjeeling)

1 tablespoon loose gunpowder tea leaves (or another green tea, such as Sencha)

3 to 4 tablespoons granulated sugar

1 cup (20 g) fresh mint leaves *(tough stems removed)*

Put the peanuts in a small frying pan and toast over medium heat, tossing or stirring frequently, until fragrant and golden, about 5 minutes. Transfer the peanuts to a bowl and set aside to cool.

Combine the water, black tea leaves, and gunpowder tea leaves in a small saucepan, bring to a boil over high heat, and boil, stirring occasionally, until the tea is dark and the liquid has reduced slightly, 5 to 8 minutes.

Stir in 3 tablespoons sugar and the mint leaves, then remove the pan from the heat, cover, and allow to steep for 5 minutes.

Taste the tea and stir in another tablespoon of sugar, if desired. Strain the tea through a fine-mesh strainer into a teapot or other vessel, gently pressing on the tea leaves and mint to release all of the liquid.

Serve in small heatproof glasses: Add a generous sprinkle of peanuts to each glass, pour the tea over the top, and serve hot.

MENUS

Shabbat Dinner

Shabbat (the Sabbath) is the Jewish day of rest, which occurs every week from Friday at sunset until Saturday at sundown. Families and friends typically gather on Friday nights for a festive meal, and home cooks pull out all the stops for their guests.

ROMAN-INSPIRED MENU

Roasted Tomato Halves *(Pomodori a Mezzo)*, page 65

Slow-Braised Beef Stew *(Stracotto di Manzo)*, page 235, served with rigatoni

Sautéed Dandelion Greens *(Cicoria Ripassata)*, page 76

Roasted Cipollini Onions *(Cipolline al Forno)*, page 73

Chocolate and Almond Cake *(Torta di Mandorle e Cioccolata)*, page 284

LIBYAN-INSPIRED MENU

Savory Tomato Spread *(Merduma)*, page 68

Garlicky Pumpkin Spread *(Cershi Bel Hal)*, page 87

Spicy Tomato-Poached Fish *(Haraimi)*, page 212

Beef and White Bean Stew with Cumin *(Lubia Bel Kammùn)*, page 121, served with couscous

Vegetable Stew for Couscous *(Zuppa per Couscous)*, page 204

Teatime Shortbread *(Greiba)*—page 282

Purim

Purim is a joyous late-winter holiday that honors Queen Esther—a brave Jewish woman who became the queen of ancient Persia and saved the Jewish people from annihilation at the hands of her husband's wicked advisor, Haman. Purim is full of merriment, and Jewish communities around the globe celebrate with parties and by making and sharing delicious sweets.

PURIM SWEETS MENU

Haman's Ears *(Orecchie d'Aman)*, page 302

Syrupy Fried Pastry Roses *(Debla)*, page 304

Syrupy Semolina Cake *(Safra)*, page 289

Chewy Almond Cookies *(Amaretti / Abambar)*, page 265

Chocolate Marzipan *(Marzapane al Cioccolato)*, page 308

Dried Fruit and Nut Bar Cookies *(Pizza Ebraica)*, page 273

Mint Tea with Roasted Peanuts *(Shai Cacauia)*, page 314

Passover

Arriving with the spring blossoms (and, in Rome, peak artichoke season!), Passover marks the Exodus of the Israelites from enslavement in ancient Egypt. During Passover, Jews traditionally refrain from eating chametz, which are leavened foods made from wheat, rye, oats, barley, and spelt. People join together for the seder, where they retell the Passover story and enjoy a lavish meal. Roman Jews' Passover traditions are unique, unlike those of any other Jewish community (see page 252).

PASSOVER SEDER MENU

Roman-Style Haroset *or* Libyan-Style Haroset *(Lalek)*, page 309 or 310

Roman Egg Drop Soup *(Stracciatella)*, page 116

Garlic and Rosemary Roasted Lamb *(Abbacchio alla Giudia)*, page 248

Chicken with Peppers *(Pollo con Peperoni)*, page 222

Roman-Style Braised Artichokes *(Carciofi alla Romana)*, page 48

Stuffed Tomatoes with Rice *(Pomodori con Riso)*, page 174

Honey-Soaked Matzo Fritters *(Pizzarelle con Miele)*, page 149

Lemony Almond Cake *(Bocca di Dama)*, page 286

Shavuot

Beginning seven weeks after Passover, Shavuot commemorates the biblical story of God revealing the Torah to the Israelites at Mount Sinai. It also marks the end of the barley harvest in Israel and the beginning of the wheat harvest. Some communities serve foods made with dairy on Shavuot, in honor of Mount Sinai's alternative name, Har Gav'nunim (Mountain of Majestic Peaks), which sounds like the Hebrew word for cheese—gevinah.

SHAVUOT MENU

Fennel Gratin *(Finocchi Gratinati)*, page 79

Semolina Gnocchi Gratin *(Gnocchi alla Romana)*, page 165

Spinach Frittata with Raisins and Pine Nuts, page 196

Sour Cherry Ricotta Pie *(Crostata di Ricotta e Visciole)*

and/or Ricotta Cheesecake *(Cassola)*, page 291 and/or 283

Rosh Hashanah

Rosh Hashanah, or the Jewish New Year, is regarded as the spiritual head of the year. It arrives just as summer is softening into autumn, and it launches a season of spiritual contemplation and introspection. Families and friends gather for festive meals and set intentions for sweetness and joy in the year ahead.

ROSH HASHANAH MENU

Spiced Apple Preserves *(Mele Marmellata)*, page 311

Pasta Squares and Spinach in Broth *(Quadrucci in Brodo con Spinaci)*, page 112

Slow-Braised Beef Stew *(Stracotto di Manzo)*, page 235, served with rigatoni

Roast Chicken with Rosemary, Garlic, and Potatoes *(Pollo Arrosto)*, page 220

Sautéed Spinach with Pine Nuts and Raisins *(Spinaci con Pinoli e Passerine)*, page 69

Braised Peas with Onion *(Piselli in Tegame)*—page 70

Jam Tart *(Crostata di Marmellata)*, page 296

Yom Kippur

Yom Kippur, which falls ten days after Rosh Hashanah, is considered the most sacred day of the Jewish calendar. It is a time of repentance, when Jews ask one another and God for forgiveness. Although it is a holiday defined by fasting (observant Jews refrain from eating and drinking during the twenty-five-hour holiday), there are two meals associated with Yom Kippur. The first is a pre-holiday meal, eaten just before the fast begins. The second is a "break fast," where, after a day focused on prayer and spirituality, people re-enter the physical realm with a nourishing meal.

LIBYAN-INSPIRED YOM KIPPUR PRE-FAST MENU

Garlicky Pumpkin Spread *(Cershi Bel Hal)*, page 87

Braised Chicken and Chickpea Stew *(Tbeha con Ceci)*, page 232, served with couscous

Saucy Stuffed Vegetables *(Mafrum)*, page 257

Syrupy Semolina Cake *(Safra)*, page 289

ROMAN-INSPIRED YOM KIPPUR BREAK-FAST MENU

Stuffed Pasta in Broth *(Carcioncini in Brodo)*, page 110

Whole Roasted Fish with Raisins and Pine Nuts *(Triglie con Pinoli e Passerine)*, page 211

Sautéed Dandelion Greens *(Cicoria Ripassata)*, page 76

Lemony Almond Cake *(Bocca di Dama)* *with* Caramelized Fruit *(Frutta Caramellata)*, pages 286 and 311

Sukkot

Sukkot commemorates the forty years the Israelites wandered in the desert after the Exodus from ancient Egypt. It is also the Jewish calendar's harvest holiday, celebrating the abundance of autumn. Jewish households traditionally build a temporary outdoor hut called a sukkah and enjoy alfresco meals with family and friends throughout the week-long holiday. Warm, comforting dishes—as well as foods that travel easily from the kitchen to the sukkah—are de rigueur.

SUKKOT MENU

Chicken and Veal Meatballs in Tomato-Celery Sauce *(Polpette di Pollo Con Sedani / Ngozzamoddi)*, page 226

Stuffed Zucchini *(Zucchine Romanesche Ripiene di Carne)*, page 242

Sautéed Spinach with Pine Nuts and Raisins *(Spinaci con Pinoli e Passerine)*, page 69

Tomato Rice Pie *(Tortino di Riso)*, page 179

Roasted Cipollini Onions *(Cipolline al Forno)*, page 73

Crunchy Chocolate Orange Cookies, page 278

Hanukkah

Roman Jews welcome Hanukkah, which falls in the depths of winter, the same way Jewish communities around the world do: by eating fried food. The oil symbolizes the miracle of the Hanukkah story, when a small Judean army, called the Maccabees, recaptured the Holy Temple in Jerusalem from the ancient Greeks. The Maccabees found only enough oil to light the Temple's menorah for one night, but it miraculously lasted for eight days and nights. There is no shortage of deep-fried goodies in Roman Jewish cuisine (see page 132), so view this menu as a "choose your own adventure."

HANUKKAH MENU

Mixed Fried Vegetables *(Pezzetti Fritti)*, page 130

Fried Fresh Anchovies *(Alici Fritte)*, page 138

Fried Salt Cod *(Filetto di Baccalà)*, page 134

Fried Mozzarella *(Mozzarella Fritta)*, page 135

Jewish-Style Fried Artichokes *(Carciofi alla Giudia)*, page 128

Apple Fritters with Vanilla Sugar *(Mele Fritte)*, page 150

Cozy Weeknight Dinner

Sharing sumptuous meals on holidays is lovely, but weeknights deserve the star treatment too. Roman Jewish cuisine has your random Tuesday dinner all sorted out.

DINNER MENU

Brothy Turnip and Rice Soup *(Rape e Riso)*

or Romanesco Broccoli Stew with Pasta *(Minestra di Pasta e Broccoli)*, page 105 or 96

Spaghetti with Artichokes and Bottarga *(Spaghetti con Carciofi e Bottarga)*, page 162

Sole with Lemon and Herbs *(Sogliole al Limone e Erbetta)*, page 208

Cinnamon Almond Cookies *(Biscottini con le Mandorle)*, page 268

Al Fresco Picnic

Pack a blanket, a bottle of something bubbly, and these summery, easily transportable dishes for a standout picnic.

PICNIC MENU

Spaghetti with Tuna and Tomato *(Spaghetti Tonno e Pomodoro)*, page 171

Onion Frittata *(Frittata di Cipolle)* *with* Roman Flatbread *(Pizza Bianca)*, pages 186 and 190

Silky Marinated Zucchini *(Concia)*, page 44

Roasted Summer Vegetables *(Verdure al Forno)*, page 74

Dried Fruit and Nut Bar Cookies *(Pizza Ebraica)*, page 273

ACKNOWLEDGMENTS

Writing a cookbook in the middle of a global pandemic had its unique challenges. But despite the extra layers of struggle and isolation, creating this book was a joyful process. I am so grateful to all of the incredible people who brought life and vibrancy to these pages.

First and foremost, I would like to thank Micaela Pavoncello of Jewish Roma Walking Tours for being a true expert on Rome's Jewish history and community. Thank you for sharing your scholarship and wisdom, your humor, and your friendship.

Another huge debt of thanks goes to my assistant, Megan Litt, for her invaluable help with research, translation, volunteer coordination, and recipe development. Thank you for being a sounding board throughout the entire process.

To all of the people in Rome and beyond who shared their family stories, helped to track down hard-to-find cookbooks, and opened their restaurants and homes to me (virtually and in-person) to cook together or share a meal, thank you, thank you, thank you. You are the heart and soul of this book: Giulia Bassan, Marco Bassan, Massimo Bassan, Italo Camerino, Letizia Della Seta, Angelo di Porto, Stefania Gai, Daniela Gean, Ghily Guetta, Hamos Guetta, the staff at the Museo Ebraico di Roma, Silvia Nacamulli, Roberta Nahum and the members of ADEI-WIZO, David Pacifici and the staff at torah.it, Michele Pavoncello, Umberto Pavoncello, Laura Raccah, Laura Ravaioli, Giorgia Renato, Menasci Renato, Ghila Ottolenghi Sanders, Marco Sed, Yael Sed, Angelo Spizzichino, Graziano Spizzichino, Miriam Spizzichino, Claudia Spizzichino, Italia Tagliacozzo, Giovanni Terracina, Mino Zarfati, Miriam Zarfati, and Rachel Zarfati.

Thank you to chef Marc Vetri (Vetri Cucina), chef Steve Samson (Rossoblu), and chef David Nayfeld (Che Fico) for sharing their passion for cucina Ebraica with me.

Thank you to Elizabeth Minchilli, Katie Parla, and Maureen Fant for being inspirations, and for your generous support and guidance along the way.

Thank you to my agent, Meg Thompson of Thompson Literary Agency, for encouraging me to submit a book proposal—in the middle of a pandemic!—and for helping to shepherd it through to publication.

Thank you to everyone at W. W. Norton & Company, especially my kind and talented editor, Melanie Tortoroli, whose wise questions and suggestions strengthened every page. Thank you to everyone who helped make the book visually stunning, particularly photographer extraordinaire Kristin Teig and food stylist Carrie Purcell for bringing the recipes to life so beautifully, Brooke Deonarine for the pitch-perfect prop styling, and Laura Palese for the compelling book design.

Thank you to the incredible roster of volunteer recipe testers who tried out recipes in their own kitchens and shared invaluable feedback: Dafna Adler, Rebecca Alpert, Philip Aspin, Sydney Baer, Shylie Bannon, Bonnie Benwick, Laura Berger, Aaron and Asher Bisman, Rebecca Blady, Felice Bogus, Jenn Book Haselswerdt, Michelle Bottner, Lauren Broomham, Rose Brown, Marissa Renee Campos, Karen Cattan, Aviva Clayman, Michele Cohen, Will Cooper, Hannah Delaney, Alan Divack, Natanya Eskin, Sylvia Fallas, Liz Feinstein, Rachel Fish, Liz Fisher, Karen Folz, Rachel Forth, Karen Fox, Sandra Fox, Benjy Fox-Rosen, Emily Freed, Georgia Freedman, Pamela Freedman, Sasha Frieze, Ora Fruchter, Temim Fruchter, Debs Gardner, Gabriella Gershenson, Naomi Gofine, Adele Goldberg, Leah Goldberg, Ilene Goldman, Shelley Goldman, Jami Goldstene, Judith Goodman, Rachel Goodman, Jessica Grosman, Mimi Gross, Rebecca Guber, Anna and Naf Hanau, Shira Hanau, Jennifer Handy Hayat, Margaret Hathaway, Courtney Hazlett, Magdalena Hutter, Daniel Infeld, Jared Ingersol, Madison Jackson, Adam Jacobs, Serena Jenkelowitz, Elizabeth Kamens, Arielle Kane, Shayna Kessel, Shira Koch Epstein, Carol Koenig, Sandra Kofman, Sandra Kogan, Tamar Kornblum, Hannah Giles, Abbie Kozolchyk, Faith Kramer, Christiana Kugel Rob Kutner, Sherri Lerner, Jeyn Levison, Joshua Lichtman, Patricia Lurie, Elisheva Margulies, Maskit Maymon, Eliana and Lev Meirowitz Nelson, Marni Mendelsohn, Rebecca Milzoff, Sarah Mina Gordon, Fred Mogul, Avia Moore, Lindsey Paige, Mary Rose Perez, Allie Plotsky, Carey Polis, Deena Prichep, Debbie Prinz, Jesse Rabinowitz, Gil Raviv, Elizabeth Richman, Avery Robinson, Amy Rogers, Bara Sapir, Olive Sasaki, Lauren Schreiber, Lisa Schwartz, David Segal, Ilana Sichel, David Siegel, Rebecca Silber, Joe Silberlicht, Fiona Smith, Amy Sowder, Gayle Squires, Roberta Stewart, Aleza Summit, Carly Sutherland, Audrey Tatro, Ilene Tatro, Emily Teel, Mira Toister-Achituv, Kath Vincent, Aliyah Vinikoor, Alix Wall, Aliza Robyn Wasserman, Mara Weber, Rachel Weber, Talia Weidberg, Marilla Wex, Susan Yarnall, Valerie Yasner, and Jill Zenoff.

Thank you to my Koenig and Fruchter families for your love and support. Endless love and thanks to my husband, Yoshie Fruchter, and to our children, Max and Beatrice, for inspiring me every day.

SELECTED BIBLIOGRAPHY

Ascoli Vitali-Norsa, Giuliana. *La Cucina nella Tradizione Ebraica.* Casa Editrice Giuntina, 2010.

Goldstein, Joyce. *Cucina Ebraica: Flavors of the Italian Jewish Kitchen.* Chronicle Books, 1998.

Guetta Hassan, Linda. *La Cucina Ebraica Tripolina.* Gallucci, 2006.

Limentani Pavoncello, Donatella. *Dal 1880 ad Oggi: La Cucina Ebraica della Mia Famiglia.* Carucci Editore, 1982.

Machlin, Edda Servi. *Classic Italian Jewish Cooking: Traditional Recipes and Menus.* Ecco, 2005.

Malizia, Giuliano. *La Cucina Ebraico-Romanesca in Oltre Cento Ricette Tradizionali.* Newton Compton Editori, 1995

Marks, Gil. *Encyclopedia of Jewish Food.* Houghton Mifflin Harcourt, 2010.

Minchilli, Elizabeth. *Eating Rome: Living the Good Life in the Eternal City.* St. Martin's, 2015.

Parla, Katie, and Gill, Kristina. *Tasting Rome: Fresh Flavors & Forgotten Recipes from an Ancient City.* Clarkson Potter, 2016.

Roden, Claudia. *The Book of Jewish Food: An Odyssey from Samarkand to New York.* Knopf, 1996.

Sacerdoti, Mira. *Italian Jewish Cooking.* Hill of Content, 1992.

Tedeschi, Bruna. *La Mia Cucina Ebraica Romanesca.* Logart, 2008.

Toaff, Ariel. *Mangiare alla Giudia: La Cucina Ebraica in Italia del Rinascimento all'eta Moderna.* Il Mulino, 2000.

Zanini De Vita, Oretta. *Popes, Peasants, and Shepherds: Recipes and Lore from Rome and Lazio.* Translated by Maureen Fant. University of California, 2013.

INDEX

Note: Page references in *italics* indicate photographs.

Q

R

S

T

ABOUT THE AUTHOR

Leah Koenig is the author of seven cookbooks that explore the world of Jewish cuisine, including the acclaimed *Modern Jewish Cooking* and *The Jewish Cookbook*. Her writing and recipes have appeared in the *New York Times*, *New York* magazine, the *Wall Street Journal*, the *Washington Post*, *Food & Wine*, *Taste*, and *Food52*, among other publications. And her newsletter, *The Jewish Table*, reaches thousands of subscribers each week. In addition to writing, Leah leads cooking demonstrations and workshops around the country and world. She lives in Brooklyn, New York, with her husband and two children.

www.leahkoenig.com